Sustainable Rural Development

Also by Andrew Shepherd

PREVENTING FAMINE (*with Donald Curtis and Michael Hubbard*)

WATER PLANNING IN ARID SUDAN (*with Malcolm Norris and John Watson*)

Sustainable Rural Development

Andrew Shepherd

First published in Great Britain 1998 by
MACMILLAN PRESS LTD
Houndmills, Basingstoke, Hampshire RG21 6XS and London
Companies and representatives throughout the world

A catalogue record for this book is available from the British Library.

ISBN 0–333–66484–1

First published in the United States of America 1998 by
ST. MARTIN'S PRESS, INC.,
Scholarly and Reference Division,
175 Fifth Avenue, New York, N.Y. 10010

ISBN 0–312–17763–1

307.72/

This book is printed on paper suitable for recycling and made from fully managed and
sustained forest sources.

10   9   8   7   6   5   4   3   2   1
07   06   05   04   03   02   01   00   99   98

Printed in Hong Kong

Contents

List of Figures and Tables

Figures

Tables

Preface and Acknowledgements

Writing books is almost a luxury at the end of the twentieth century. The next generation may be writing interactive computer programmes. This book might have been better as an interactive programme, as in the kind of a paradigm shift currently under way in rural development there is so much to discuss and debate, and so many people are qualified to contribute. The process which went into writing the book has certainly been an interactive one over the last twenty years. It started in northern Ghana in 1976, where I went with my family to do fieldwork for a PhD on the development of large-scale mechanised rice farming. It continued with twelve years' work, on and off, in the Sudan, including a spell as a UNICEF officer. During those years I worked as an academic on famine and food security, rural development programmes, pastoralism and irrigation schemes, and the development of large-scale mechanised sorghum production. For UNICEF I developed a women's development programme and had involvements with health, water and sanitation and relief work. Again my family were with me. In the early 1990s I worked more widely in the Horn of Africa on food security and development in conflict situations. Since then my major focus has been on public sector rural development in India. I also spent many days between 1991 and 1995 working as a committee member for Comic Relief's Africa Grants, giving me an insight into the operations of NGOs. During most of this time I have been a part-time small-scale organic farmer in the Welsh borders with my partner, Hilary, who has served as secretary to British Organic Farmers: this experience has also helped form some of the ideas in this book.

In all this I have been fortunate enough to mix teaching, research, consultancy and practical roles, so that my work has always had a practical orientation. I have also been fortunate to interact with a very wide range of people involved in development over the twenty years, from countless villagers, men, women and children, through fieldworkers and programme managers to policy-makers in government and aid. It is this experience, together with the background reading for course preparation and research projects, which is the basis for this book. There are many people who should be thanked for their help down the years, but here I will mention only a few. First of all, my family – Hilary, Tom, Owen and Penny – who have borne my endless coming and goings, who have lived with me in difficult places, and suffered the indignities of being 'animated baggage'. Secondly, my colleagues at Birmingham University's Development Administration Group, my professional home on and off since 1977. Many of the ideas about projects, institutions and management are ideas which have emanated from discussions and debates there. Particularly formative in different ways and at different times have been: Donald Curtis, Richard Batley, Michael Hubbard, Tina Wallace, Richard Slater, Robert Leurs, Ita O'Donovan, and Sarah Crowther. Some DAG alumni have also played a role: Mark Bradbury, Desi Fernanda, Nsaba Buturo, to mention a very few. Thirdly, there are too many people with whom I have worked overseas to thank each one. I will select only a few who played critical roles in my intellectual development, such as it is. These are: Abdul Rahman Abbakker Ibrahim, Asha Mustapha el Neima, Cole Dodge, Ahmed Musanna, Samtup Lepcha, Keith Virgo, Sumitra Gurung, Nasir Tyabji. Fourthly, I would like to thank several people who have read and commented on all or parts of the book: Donald Curtis, Iker de Luisa, Robert Leurs, Michael Willson, Nancy Godfrey, Ita O'Donovan, Lorraine Thorne, Alka Pathak, Mark Bradbury, John Watson, and my publisher's anonymous reviewers. Finally, in preparing the manuscript, Jenny Chapman ably put together the bibliography from sundry sources. Some of these people might disagree with the conclusions I have come to; these are my responsibility!

ANDREW SHEPHERD

The author and publishers wish to thank the following for permission to reproduce copyright material: Routledge for two figures from Jack Ives and Bruno Messerli, *The Himalayan Dilemma*; Intermediate Technology Publications for a table from *Challenging the Professions* by Robert Chambers; FAO for Figures 8.1 and 8.2; Elsevier Science for a table from its journal *World Development*; and Wiley for material from Peter Checkland and Jim Scholes, *Soft Systems Methodology in Action*. Every effort has been made to contact all the copyright-holders, but if any have been inadvertently omitted the publishers will be pleased to make the necessary arrangement at the earliest opportunity.

List of Abbreviations

ASCRA	Accumulating Savings and Credit Association
ATO	Alternative Trade Organisation
BMA	British Medical Association
CBA	Cost–Benefit Analysis
CBO	Community Based Organisation
CPR	Common Property Resource
EIA	Environmental Impact Assessment
EIS	Environmental Impact Statement
FAO	Food and Agriculture Organisation of the United Nations
FSD	Farming System Development
FSR	Farming Systems Research
GATT	General Agreement on Tariffs and Trade
GNP	Gross National Product
GR	Green Revolution
HYV	High Yielding Variety
IARC	International Agricultural Research Centre
IBPGR	International Board for Plant Genetic Resources
IFAD	International Fund for Agricultural Development
IFPRI	International Food Production Research Institution
IIED	International Institute for Environment and Development
ILO	International Labour Organisation
IMF	International Monetary Fund
IMR	Infant Mortality Rate
IPM	Integrated Pest Management
IRD	Integrated Rural Development
IRR	Internal Rate of Return
LDC	Less Developed Country
LFA	Logical Framework Analysis
MV	Modern Variety
NGO	Non-Governmental Organisation
NIA	National Irrigation Administration
NPV	Net Present Value

NIC	Newly Industrialised Country
ODA	Overseas Development Administration
ODI	Overseas Development Institute
OECD	Organisation for Economic Co-operation and Development
PHC	Primary Health Care
PLA	Participatory Learning and Action
PRA	Participatory Rural Appraisal
R&D	Research and Development
ROSCA	Rotating Savings and Credit Association
RRA	Rapid Rural Appraisal
SAP	Structural Adjustment Programme
SARD	Sustainable Agriculture and Rural Development
SMS	Subject Matter Specialist
SSE	Small Scale Enterprise
SSM	Soft Systems Methodology
T&V	Training and Visit
TNC	Transnational Corporation
TV	Traditional Variety
UN	United Nations
UNCED	United Nations Commission on Environment and Development
UNDP	United Nations Development Programme
UNICEF	United Nations Children's Fund
UNEP	United Nations Environment Programme
UNNGLS	United Nations Non-Governmental Liaison Service
UNRISD	United Nations Research Institute for Social Development
USA	United States of America
USAID	United States Agency for International Development
UK	United Kingdom
WCED	World Commission on Environment and Development
WDR	*World Development Report*
WHO	World Health Organisation
WMD	Watershed Management Directorate
WUA	Water Users Association

1

Towards a New Paradigm

Rural development is the set of activities and actions of diverse actors – individuals, organisations, groups – which taken together leads to progress in rural areas. Progress is defined differently by different people: historically, material progress – growth of incomes and wealth, poverty alleviation – has been the main consideration in development theory and practice. Today other indicators of progress – cultural, spiritual, ethical – are increasingly taking their place beside the material in a reformulated, more holistic concept of development. In the very definition of development there is then evidence that old paradigms are breaking down, and a new one formed.

The old paradigm

Conventionally rural development has been a part of the modernisation paradigm. There is a whole literature on modernisation, and a half century of development has been based on it. Very roughly, modernisation equates development with four basic processes: capital investment, which leads to productivity increases; the application of science to production and services; the emergence of nation-states and large-scale political and economic organisation; and urbanisation. These processes are linked to changes in values and social structure. Modernisation has flirted with models (or stages) of development through which countries pass to reach some developed state, usually equated with wealthy western societes. The most recent fashion has been to propose the trajectory of the Newly Industrialising Countries (NICs) as a model. However, as with previous models, there is now widespread agreement as to the specificity of this and of any particular development path. There is

1

no uniform process of development. Indeed, the equation of developed with materially prosperous western societies has come under question, with the focus on their negative environmental impacts and social deterioration.

The modernisation paradigm has evidently failed on a number of counts. Poverty and insecurity are still there in many poor countries, as well as some resource-rich ones, despite four or five decades of independent government and development policies and programmes. Worse still, the majority of rural populations are still marginal to their societies' development path: institutionally they are not incorporated. As a result societies are disintegrating, and states are struggling to maintain the political status quo. And finally, there has been the most rapid environmental degradation the world has ever seen. Of course the picture is not entirely bleak. Many countries have been able to improve average levels of some socio-economic indicators, but often the poor have remained absolutely poor and insecure as well as relatively worse off, while other sections of the population have improved their position markedly.

The conventional paradigm in rural development has focused almost single-mindedly on growth in production and the expansion of the market economy (or in state socialist countries, the expansion of nationally controlled production and services). If redistribution was part of the agenda, it was to be controlled by the state. The assumption has been that growth and markets are best promoted by the state and by a range of external interveners, donors and non-governmental organisations (NGOs) who know best about the kind of production and markets required. Rural modernisation was to be achieved by big, bureaucratic organisations, with (mostly male) professionals and administrators in command of the process. Economic criteria dominated decision-making; social, environmental, political 'factors' were relatively unimportant, and participation of the 'beneficiaries' of this development was only included as an afterthought.

In rural development the modernisation paradigm has proved mechanical and inflexible. In many countries it has not helped remove material poverty nor conserve valuable social and environmental resources. It is not capable of promoting sustainable development. Its outputs have too often been both environmentally and institutionally unsustainable. Sustainable development refers to improvement in livelihoods which does not undermine the livelihoods of future generations (environmental sustainability) (WCED,

1987), and which can be sustained over time (institutional sustainability). Livelihoods refer to more than just income and wealth: quality of life and of society, security, and dignity might be just as important to those whose livelihoods need improving. The modernisation approach has not succeeded in being inclusive: the very poor, and the occupationally, ethnically, racially, religiously or geographically marginal have remained marginal, or lost out; women have been excluded, or subsumed into the household, which was assumed to operate on altruistic principles, unlike the rest of the economy. The intangibles of development – autonomy, freedom, dignity, peace – were omitted.

Two major developments have occurred within the old paradigm during the 1980s and 1990s. These are the imposition of structural adjustment programmes (SAPs), and moves to trade liberalisation. To what extent have these modified the impact and failures of the old paradigm?

Structural adjustment

Perhaps the most extensive debate about development since 1980 has occurred over the concepts and practice of structural adjustment programmes (SAPs). Very crudely, these have attempted to stabilise inflation-prone economies through deflationary measures: devaluing the currency, reducing the money supply, reducing public expenditure, shifting the balance between public and private sector towards the private in all sectors, and increasing exports and reducing imports. These programmes look set to guide the overall practice of development in poorer countries for the foreseeable future. It will be important to assess how far the new rural development paradigm is compatible with or even determined by this dominant version of achieving progress.

SAPs should have much to offer rural societies and economies. They seek to unravel state interventions which built bureaucracies, taxed rural producers excessively, and offered little by way of services in return because the benefits of state investment and expenditure were largely urban. Currency devaluation and the reduction of subsidies should not only give producers of exported crops a fairer return, but would also make more expensive the importation of agro-chemicals, petroleum and machinery, leading to employment and sustainability benefits. The withdrawal of the state from playing the role of direct provider of services – which it could do effectively only in limited, usually urban or wealthy areas – creates space for devolved and citizen-based modes of action, as well as the private sector. At its best, structural adjustment can be seen as a framework for the responsible exercise of choice by individuals, groups and collectivities, and a set of constraints on the self-protecting actions of elites who use political power to achieve their own economic ends.

There is a lack of consensus about how much SAPs do these positive things, or indeed achieve their basic objectives of reducing economic instability and recreating the conditions for growth. The evidence is weak; in Africa, where most countries have been through SAPs, the results generally seem to be disappointing: SAPs neither generate growth nor deal with poverty. Optimists conclude that a persistently implemented SAP is correlated with greater stability and growth (Demery, 1994: 36). The only clear success is with promoting traditional export crops and reducing trade deficits despite adverse terms of trade for those major exports (Demery, 1994: 42–3). Most commentators agree that SAPs alone cannot transform the gloomy economic prospects of the African continent (Stewart, 1994: 98ff).

However, SAPs have been criticised on the grounds that they harm the interests of the poor and not only the urban poor; but also the rural poor and women in particular. This is the opposite of what should happen according to the proponents. They argue that the reforms should work to the benefit of rural small farmers and workers, and that overvalued exchange rates, protection, quotas and subsidies tend to benefit the urban rich, who therefore resist the full implementation of SAPs. Even existing patterns of pubic expenditure in health and education are biased to the tertiary (hospital, and university) sector, which benefits the poor much less than the rich. The evidence, again from Africa, is that per capita spending on health and education stagnated in the 1980s, but that SAPs failed to restructure expenditure to benefit the poor, due to elite pressures.

As markets for exported primary products were liberalised, and state monopolies removed, those farmers producing exports may have benefited for a while. However, as the terms of trade for primary products continued to decline as more and more were produced, and due to institutional and infrastructure weaknesses which meant that rural producers were not producing in or for competitive markets (Sahn, 1994: 292), these benefits have often not been very substantial. Credit and transport in particular are held up as inadequately available. Duncan and Howell conclude from a review of five countries' experience that

> there is nothing in these programmes inherently incompatible with the interests of poorer smallholders or the rural poor generally. . . If, however, the aim of sustaining a broadly based growth of production and incomes is to be achieved, the price changes that are at the heart of adjustment programmes need to be accompanied by improvements in the framework of institutions and public investments needed by farmers if they are to take advantage of the opportunities created. (Duncan and Howell, 1992: 208)

One of the problems of assessing the degree to which poverty is affected by structural adjustment is that much of the life of the rural poor is not touched by a SAP as it lies outside the officially recognised and measured economy. Poor farmers make little use of formal credit, fertiliser or other inputs; food crops are often privately traded anyway in open markets, and subsidised commodities do not reach the poor. In Africa at least (but this would also be true of big economies like China's) many of the poor are still self-provisioning to a substantial degree. There are also many aspects of human development which are not strongly related to economic growth, but which nevertheless are an important aspect of poverty. Health and nutrition would be a major example (Sahn, 1994: 293). There has been an inconclusive debate about the implications of SAPs for women, the major providers of health and nutrition: on the one hand, if women are forced on to the labour market by economic pressures they have less time for child care; but also the greater incentives for export cropping generally benefit men, and may reduce women's control over income. This can be significant, as women spend more on food, health and children (ibid: 294)

The world's financial and donor institutions seem to have accepted that adjustment is a long-term agenda, and to have embarked on a new and deeper series of reform measures, reducing and changing the role of the state to one which enables and regulates rather than provides, formulates policy and legislates rather than implements, leaving the private and non-profit or community sectors to take up many of the roles the state had been playing. There is a broad consensus that a wide spread of reform measures are needed: better infrastructure, financial markets which can reach the masses of credit-hungry, research and development especially in agriculture, environmental protection, and support to private sector producers of services.

This agenda for state action is very different from the prescriptions indicated by the successful 'tiger' economies of Asia (South Korea, Taiwan, Singapore and Hong Kong). There the state not only promoted the market and international investment but also invested heavily in industry, protected agriculture, offered subsidised credit and developed social security systems, a very similar set of policies to those pursued from the 1950s through to the 1980s in the majority of countries now undergoing SAPs. The reasons for this success are strongly debated between the neo-liberals who see it as a validation of market-based strategies, and the statists, who see these successes as the result of a strong state role in development – the 'developmental state'. In fact the successes of these economies was in large part due to their particular and historically specific relationships with the world economy, relationships which are no longer possible in today's reconfigured global economy. It may be that the price of their success – the ecological degradation, the repression and damaged society – is also too great for much of today's world.

Both sides of the debate about structural adjustment and trade liberalisation are marked by the limitations of the conventional paradigm. SAPs are designed and evaluated without cross-disciplinary assessment of their potential impact, on the environment, on the polity, on society (especially vulnerable groups). Early criticism of structural adjustment, for example the publication of UNICEF's critique (1987), made the World Bank include social and poverty alleviation objectives in SAPs. The resulting programmes to mitigate the social consequences of SAPs apparently brought few results, however. Despite the existence since 1987 of an Environmental Department within the World Bank, no serious examination of the environmental implications of SAPs was undertaken (Reed, 1996). There are widely perceived negative environmental consequences of SAPs, as countries are encouraged to exploit their natural resources in order to balance trade accounts or repay debts.

SAPs are designed with only one basic aim in mind: the removal of internal (and mostly macro-economic) constraints to growth in the country concerned. In conception they are thus stuck in a thoroughly simplified causal picture of reality. The inevitable criticisms usually invite adjusters to take other single issues into the analysis, and small shifts in the design of SAPs can be seen as a result. Sometimes critics choose to focus on the external constraints to growth, but the complexities of this issue have been swept aside by the liberalising world trade negotiations. Policy formulated within a structural adjustment framework is inevitably growth obsessed, and rarely sensitive to the quality of growth, despite pronouncements to the contrary. As such it is hostile to the new paradigm; nor can it be turned around through piecemeal changes.

Nevertheless, there is within the structural adjustment arena scope for positive change and the search for an alternative approach. The paradigm shift mapped in this book would be compatible with and would indeed contribute positively to an SAP which provided an umbrella for devolution: the promotion of small competitive farms and enterprises and co-operation among them; for research and development on indigenous technology and with indigenous technologists, and for common property and service institutions where small scale is a disadvantage. The new paradigm is not anti-growth (just as it is not anti-science): it is a question of the quality of growth, not just distributionally, but also environmentally. It is also a question of who is directing that process of growth. The mission of rural development is to involve the rural poor in these processes.

SAPs, by contrast, are generally more narrowly concerned with promotion of private sector firms as an alternative to the over-developed state. As far as rural development is concerned, this framework is probably more conducive than the previous one of heavy state intervention. In all but a few cases where there was political discipline, this inevitably led to abuse of power, inappropriate development strategies, and accumulation of assets in the hands of the wealthy and powerful. The poor are better off facing the market. However, the tendency now is to reorient the machinery of state to serve the large-scale, well-organised, often international private sector. This can probably look after itself, while the real focus of state attention should be to support more localised enterprise and the local provision of infrastructure and common services. As far as many rural people are concerned, privatisation has limited benefits: private investment simply will not materialise in many rural areas as there are better opportunities elsewhere. What is required is local institutional development in rural areas, including the development of market institutions and enterprises, but also infrastructure, services and governance. Without strong civic associations and local organisations the world's powerful economic corporations will ride roughshod over local interests. The state should have a strong role in protecting and promoting organisations of civil society.

Trade liberalisation

One of the chief limits on the success of SAPs has been the world trade environment. The success of SAPs in promoting traditional exports has on occasion contributed to gluts in supply which cause reduced world prices. An example was Ghana's increased cocoa exports in the early 1980s which helped to oversupply the market, and meant that export earnings did not recover as expected (Kofi, 1995). Of course, this policy is nothing new: industrial countries and the world's financing institutions have been encouraging greater competition among primary producers where consumption is relatively inelastic for a long time. What is needed rather is for producer countries to associate together, limit expansion, and diversify their exports (Stewart, 1994: 111).

The new deal in the GATT Uruguay round of international trade negotiations has likewise been heralded as of benefit to agricultural commodity exporting countries, including most developing countries. However, the actual picture is more complicated, and less optimistic. The negotiations centred around the reduction of tariff and non-tariff barriers to trade. The winners are therefore producers of goods which had high tariffs and other barriers. These include cheap labour producers of garments and southern producers of temperate agricultural products. The losers include the many developing countries with specially negotiated trade preferences for exporting their products, and importers of low-priced food from northern over-producers. Regionally,

> Africa gains little or loses from almost all the changes. . . South East and Eastern Asia gain most immediately. They have fewest preferences to lose, and have probably reached the stage at which they need cheap access to technology. Exports are highly important to those countries and most companies: they will need and are mature enough to exploit the new market access. The poorer countries will gain less. Those with the cheapest labour will probably become the new centres of the clothing trade, but those which only offered the advantages of quota dispersion [under the

multi-fibre agreement, to be phased out by 2004] (e.g. Bangladesh) may lose. (Page, 1994: 19)

Reluctantly, it has to be concluded that there is not much in the world trade agreement to brighten the future of small farmers and rural workers in many poor countries.

Clearly, countries which can diversify their exports away from the traditional ones will have a better chance of competing and paying their producers well (Wangwe, 1994). Diversification towards regional markets is also likely to provide opportunities. However, the dynamic world trading system will no doubt not take long to catch up with the small successes which many poor countries will be able to achieve. They will be temporary unless the economy itself becomes so dynamic that it can opportunistically switch from one product to another with ease. It is difficult to see many poor countries even beginning to do this in the foreseeable future. The cases where it has happened are based on decades of investment and market development (Jaffee and Morton, 1995). There is therefore an urgent need for an alternative trading system which offers poor producers better prices and more stable markets.

That alternative system exists in embryonic form: the fair trade movement. There are now tens of NGOs around the world devoted to facilitating fairer trade, especially between northern consumers and poor southern producers. This trade relies on the growing criticism among northern consumers of trading structures, and is a new chapter in a long history of the consumer movements in the north. Alternative trade organisations (ATOs) have grown up to challenge the low prices and poor working conditions experienced by many third world producers. They have selected products which have potential for raising poor producers' incomes. Handicrafts are an example: they add value to local raw materials, help women earn income, they do not undermine food production, and pricing them allows account to be taken of the hours of work put in. Honey, herbs, spices and nuts from the forests are other examples, all of which help to conserve forests as well. ATOs help small producers to organise and to obtain finance to pay producers and they extend information to small producers and set up information channels, then present and promote their products professionally. They are gradually building up networks based on partnerships among equals. There is considerable demand for products traded in this way, and a number of trade marks have emerged to give consumers confidence that products have been fairly traded (Barratt Brown, 1993).

Barratt Brown (1993, 169ff) presents a challenging agenda for the further development of fair trade out of the niche it now occupies. This is based on the use of electronically transmitted information through networks of networks, a 'clearing union' linking together the growing number of producer–consumer unions around the world, with ATOs. The major constraint in the growth of fair trade is currently the small scale of supply. Since this is also true of sustainably produced agricultural products, there is enormous scope for linking these two movements.

The paradigm shift

The central proposition of this book is that there is a paradigm shift in the theory and practice of rural development. The shift can already be seen in the fields of agriculture, project analysis and procedure, gender issues and local level institutional development. It is incomplete, in process, and the book aims to contribute to this process.

The paradigm shift represents a move from an industrial (technical fix) approach to technology development to an organic or holistic approach, with sustainable improvement replacing profit as the implicit objective; from a technocratic and exclusive to a participatory and inclusive approach to development management; and from resource control by big organisations to local resource management, often with a strong common property aspect. There are four fields where substantial conceptual advances have been made: these are the substantive starting points for this book.

Moves to sustainable agriculture

There is a paradigm shift taking place in thinking about agriculture throughout the world, and particularly in developing countries. It is important to document this in detail since it is one basis on which the whole development paradigm is beginning to shift. The new paradigm, drawing strongly on sociology and anthropology, celebrates indigenous knowledge and farmers' science and respects farmers' perceptions and objectives, recognises that many farmers are women, with possibly different objectives and perceptions, looks to avoid reliance on external inputs where possible, looks for energy-efficient farming systems, tries to integrate conservation into production, and above all treats farms as whole units in interaction with their environment both physical and institutional. Whereas agricultural economists used to use crude models of the peasant economy – seeing peasants as profit maximisers, or resistant to change – they now have a much more sophisticated set of models to draw on, dealing with the choices and risks which farmers have to face in reality, and the varied and innovative ways they can face those realities. Whereas past economic models used the notion of the household as their basic unit, it is now recognised that assumptions of altruism within the household are often not valid, and that the different objectives and strategies of individuals (men, women, children, the elderly) within households are important (Ellis, 1993: 163–88; Kabeer, 1994: 95–135).

In development practice we have seen the rise of farming systems research, incorporating social sciences alongside natural sciences in the exploration of technology with farmers; FAO has developed a new participatory, holistic approach to extension known as farming systems development, an answer and an alternative to the World Bank's ultra-conventional Training and Visit system; we have seen governments and donor agencies reducing subsidies on foreign exchange, agro-chemicals and mechanical devices, and a renewed interest in low external input systems among farmers. Public sector extension practice has generally been slower to catch on to the new approaches.

In the west, environmental and health concerns have led to a rapid development of 'alternative agriculture', focused on the need to reduce reliance on or eliminate chemicals from farming systems and thus, at least partly, from the food which people buy and from farm wastes. Here the standard-bearer is the 'organic/biological farming' movement, which has gained respectability in Europe, North America and Japan during the last decade. There are increasingly links between European (and North American) organic movements and related NGO efforts in developing countries. The use of chemicals in developing country agriculture and awareness of damaging effects is less advanced, but growing rapidly. This may not always be the most pressing issue in the search for sustainability in agriculture; but a serious health and environmental issue it is now known to be, at least in Green Revolution (see Chapter 2, pp. 33–8) areas where large numbers of farmers and farmworkers die each year from exposure to agro-chemicals. More broadly, the existence of chemical-based agricultural development strategies prevents solutions and progress being sought across a wider range of (more sustainable) technologies for a wider spread of geographical areas.

In poor countries, sustainable agriculture is an economic as well as an environmental necessity. Poor farmers and countries cannot afford technologies and production systems where waste accounts for a large part of production costs. Farmers have been led towards wasteful systems by public research and extension: if these organisations now listen to farmers, the messages are clear. They want technologies which do not pollute, which minimise cash costs and maximise returns to farm-household labour. In the increasingly less isolated consumer markets of poor countries the message is also changing: from an exclusive concern with price and quantity to a concern for taste and healthy food.

These wider concerns are an illustration of the recognition that growth must be evaluated qualitatively as well as quantitatively. Concern with the social, health and environmental impacts of agricultural growth is reflected in other sectors.

Sustainable local institutions

The second field in which a paradigm shift is evident is institutional development, and within this field it is local, indigenous, participatory institutions which have experienced the greatest positive re-evaluation. The conventional paradigm did not even recognise their existence in its hurry to impose 'modern' institutions like co-operatives, and new, western legal frameworks.

The understanding of how organisations work has matured greatly over the last three decades. In particular the study of common property resources and their management by economists and anthropologists has resulted in useful and schematic insights based on a political economy of local organisation. This has led to a clarification of the role of individuals and households in collective endeavour. In essence the prescriptive argument is for *subsidiarity* – leaving decisions and activities to the smallest group possible, minimising co-operation, retaining it only where necessary, and then being highly flexible about the form it should take. This positive appreciation of the potential of organisations evolved by members themselves has complemented the largely negative analysis and experience of community development and collectivist programmes inspired by state socialism.

Local-level organisation is a field where greatly improved academic understanding has often not been translated into practice. 'Naive' community development, idealistic notions about the degree of co-operation possible in community ventures, and the incentives which individuals have to contribute, still prevail, perhaps especially in Africa, and among NGO personnel. In Asia greater social stratification has often made it impossible to hang on to outdated concepts of community and unity. Development work is still rarely led by social scientists, and agriculturalists, engineers and other technically skilled professionals rarely have enough training in the critical social and organisational aspects of development work. Nevertheless, the widely experienced failures of modernisation have encouraged even the highly sceptical to be more favourably disposed towards existing local organisations which work.

Appreciation that women have been excluded, and have even lost out, from much development has led to a widespread attempt to include them through establishment of women's groups and organisations managed by rural women. These initiatives may have been propelled by a variety of motives – making programmes effective, or more efficient; achieving equity; empowering women (Moser, 1989) – and they may have had varying results, but their overall result has been to draw attention to the possibility that excluded, marginalised groups of people can come together, organise themselves, and decide how they want to improve their lot. Sustained efforts on this issue by many organisations have led the way in greatly expanding the scope for people's organisations in development.

Revolutionising the project

The ubiquitous 'rural development project' has been the major institutional instrument for disbursing aid to rural areas. The project started out as a planner's tool to reshape the world. The dominance of aid (and aid-like processes) in rural development has created a project culture based on notions of management by objectives and cost-effectiveness. Projects have, however, proved immensely problematic in the context of rural development, and the old project cycle has all but collapsed with the development of notions of process projects. However, the inertia of aid, government bureaucracies, and even some NGOs should not be underestimated. The project (or logical) framework has emerged as a planning tool which is held to be capable of reconciling the demands of bureaucracies with those of process and people's participation. This has revitalised the project in some organisations. Generally, interest in the development industry shifted in the 1980s to programmes (especially of the structural adjustment variety), and the policy conditions which accompanied programmes, and international trade.

The challenges for the project as the major form of development have been: to move from a blueprint to a process approach (with analytical techniques to match – the logical framework, Participatory Rural Appraisal, etc.); and to incorporate environmental, social and political analysis into a holistic approach. Changes in project approaches reflect change in the concept of rural development: moving from a transformation to an improvement approach, in which people become the subject of development, and it is seen as a long-term, multi-faceted process, with many intangible as well as tangible results. Once again, gender issues have been at the cutting edge in transforming the project approach: normal objectives and explicit and implicit assumptions have been challenged by the incorporation of women's as well as men's perspectives, together with an analysis of the power relationships between them. All this has stretched the project as a form of organisation to breaking point. An alternative approach to development organisation is needed. The learning organisation in rural development should be more evaluative, adopt a holistic perspective, be managed strategically, and be close to the rural society it serves.

Gender perspectives

As already hinted, debate and practice about the relative roles and powers of men and women in development has challenged the foundations of conventional development approaches. The issue of 'who benefits by comparison with who contributes' has been raised powerfully by evaluations of development focusing on the differences between men and women. Once women are incorporated in the process of development, and the issues of power relationships between men and women are addressed, it should be easier to include also other marginal groups. The inclusion of women challenges some of the bases of the dominant economic theories: the altruistic household, which allows development interventions to be targeted unthinkingly at the (usually male) head of household; the notion of shared poverty: when in fact poverty may be experienced quite differently by men and women; and the valuation of development itself (Kabeer, 1994). Here the environmental critique combines with the gender critique to question the reduction of all values to the economic in the end. Intangibles – autonomy, dignity, peace, equity, freedom, justice, the quality of the environment – have taken their place alongside material progress as worthy objectives of development.

The gender perspective powerfully (and universally) introduces the element of human rights into development discourse at a very basic level. Development can no longer be insulated from the debate about human rights: widespread violations of human rights can no longer be tolerated in the name of development.

The gender perspective also helps to focus attention in rural development on the restructuring of development agencies as a key aspect of the task. Gender (and broader human rights) issues cannot be addressed by development organisations unless they themselves are transformed.

Institutional implications

The institutional implications of these arguments include a shifting balance of professionals involved in rural development: from economists, planners, agriculturalists and engineers to a greater involvement of other social scientists and management specialists. There has also been some acceptance of the need for 'new' professionals – professionals with different attitudes, work patterns and allegiances (Chambers, 1993). Indeed, all the professions historically most influential in rural development are experiencing substantial changes: economists are increasingly concerned with environmental and social costs and benefits as well as financial; they are also developing an exciting new branch of economics – institutional economics – which focuses on the application of economic logic to behaviour in and of institutions. The biggest institutional implication is that ordinary people are in or closer to the driving seat of the activity (or project). Achieving this, while continuing to achieve other objectives is the major task ahead. To do these things, organisations need to change many aspects of their structures and procedures.

These fundamental issues also raise questions about the appropriate institutions to lead rural development in the new paradigm.

Ideas and institutions are of course inextricably intertwined – an institution cannot simply 'adopt' a new ideology or guiding framework unless the constellation of interests surrounding it is favourable. The World Bank has undoubtedly been the lead institution in conventional rural development as in so many other spheres of development. Given the depth of the paradigm shift, illustrated in Table 1.1, it is unlikely to be in a position to retain this intellectual leadership. In the 1980s in any case it reduced its lending in rural development considerably, refocusing on large-scale infrastructure development. Its structural adjustment programmes are also having the effect of reducing the role which its client public sector organisations can play in rural development (and development generally).

It would be logical that it should lose its leadership position to NGOs, in alliance with some bilateral agencies, and a potentially powerful network of new professionals, environmentalists and rural people around the world. However, the World Bank, like other donor agencies, is making efforts to involve NGOs in its programmes, in the belief that they will promote participatory development better than governments. To an extent it has shown itself willing to be lobbied and influenced – most notably over its investments in big dams. With the resources still at its disposal it is not easy to challenge its intellectual hegemony. This can perhaps only be done by coalitions of southern citizen movements, with support from wherever they can get it in the north. Northern NGOs, increasingly dependent on official donors, however, are quite likely to be co-opted by the World Bank and the official donor community.

The roots of the new paradigm

How does the present paradigm shift relate to development theory? Clearly, it is distanced from the universalistic theories of development (or underdevelopment) which dominated the period 1950–80. Modernisation theory and its antitheses, dependency theory, and Marxist theories of underdevelopment, were all attempts to develop laws which would work almost irrespective of place and time. These theories correspond to the preference for universalistic solutions to varied problems: they resulted in state-run development schemes and services with (in theory, but often not in practice) equal treatment for different people. The search for pattern and uniformity which can be replicated is still a concern in many development agencies.

TABLE 1.1

A summary of the paradigm shift

The old paradigm	The new paradigm
Economic growth at all costs	Quality growth: environment-enhancing, socially just and acceptable; contributing to peace
Redistribution, if any, by the state	Process of inclusion of the excluded in decisions
Authoritarianism tolerated as price of growth	Intangibles valued: freedom, autonomy, dignity
Subsidies for small enterprises, provided by the state	An 'enabling environment' for enterprise growth
State-provided social (and other forms of) security	Local institutional development for security
Transfer of technology from rich countries	Value local technology and knowledge; participatory technology development
Transfer of valuable assets (eg genetic resources) to rich countries	Institutions to protect assets of poor communities
Tangible, economic valuation of development: governments to define it	Development as multi-faceted, and often intangible: people to define it
Privatise/nationalise common properties	Affirm common properties as common, and expand field of goods seen as common
Build large powerful organisations for development: focus on government and large NGOs	Polycentric institutional arrangements: people's organisations, frameworks of governance
Planning = central thought process	Evaluation = central thought process
Organisation hierarchical: to implement plans	Non-hierarchical learning organisation
Compartmentalised	Holistic
Role of the state: major producer, provider and regulator	Role of the state: creating enabling legal frameworks, devolving power. encouraging associations

By contrast the new paradigm is more in the substantivist tradition of social science (Hettne, 1995: 254), rejecting grand theory and universal explanations and prescriptions. It upholds the variety of experience of development in time and place, and the need to search out what is appropriate and relevant, both in terms of explanations as well as prescriptions. It admits that standards of provision will not be uniform, but would tend to the position that other things are more important. The new paradigm does not have clearly competing theories of global significance: it will have sets of meta-theories for much more historically and geographically specific circumstances. In this sense, writing a textbook is a hazardous enterprise. A colleague asked me whether I could incorporate many more 'practical tips': I think, however, that the book may already be too prescriptive, and that there are not enough gaps into which people can enter their own thoughts. Perhaps this is the difference between a book and an interactive computer programme, which I would have written had I been capable. Nevertheless, the lack of overarching theory is consistent with theories of development today: there are no clear theoretical positions with widespread acceptance: development theory has become fragmented. Perhaps only the monetarists and free trade proponents, whose theories lie behind structural adjustment and liberalisation policies, have been able to exert an overriding influence during the last fifteen years. Even this is on the wane.

Like much development theory, what I have written is value-based, in the 'normative' tradition, showing how development should be. It is an attempt to go beyond the structural adjustment agenda, and propose a new agenda. The latter is derived partly from research and experience, but partly also from the evolution of concepts about development in the development discourse. In terms of theoretical traditions the new paradigm sits most easily in the 'Another Development' mode (Hettne, 1995: ch. 4). This tradition, at its broadest, operates with three principles: territorialism, cultural pluralism and ecological sustainability. Territorialism refers to the fact that elements in the analysis (or strategy) are rooted in space and with particular people – a community, a group. The strategy aims to improve the situation of that group, not to increase GNP or any other macro-indicator. Cultural pluralism refers to the fact that 'different communities in the same society have distinctive codes of behaviour and different value systems' (Hettne, 1995: 202). This has given rise to the concept of ethnodevelopment, which reinforces separate ethnic identity rather than attempting to submerge it into a national culture. The next step may be self-determination, where an ethnic group seeks to govern itself to some degree. Ecological sustainability refers to development patterns which are sustainable in particular places: this may rule out of court the achievement of certain improvements in consumption levels, for example. This challenges the whole notion of development as a progression towards some pre-defined state of existence.

This tradition of thought (and less often, practice) is a hard one to follow. But it is not one which rejects other aspects of the development discourse: macro-economic management, for example, provides a context in which the principles of Another Development, or the practicalities of the new rural development paradigm are situated. Macro-economic management brings benefits and opportunities as well as suffering and obstacles.

Language

An early note of caution is appropriate. Rural development, like other creatures of the 'development industry' (donor agencies, governments, consultants' firms, NGOs, academics), is prone to jargon and the extensive use of buzzwords. Sustainable development, sustainable agriculture, participation, women's involvement, indigenous knowledge, integration, are all examples of phrases which are uttered ritualistically when the need arises. At the same time, these phrases and words are not there by chance, but because they represent dimensions of the development process which are significant. They fall easily off the tongue or from the pen, but are less easily translated into reality, precisely because they are difficult (but not impossible) for the development industry to realise.

Project documents are peppered with buzzwords. These are required by financing organisations which must account for their spending or lending in the most up-to-date or fashionable terms. The buzzwords are often used by people with little understanding of what they might mean – so they take on a hollow, artificial tone. Thus any document which states that women will be involved in all activities, but fails to state how this will be achieved, how the constraints previously experienced in involving women will be removed or reduced, is contributing to a mystification of the involvement of women. Talking or writing about it becomes a substitute for doing it, or making it happen.

Buzzwords can be so loosely used as to be meaningless. An anecdote illustrates. A recent meeting of the Nepal Economic and Social Development Council heard a presentation by the Planning Commission on sustainable agriculture, which argued the need to focus agricultural development efforts on increasing the use of chemical fertiliser. A Council member pointed out that this was against the spirit of 'sustainable development' which includes the notion of relying on own resources, on farm, or at the national level. The paper was rewritten as a result.

Language can also easily prevent understanding. Frequently outsiders and insiders think of a phenomenon in quite different ways. If the outsider has power to impose his or her thinking, unfortunate consequences may follow. For example, again in Nepal, landslides are generally considered a problem by 'environmental managers' and development agents who try to prevent them. However, farmers may benefit from the possibilities of creating new farm land from a landslide. Certain farmers even go so far as to create mini-landslides, using water, so that they can build up new terraces (Gurung, 1988). Imposing the outsider's perception could lead to excessive investment in preventing something farmers see as beneficial.

There is, then, a particular problem in writing this book. The buzzwords express a response to legitimate, pressing concerns. They have come about, usually, as a result of sustained concerns. This book goes beyond the individual concepts and searches for the links among them, and between them and the reality of rural people, rural areas, and rural developmental processes. Individual concepts do not make sense by themselves, but only within a reordered paradigm.

Paradigms

The notion of paradigm and paradigm shift was popularised by Kuhn (1970) in the context of the 'hard' sciences. Since the 1970s the development process has witnessed the gradual breakdown of its conventional paradigm, though it has proved resilient in the face of criticism and negative experience. We would appear to be still in what Kuhn calls the 'pre-paradigm period', which 'is regularly marked by frequent and deep debates over legitimate methods, problems and standards of solution, though these serve rather to define schools than to produce agreement' (ibid: 47–8). However, in social science paradigms co-exist, in the same way that social or political ideologies co-exist in public life. It is not clear that social scientists ever escape the pre-paradigm period. Nevertheless, there are dominant paradigms: in the 1980s neoclassical economics with its advocacy of the unfettered market re-emerged as the dominant social science paradigm, through its influence in governments, especially the USA and the UK, and through them the multilateral donor institutions, especially the IMF and World Bank.

Whereas in the 1970s, when I first started to work on rural development, 'taking the part of the peasant', as Williams (1981) expressed it, was only really possible by criticising existing theories and practice, it is now possible to work in an alternative development tradition. This has been elaborated gradually, at a rather abstract global level, reflected in the journal *Development Dialogue* (among others), as well as in local practice and new meta-theory based on local practice, for example the focus on indigenous knowledge, and the elaboration of notions of participation into sets of participatory planning techniques. What is significant from the late 1980s onwards is that the shift of perception ('world view', in Kuhn's terms) is beginning to enter the mainstream of projects and programmes and the thinking of administrators and financiers.

Structure of the book

The rest of the book maps the paradigm shift in detail, establishes the interconnectedness of its different elements, and examines the difficulties involved in shifting to it. Three chapters (2 to 4) focus on the contents of rural development, another three on the processes involved (Chapters 5 to 7), and two further chapters take a close look at the changes required in the organisations which work in rural development (Chapters 8 and 9). Finally, the conclusion (Chapter 10) examines the point in the paradigm shift we have reached today, and the direction rural development is likely to take in future.

Conclusion

This opening chapter has made a claim which has yet to be substantiated: that the conventional rural development paradigm is facing a serious challenge from an alternative set of ideas focusing on justice, and environmental and institutional sustainability. The starting points for this alternative paradigm are the emergence of sustainable agriculture, a deep and widespread dissatisfaction with the project as a framework for most rural development, including its exclusion of women, and the emergence of radical new propositions about how grassroots development organisations work. The new paradigm is not inconsistent with the current macro-economic emphasis on good housekeeping (structural adjustment) and trade liberalisation, but would extend these sets of ideas to include a clearer focus on institutional development beyond the private sector, and a need to explore new markets and ways of organising markets which are fairer to poor producers.

The new paradigm is thus ambivalent about both state- and market-led versions of development. The state has often not served rural people well, especially the poorer and more marginal among them. Indeed it has often been the chief exploiter and represser of rural people and organisations. But states are there, part of the setting for rural development. On the other hand, recognising their very real limitations, they could become the facilitator and protector rural people would like to see. For the state to promote the market alone is not enough, as the powerful market organisations can be equally exploitative, and can harness the state to the defence of their interests above all else. For markets to work they need to be competitive and adequately supported by infrastructure, both physical and institutional. Making sure these are in place is a clear and widely accepted role for the state. Beyond that, however, there is a need to promote participation in the market by rural actors and organisations themselves, to strengthen their bargaining position with big capital or well-organised urban and industrial interests. This is a further clear role for the state; if achieved there is a chance that growth will be high quality growth.

2

Sustainable Agriculture

History of agricultural development

In very general terms rural development can be seen as the outcome of a history of struggle between the forces of expanding capitalisms (colonial and North American) and rural populist or nationalist movements. The principle threads are: colonial development and conservation programmes; the experience of the US in reconstructing shattered economies, at first in the southern US after the civil war, and later in China, Japan, South Korea, and India. These threads, in particular the latter, have shaped the dominant approach.

Colonial rural development was narrowly focused either on securing labour supplies for mines or commercial agriculture from rural areas, which were sometimes kept in a backward state as labour reserves, or on developing a class of 'yeomen farmers' who would produce raw materials cheaply for the metropolitan industries. In the years leading up to independence there was more effort made to broaden the concept and the benefits of development, notably in the community development movement. Large-scale, centrally controlled irrigation projects were a feature of some key colonies; as was the notion of a Famine Code – a basket of measures to prevent famine. Villageisation, soil conservation measures and settlement schemes were also common and often unpopular interventions.

From the 1950s it has been American ideas which have dominated. These originated in the reconstruction of the American south after the civil war (Cleaver, 1975) when northern industrial foundations (especially the Rockefeller) began to consciously restructure the southern economy and society in a movement called 'scientific philanthropy'. This agricultural education aimed to transform southern farmers into businessmen who could distinguish which farming techniques would benefit their balance sheets. These efforts relied on 'progressive farmers' as the agent who would transform the whole social order.

The key ingredients of this private-sector-led programme were to become the components of American-led rural development efforts in the third world. These were: an extension system closely linked to private sector input provision and bank credit; a focus on home economics to promote consumerism, and business skills so that farmers could analyse profitability; the development of progressive farmers' organisations which could finance agricultural extension; boys' and girls' clubs to educate future farmers and farmers' wives; basic education for the rural poor and a modern education for the elite. These ideas were most extensively tried out in China, where they failed just as they had failed in the southern USA. In China the Americans learned that land reform was vital to stave off revolution. Land reform became the centrepiece of reforms in Japan and South Korea in the 1940s and 1950s, complementing the extension, education and public health components.

During and after the Second World War the Green Revolution was supported in Mexico, the Philippines and India from the 1940s through to the 1960s by Rockefeller, the Ford Foundation and the US government, with the US government becoming increasingly important in the whole picture. Promoting technical change in agriculture has been its main rural development strategy since then, supplanting the broader, almost integrated approach of the Rural Reconstruction movements. The advent of the Green Revolution was a powerful technical alternative to the unpalatable imperative of land redistribution.

What was the Green Revolution (GR)? The most common definition refers to a combination or 'package' of High Yielding Varieties (HYVs), fertiliser, other agro-chemicals, and moisture control. Used in this narrow sense, GR technology may only be applicable to favourably endowed areas, where accurate soil moisture conditions can be economically created. However, the GR has outgrown this early concept as varieties for many different environments, and with many different characteristics (drought/flood resistance, pest/disease resistance, etc.) have been developed by plant breeders.

Pearse (1980: 158) wrote of 'an essential change sequence' in agronomic practice, leading to increased yields, increases in marketed surplus and a greater purchase of agricultural inputs, all implying a greater involvement of the producer with the market. An even broader definition would talk about the use of technologies by an interventionist state to promote agricultural growth, via commercialisation and industrialisation of agriculture and especially peasant economies (Mosher, 1966: 183). The more humanitarian thinkers emphasised the GR's potential for reducing world hunger (Brown, 1970).

These ideas fitted very well into an era of development characterised by the urban and industrial bias of industrial import-substitution strategies. Cities were growing rapidly and needed feeding. Lack of food in the market led to social unrest. Social unrest could lead to communism, ran the line of thinking. So the Green Revolution became a prime anti-communist development strategy – one which was capable of winning the hearts and minds of the masses, urban and rural. At the same time, the Green Revolution became the major strategy for expanding the market and to undermine the self-sufficiency of economies of the world which traded very little.

The achievements of the GR have been substantial, if hard to measure, especially against investment costs. In LDCs (excluding Mexico, Taiwan and centrally planned economies), 15–16 million hectares of HYV rice and wheat had been planted by the mid-1970s. Ninety per cent of this was in Asia, of which nearly half was in India. Since this time there have been no really meaningful statistics, since practically all governments have HYV seed programmes, and their use has become so widespread (Pearse, 1980: 37–8). It is now more precise to speak about Modern Varieties (MVs) (Lipton and Longhurst, 1989), since high yield is not always the prime characteristic of the seeds or technological packages produced.

The Green Revolution marks the second phase in the history of modern agricultural development. Since the 1980s we have begun to enter a third phase of global agricultural development: the search for sustainable agriculture. This has arisen from the growing multidimensional critique of the Green Revolution. The early critique of the GR focused on the way that the new technology created or reinforced inequality between areas and social groups, and was likely to lead to conflict. Later criticism emphasised the health and environmental risks. Finally there are serious questions about the extent of public benefit from public investment in the GR.

The critique of the Green Revolution

Geographical inequalities

Geographically the GR had limited applicability. This has operated continentally and regionally. The process of setting up adaptive research institutions capable of adapting internationally produced technical packages to the varied environments of LDCs has been long, slow, and not always linear. Progress has been made notably in India (Farmer, 1984), China and elsewhere in South East Asia. In Africa there are fewer cases of dramatic technical success, the major exception being maize in Eastern and Central Africa (*Journal of International Development*, 1989). A major constraint in Africa may be the underdevelopment of the wage labour force (Lawrence, 1987), compared to Latin American or Asian countries. Without adequately functioning labour markets capital investment is constrained, as there will be many enterprises or geographical areas where returns to capital will not offer incentives to investors.

The dramatic yield increases that are possible in well-endowed areas have not been repeated in more risk-prone or marginal areas, but there are nevertheless many modern varieties now available which expand farmers' choice in those areas. It is widely agreed in the vast literature on the impact of the GR that inter-regional inequalities have significantly increased (Freebairn, 1995: 277). These inequalities – between Punjab, Haryana and western Uttar Pradesh on the one hand and eastern India on the other, between central and peripheral Kenya, between communal and commercial farming areas, north and south in Zimbabwe, central and north-eastern Thailand, central and peripheral Sudan, and so on – have generally remained and become structural.

Socio-economic inequalities

Inequality among farmers in resource (land, capital, labour) endowment led to a 'structured differential propensity to innovate' (Pearse, 1980). Adoption of GR technology required an ability to take risks, access to fixed and working capital (equipment, irrigation, drainage, seeds, fertiliser, etc.), access to land, and possibly an ability to employ wage labour.

The 'diseconomies of smallness' (ibid) were not that HYVs were necessarily inappropriate for small farmers, nor that small farmers are peculiarly risk-averse (anyone is sensibly risk-averse), nor that they do not have the skills. They are: problems of access to water, tillage power, inputs, credit and the time to develop marketing links. The new technology spread more effectively to the extent that inequalities were less, or that these problems of small farmers could be mitigated. So it spread more effectively in Java because, fundamentally, landholdings were relatively equal, and equally endowed (Pearse, 1977).

The problem was often not that small farmers could not adopt new technology – they did in millions. But they did so later than bigger farmers, once access to the technologies was easier. By this time, much of the financial advantage of turning to the new, more productive systems had already been exhausted by the earlier adopters. Mass adoption often contributed eventually to declining real crop prices, a sign of success for most governments or big employers. Bigger farmers were in a better position to cope with this problem through cutting costs of production, or diversifying again.

A recent collation of the diverse literature on the GR and inequality among farm households has observed that most studies which have a conclusion conclude that inter-household inequality has increased. However, the proportion of studies making this conclusion is lower in India and the Philippines, and among Asian authors compared to others. Nevertheless, these subtleties do not undermine the overall conclusion much: though they do suggest some consistent geographical differences. The literature remains at odds with the continued heavy promotion of the GR by development agencies in the belief that it helps to reduce poverty and inequality (Fairbairn, 1995).

In many cases the new technologies were introduced with substantial subsidies by states anxious for rapid adoption, in order to prevent recurrence of famine (India) or perceived threats to social order. Inputs were often scarce relative to demand; usually the more powerful individuals were able to corner the market. Smaller farmers often had to buy the inputs on the parallel market at inflated prices. Fortunately, under structural adjustment programmes, state subsidies and delivery systems are usually being abandoned – ironically they had done little for small farmers, who do not typically have, nor are they usually able to develop close relationships with the Agriculture Ministries or project organisations allocating scarce inputs. Officials are usually socially aligned with bigger farmers, or if not, their material or venal interests can more often be satisfied by serving larger rather than smaller producers. Many small farmer programmes the world over have struggled with these issues in the last twenty years.

With structural adjustment, subsidies have had to go – the obvious ones, on chemicals, seeds and other inputs, and the less obvious ones, on irrigation water, credit and imported goods including machinery and fuel, undervalued by overvalued currencies. Rapid agricultural modernisation has been fuelled by these policies, policies which have generally benefited the wealthier farmers and urban industrial or consumer interests as expressed in Lipton's theory of urban bias (1977) and Bates's study of African agricultural political economy (1981). To the extent that subsidies have been an important element in determining the pattern and pace of agricultural growth, it is likely that the trend and pattern will change. So, in the West African savannah areas easy access to land enabled businessmen farmers with access to subsidised seeds, fertiliser, pesticides, machinery and fuel to greatly expand their farms in the 1970s and 1980s. By the 1990s, after SAPs had reduced subsidies, many had withdrawn from large-scale cereal production after accumulating losses and bad debts, leaving the field open for peasant producers.

There was much talk about 'delivery systems', bringing inputs to the farmer. However, in reality the term was often far from an accurate description of what happened. Farmers had to go from agency to agency looking for the technical bits and pieces required to run a farm system based on modern varieties. Agencies were rarely co-ordinated in their actions. There were bureaucratic and social obstacles for small farmers at each agency, as well as requirements to pay kickbacks to officials presiding over scarce resources. The time involved in accessing the Green Revolution often put it out of the reach of smaller farmers until the inputs were readily available through the market. The biases of extension agencies, in particular their reliance on male extension agents, often put women farmers at a disadvantage.

Much of the impact of the new farming technology on socioeconomic inequality depended on the structure of property relationships. In Japan in the inter-war period access to land and other resources was fairly equal. Small and medium farmers were politically important and demanded the generation of relevant research results. This led to the adoption of new technology across the board, and probably to a rise in wage rates as labour was increasingly scarce due to rapid industrialisation. This beneficial cycle may have been repeated elsewhere in East and South East Asia – South Korea, Taiwan, central Thailand, central Luzon in the Philippines, Java, and parts of China. These are exceptional cases, however.

The creation of landlessness is perhaps the most severe criticism laid at the door of the Green Revolution. Just as it is difficult to lay the blame for increased inequality in many rural societies at the door of the GR alone, so it is with landlessness. The growth of landlessness is more related to displacement by large-scale development (dams, large-scale mechanised farming) and the ending of tenancy and sharecropping relationships as landlords took land in hand as a result of changing levels of profitability of farming. While all these are tied up with the GR, changing profitability is determined by a wide range of factors – government policies on prices and subsidies, the returns to mechanisation and economies of scale, and the returns to alternative investments in the economy. The technology of farming is merely one factor.

Employment and wages

Poverty remains in countries with substantial Green Revolution successes, and even in the Green Revolution regions themselves, after decades of agricultural modernisation. This is Lipton and Longhurst's 'mystery'. Its explanation (1989: 204–6) is that, due to population growth, geographically uneven development, and the consequent tendency for the poor to migrate from marginal to prosperous areas in search of paid work, the share of labour in the increased income which accrues to Green Revolution farms and areas actually falls. Labour is plentiful, while land and possibly inputs are scarce: economically it is logical that rewards to landowners and input purveyors would increase, while returns to labour are depressed.

The share of income going to labour falls even though the development of quick maturing seeds and better irrigation has enabled widespread double cropping, where only one crop a year was taken previously. There is a sequential development in the labour market: initially demand for labour increases, especially at particular seasons (e.g. the main crop harvest, and the first weeding of the second crop); this attracts labour migrants, and also persuades farmers to invest in labour-displacing mechanisation. Both depress wages in the medium to long term, and rob workers of their share of increased incomes.

Within that share of income going to labour, there are many documented cases where the share going to women in particular has declined, as a result of mechanisation and income-generating tasks being taken over by men in new labour relationships. However, women may also experience increased demand for female labour in particular circumstances.

The decline of the share of income going to labour is the kernel of Lipton and Longhurst's important book, and could lead to the formulation of some radical conclusions about agricultural development policy: that it is influences on agricultural wages which are critical in the fight against poverty and hunger; that rural workers' organisations and negotiating power are vital; that land and other asset redistribution may be the keys to poverty alleviation. The book's conclusions are far more anodyne, if worthy: the authors look for answers in population policy, reallocation of agricultural research funds, and targeted employment and nutrition programmes. All of these are not at all straightforward. For example, in agricultural research the criticism of scientists and especially the International Agricultural Research Centres is that they have not used their limited but real autonomy from hegemonic political and economic interests to adequately research the links between 'modern varieties' (MVs) and the interests of wage labourers, who form the majority of the poor in South and South East Asia, Latin America and increasingly in Africa too.

Researchers have not always understood the situations faced by poor farm families, who may, for example, often have more family labour available per hectare cultivated than wealthier families. As a result their strategies may be very different: they might prefer mixtures of crops rather than single stands, for example. Scientists have to decide whose scarcities and priorities they work on. And they also have to try to predict what priorities will be in ten or twenty years' time, when the results of research done now becomes available. Generally speaking, scientists are under pressure to produce results and so work on the most uniform conditions, and simplify the environments at which they direct their research. They find it difficult, for example, to deal with complicated crop mixtures and crop–livestock interactions; or long-term disease-proneness. So the difficulties of serving the poor through research on modern varieties are inherent (Lipton and Longhurst, 1989: 40–1).

Conflict

The Green Revolution has been associated with social conflict. Perhaps the best-known case of violent conflict emerging from the GR is that of the Indian Punjab where a farmers' protest movement against low state procurement prices and growing farmer indebtedness was converted in 1984 by the Indian Army's attack on the Sikh Golden Temple into a religious dispute, with well-known and terrible consequences for Punjab and India since then (Shiva, 1991a: 182–3). Here, as in many cases, the Green Revolution was closely tied up with state food security policy, and farmers have often been asked to bear the brunt of this in terms of price squeezes.

Conflict has also arisen because of the uneven spread of the Green Revolution and commercialised agriculture. Where successes have occurred entrepreneurial groups have often been quick to seize opportunities, grab land on the land frontier and squeeze out traditional users of the land. This has happened widely in Latin America and Africa. The laws and institutions of the state have often supported (indeed instigated) this process through granting land leases where traditional users' title to land is not well recognised in national law, and by providing all kinds of services to the colonising farmers (credit, extension, security). The process forms part of the development of a business class in many countries, and resembles the forcible appropriation of land which occurred in Europe and North America prior to industrialisation. Despite this dimension of class formation, the displaced people have often belonged to different ethnic groups, and conflict between them and the colonisers has taken on an ethnic dimension.

In northern Ghana, for example, several years of conflict in the 1990s can be traced back to the GR which occurred in rice production there in the 1970s. The allocation of land by the state to commercial rice farmers from the more powerful northern tribes and from southern Ghana displaced members of several acephalous and non-landowning ethnic groups. This gave rise to an ethnic consciousness focusing on access to land. Twenty years later this focused – in violent inter-tribe conflict – on demands that these acephalous groups should have their own recognised chiefs and land to allocate.

Food security

The Green Revolution has, through much of Asia, parts of Latin America, and a few countries in Africa at least, provided those states with an interest and capacity to remove food insecurity with some of the means required, in particular the bulk-marketed, usually low-grade grain in larger quantities than would otherwise be available. This, when combined with early warning systems and effective administrations, has enabled states to prevent famine. India is the classic example (Curtis *et al.*, 1988). However, these successes have created their own problems, in particular of surpluses of grain which cannot easily be disposed of; huge capital and recurrent costs of procurement, storage and disposal; and where the state has become heavily involved in the whole process, a weak private sector and badly distorted market.

Structural adjustment programmes have attempted to reduce the degree to which states need to intervene to ensure food security, arguing that the private sector is capable of undertaking at least some of the functions which have cost states so dear. In this scenario it becomes more important that states have the capacity to purchase grain in international markets when necessary rather than accumulate it internally. In this case the production of big (even unmanageable) surpluses of relatively low-grade produce is not so critical to food security: in fact, since these are likely to fluctuate strongly from year to year, they create a demand for inter-annual storage which the private sector finds difficult or impossible to undertake as it is not profitable. Nevertheless, switching from reliance on the state to the private sector is hazardous, since the private sector rarely has the capacity to step rapidly into the state's even diminished role. This was illustrated by the famine which resulted in Zimbabwe in 1991–2 as a result of drought and a maize shortfall coinciding with the over-rapid liberalisation of trade in grain. Zimbabwe falls in the southern African maize belt which is the best example of Green Revolution technology spreading in Africa. This crisis was an illustration that the Green Revolution alone will not ensure food security.

Where the majority of the population is in farming, as in most of Africa – the world's least food secure region – food security for that majority is not necessarily well served by bulk production driving prices down. Farmers' food security depends as much on what they can earn from farming as what they have to buy. Buoyant prices are more likely to be assured by steady research on a wide variety of crops and systems over a long period than by focusing on a few crops and intensive short-term research. Farmgate prices will be one of the determinants of farm labourers' wages.

Health

In the higher-potential areas, GR methods have been applied with great success in terms of production, but at what is increasingly perceived to be enormous and unacceptable cost in terms of human health and the environment. These environmental and health costs have been amply catalogued by Conway and Pretty (1991). While death and illness which can clearly be attributed to pesticide use, in particular, is minimal in rich countries it appears to be significant in poor countries, though evidence is patchy.

The consumption of chemicals in developing countries is as yet, on average, at low levels. But it is highly concentrated in certain developing countries (e.g. in Africa, continent of lowest use and where concentration is most marked: in Kenya, Zimbabwe, Sudan, South Africa, and Egypt); and within most countries most agro-chemicals are used in GR regions and on certain crops only. The low average disguises the fact that many small farmers use little or no chemicals, while levels of use in the 'Green Revolution' areas and by big farmers may be quite substantial.

Chemical use is likely to be poorly managed too, given literacy levels, language barriers, inadequacy of handling equipment and storage facilities. Horror stories are common (see, e.g., Pesticides Trust, 1989: 29–34). In particular, vegetables sold in urban markets are likely to have high levels of residues, even of organochlorines (like DDT and dieldrin), which are still used in many developing countries.

In Kenya between 1982 and 1986 there was a substantial increase in pesticide use in the smallholder sector, mainly on coffee but also on vegetables and grain crops. Generally much larger quantities of chemicals were used on exported crops than on subsistence crops. In one local area (Othaya) there were 25 pesticides for sale in 1983, 40 a year later, and 55 in Nyeri and Othaya in 1986. Knowledge of the hazards involved in their use was almost nil, even among local

Ministry of Agriculture and Health staff. All farmers were using pesticides (Christiansson, 1991).

Many chemicals in the World Health Organisation's (WHO) categories of 'extremely hazardous' and 'highly hazardous' are in use in developing countries (Pesticides Trust, 1989: 54). Some of these substances although banned, or severely restricted in certain countries (usually richer northern countries), may not appear in the Food and Agriculture Organisation of the United Nations (FAO) or United Nations Environment Programme (UNEP) lists of chemicals whose export or import should be controlled by governments (the system of 'prior informed consent' – i.e. that the government of the importing country must give its approval based on full information from the exporting country about the regulatory status of that chemical in the country of export) (Pesticides Trust, 1989: 1–2). There is an ongoing debate about the chemicals which should be in these lists (ibid: 98–100).

Following Bull's classic study (1982) it has been estimated that deaths due to pesticide poisoning – the most dramatic health impact of chemical use in modern agriculture – have been of the order of 10,000 a year. This figure has never been established with any kind of scientific authenticity: reliable information on the health impact of pesticides or other chemicals is very scarce. Given the continued use and promotion of pesticides by the world's leading development agencies and governments, this would seem to represent to them a somehow acceptable death rate. Perhaps a cost–benefit calculation can show that the benefits of use outweigh the costs at this level, though it should be impossible to put a price tag on the loss of life.

High-quality evidence from the Philippines suggests that death rates in the Green Revolution areas of central Luzon region increased among economically active males in rural areas, while they decreased among women and children (Loewinsohn, 1987). Death was highest during the months of highest insecticide application, and was reduced following a ban on the use of one particular chemical, endrin, in 1982. Mortality from all other causes except cancer was on the decline. In central Luzon there was a 27 per cent increase in non-traumatic mortality rates among males aged 15–54 between 1961–71 and 1972–84. If this were extrapolated to other rice-growing areas in Asia many tens of thousands would be dying every year from occupational exposure to insecticides. 'The chronic effects of low doses of residues are not known with any certainty' (Beaumont, 1993: 30). There are now some serious research projects attempting to investigate the issue, whose results will not be available for a number of years. Apparently children tend to be both more exposed and less able to deal with toxic materials in the body (Beaumont, 1993: 144).

The problems are recognised by many governments which are seeking to ban or otherwise control hazardous substances. However, these countries are all

relatively poor and lack resources for effective pesticide regulation and monitoring, for provision of adequate medical facilities, for education, extension and training work for pesticide use. Information on alternative less pesticide dependent or non-chemical pest management systems is not yet widely available, although components of such systems are practised in traditional agriculture and progress has been made towards adoption of these systems, in South-east Asia in particular. (Pesticides Trust, 1989: 98)

Environment

There are many ways in which modern agriculture compromises the interests of future generations: loss of vital topsoil which can only be built up slowly and painfully; pollution of soil, water and atmosphere; deforestation; irrigation rendering soils unusable or unproductive due to salinity; massive tampering with the eco-system such that gross imbalances and vulnerabilities are created; loss of genetic diversity in plants and livestock which reduces the ability of future generations to explore genetic options to their problems. These environmental consequences are due to both the increasing intensity and the increasing extent of agriculture in the modern world.

Even Lipton and Longhurst (1989) had nagging doubts about a chemically based strategy. For the discerning reader, their apology for the Green Revolution bristles with worries about decision-making processes within the research institutions. One worry is about the tendency for crops to extract nutrients from the soil and without assured replacement (ibid: 44–8), and a strong case is made for more work on soils and moisture stress, linked with variety development. However, like many economists (and agriculturalists, for that matter) the authors view the soil as a kind of black box, a neutral medium for growing plants into which inputs go and from which outputs are taken. It is now increasingly recognised by soil scientists and ecologists that the soil is an extremely complicated medium, whose vitality can easily be destroyed through careless use of chemicals and/or cultural practices.

They also worry about the lack of research on living enemies of crops – vermin, and other wildlife – and weeds, which are often far more threatening to livelihoods than the insect pests and diseases which have been the object of so much research. The given reasons are that researchers believe they can do nothing about these problems, that damage is chronic not dramatic, evidence for damage is lacking, and the appropriate scientists have not been recruited. But there are surely other reasons for lack of such work, which are not hard to divine: this is public benefit research, as opposed to private profit. It is the kind of research one would expect public institutions to give great emphasis to in an ideal division of labour between private and public sectors. But the policies of public research institutions have been clearly subordinated to the requirements for markets of the international chemical companies. Control of wildlife is not an area of research in which they have strong interests. Indeed they have been forced to develop a 'green' image during the last twenty years, which has probably precluded this type of research.

Clearly, researchers have enormous scope for improving farmers' yields and incomes by developing resistant strains. Another doubt, however, concerns the focus of pest research on achieving 'vertical' and near-immune resistance to a specific pest, rather than 'horizontal' resistance to all types of a pest, or on achieving tolerance of pests in seed varieties, or indeed developing cultural practices which allow farmers to avoid pest attack. The problem with the vertical resistance strategy is that pests produce new virulent strains in response to seed varieties with vertical resistance. This is fine if research institutions are strong enough to keep developing new varieties when pests mutate – strong enough to stay on the 'boom and bust' treadmill. Most National Agricultural Research Systems do not have the capacity, and are thus dependent on the International Agricultural Research Centres (IARCs) (ibid: 88).

Underlying the growing pest problem is the ecology of monoculture. The very success of modern varieties (MVs) means that they tend to displace not only traditional varieties and landraces – loss of genetic stocks in the three main Green Revolution crops of wheat, rice and maize has been enormous – but also crops which cannot perform as well. Increased cropping intensity due to irrigation and quicker maturation creates a uniform environment where pests and diseases can more usually find the food they prefer. So, in the long run, the set of MVs in use becomes less stable against pests and diseases, requiring a faster pace of research to produce new varieties.

The use of MVs has displaced thousands of traditional varieties (TVs) during the last 50 years. The fact is that TVs have been selected by farmers over the years mainly for productivity, but also for pest and disease resistance at least by default – by selecting the survivors after epidemics. So, for example, Ethiopian farmers selected barley landraces over the years with resistance to many of the world's major barley diseases. In the Great Lakes Region of Africa 'most exotic bean varieties were less adapted and more affected by diseases than were the mixture of local varieties used by traditional farmers' (Thurston, 1991: 204).

Pesticides have had, and continue to have, enormous and well-documented negative impacts on wildlife. Rachel Carson's *Silent Spring* (1963) first brought this fact to a large public. Since the 1960s there has been much progress in creating less toxic and more specific pesticides. Despite this, species of birds (which control rodents), bees (which pollinate plants) and other wildlife continue to disappear at an alarming rate, attributable in part to exposure to pesticides, for example in Kenya (Christiansson, 1991: 221). Fertilisers, too, contaminate the environment, in particular water and air, and under certain circumstances can lead to eutrophication of rivers, lakes and coastal waters (Conway and Pretty, 1991: ch. 4).

Nitrogen-based and other commonly used fertilisers reduce and damage the life of micro-fauna in the soil, the very creatures which keep soils healthy and useful mediums for plant growth. So an agriculture dependent on chemicals destroys the medium it works with, and increases its dependence on those same chemicals in a vicious circle. In turn, loss of soil fauna means that organic matter does not decompose properly, soil structure degrades, and the soil is more liable to erosion. Nitrous oxide contributes to the destruction of the ozone layer and global warming (McCracken, Conway and Pretty, 1988: 47) and is emitted by fertiliser use, among other sources. Nitrates and phosphates in surface and groundwater are known human health hazards, and few poorer countries have effective regulatory mechanisms preventing damaging concentrations. Even industrial countries have tremendous difficulty controlling the diffuse sources of agricultural pollution of water, let alone air.

Industrialised agriculture also contributes to global warming through its increasing use of fossil fuels. Although other aspects of the industrial food chain (transport and processing) contribute 80 per cent of agriculture's share of carbon dioxide emissions, on-farm energy use contributes to the remaining 20 per cent (Pretty, 1995: 62). Fossil-fuel-dependent mechanisation frequently accompanies the GR. However, even in industrial countries this is a set of issues which is hardly yet on the agenda in agriculture.

There are many other direct and indirect environmental effects of industrial agriculture: the loss of soil and the loss of on- and off-farm bio-diversity are two major areas (Pretty, 1995: 69ff). The costs of agricultural pollution and environmental damage are all externalised, paid for in reduced human health, weakened soils and lost or degraded habitats. Producers of the chemicals and wealthy farmer users never pay these costs; poor farmers and consumers, and future generations, are subject to ill-effects.

Efficient allocation of public expenditure

Public investment in research and development (R&D) has driven the Green Revolution. The World Bank has attempted to calculate the costs and benefits of agricultural research, which generates the new technologies, not surprisingly coming out with the conclusion that it is generally a sound investment (1981). Countries which have invested less in agricultural research (mainly in Sub-Saharan Africa) have frequently been admonished and told to invest more on the basis of this type of analysis (Lipton and Longhurst, 1989; World Bank, 1989). However, it is not easy to evaluate the impact of this R&D, as the use of MVs tends to be accompanied by changes in farming systems – the use of irrigation, alterations in cropping systems, and so on. Comparisons should also be of systems, not only individual crop enterprises. The same case is made for comparisons between conventional and biological farms. If this is done, and comparisons are sensitive to inputs and outputs, and costs and benefits across a wide spectrum of components, the comparisons are likely to be much more favourable towards the TVs or biological systems. Thus, measuring techniques are commonly biased in favour of what the measurer seeks to protect. Comparison of systems are rare.

Special R&D organisations were created, isolated in 'ivory towers' from the real world, except for the biological raw materials which they scavenged and the outputs they produced. Experiments under controlled conditions were the key to innovation; their clients were governments and big companies capable of reorganising farm production to suit the new technologies. The agro-chemical companies have financed much agricultural research themselves, and are the patent owners of an increasing proportion of genetically engineered seed varieties. Their interests pervade much of the research carried out in public research institutions in southern countries over the last 40 years. Much of this has been 'near market' research on commercially viable processes. One would expect much of this to have been done by the private sector, since it could profit from the research: however, the argument for state intervention has been that the agro-chemical companies would not invest in the adaptive research for the underdeveloped markets of the south, and so would delay development there. However, the markets of the south are now generally open. It is in fact high time for a fundamental review of the degree to which agricultural research of the Green Revolution variety is genuinely public benefit research. As we have seen, there are so many negative externalities of this type of technological development that it is not any longer an obvious candidate.

A global paradigm shift in agriculture?

As a result of the accumulation of issues and problems, alternative approaches and technologies have begun to emerge strongly into the agricultural policy agenda, and farming practice. These have so far been disparate initiatives in the main, but it is the argument of this chapter that they now add up to a paradigm shift – a total change in the way in which agricultural development is conceptualised. Around 1990 a number of publications appeared indicating that leading world institutions, the OECD, the World Bank, the International Food Policy Research Institute, were waking up to the some of the problems of the Green Revolution. These focused particularly on its failure in Africa due to problems of delivery, of access to credit, of the development of a successful improved seed industry, or shortages of irrigation water, and generally argued that these could be solved with more of the same intensive GR inputs (Aziz, 1990; International Food Production Research Institute (IFPRI), 1990: 23; World Bank, 1989).

At the same time the FAO and UNDP (United Nations Development Programme) were beginning to develop a more searching reorientation. By 1991 the FAO and the government of the Netherlands had issued the *Den Bosch Declaration and Agenda for Action on Sustainable Agriculture and Rural Development* (FAO, 1991) which recognised that intensification in the industrialised world 'has often been accompanied by large demands on non-renewable resources, environmental pollution, problems of waste disposal, an accelerated rural exodus and the development of unsustainable production systems' (FAO, 1991: 6). There was a call for fundamental changes and adjustments, a new approach to agricultural development at national level, and eight international co-operative programmes to implement the recommendations. Chapter 14 of Agenda 21 included a series of measures which form the core of SARD (Sustainable Agriculture and Rural Development):

- the development of a coherent national policy framework taking account of structural adjustments, subsidies and taxes, laws and incentives, technologies, foreign trade, demographic trends and other factors which impinge on agriculture;
- building institutional and human capacities and devolving more decision-making authority and responsibility to the rural people while providing resource management skills;
- development of farming techniques such as green manuring, crop rotation, integrated pest management and integrated plant nutrition to reduce use of agricultural chemicals;
- improved infrastructures (credit, processing, rural services) along with cottage industries and other employment, including off-farm livelihood opportunities;
- conservation and use of land, water and animal and plant genetic resources (which in turn are essential aspects of combating desertification and loss of bio-diversity);
- adoption of policies to increase production of renewable energy and promote an appropriate mix of fossil and renewable energy use.

Agenda 21 recognised that success would depend on: participation of rural people, including women, the devolution of responsibilities to local level, change in the role of government towards better resource allocation policies, access to land, strengthened public agricultural research respecting traditional knowledge and techniques, and so on. FAO was appointed the lead agency to ensure that these changes in approach happen throughout the UN system. In addition to developing common strategies across the UN, FAO has launched a number of programmes across the developing world, often in partnership with NGOs.

The Ecologist magazine has been the most persistent critic of these reorientations. In two issues of 1991 it highlighted the following deficiencies in the SARD documentation: it ignores demands of popular movements (but argues spuriously for participation), ignores successes of traditional agriculture, does not take a radical enough line on land ownership, encourages the market against peasants' demand to stay out of it, and devotes the best land for cash/export crops (despite evidence that they are not necessarily the answer); it zones land into high and low potential and argues for intensification (including monocropping and livestock rearing) on high-potential land with strong reliance on external inputs, and resettlement programmes are recommended where there is 'overpopulation'. *The Ecologist*'s critique is that FAO is seeking to dress up its conventional dualistic agricultural strategy as an environmentally sustainable one. Its projections of chemical use, for example, are for massive increases in both fertilisers and pesticides throughout Asia, Africa and Latin America. And all this is based on population and production statistics which are widely believed to be full of error.

A more challenging statement came from UNDP (1992) in drawing up a conceptual and operational approach to sustainable agriculture and rural development. This speaks about the 'learning of very new perceptions' and the need for a global initiative to re-educate the armies of specialists in agriculture. The document lists considerations 'which should be ingrained in programme and project conceptualisation and implementation checklist' (UNDP, 1992: Ch 2.4). These included:

- farmers' involvement in technology generation;
- a participatory and gender-sensitive approach in every phase of the programme;
- the decentralisation of research from IARCs and reorient extension to farmers' needs, and to work in partnership with farmers;
- high genetic diversity of crops;
- breeding for high yields with modest nutrient levels;
- more attention to local agro-ecology;

- more imaginative use of variety of basic agricultural technologies (water and soil conservation, rotations, sequences, agro-forestry, nutrient recycling, livestock–crop mixtures, alley cropping, etc.);
- farming systems research and extension;
- participatory rural appraisal;
- put people's priorities first – deal with their livelihood issues;
- decentralise, devolve, delegate, and privatise – responses to complexity and diversity.

The picture in the 1990s, then, is mixed. The major international organisations are divided over agricultural development policy as never before. Substantial factions are going against the trend of research and development of the last five decades, and are searching for alternative principles to those of industrial agriculture. As we will see in Chapter 6, FAO has also developed a significantly new holistic (and now more participatory) approach to extension and farmer involvement in research and policy. Nevertheless, there is still a tendency to bolt on additional components to existing systems, rather than overhaul the system.

Integrated pest management

Take Integrated Pest Management (IPM). IPM's principle is to minimise pesticide use by increasing diversity of, and improving balance between, life forms in a farm system. It emphasises techniques such as crop rotation and succession, companion planting, planting pest repellants, the use of physical barriers, biological predator controls, multi-variety planting, intercropping, and a wide range of specific cultural practices to reduce pest habitats and increase predator survival. IPM advocates called for pest-resistant varietal development – and this type of research has yielded enormous benefits (Lipton and Longhurst, 1989: 80–8). They have also advocated the development of less persistent chemicals, which is now a reality with the move away from organo-chlorines and organo-phosphates and the development of optically engineered agro-chemicals, which require less of the active ingredient.

The difficulties with IPM are significant. It requires a radical redesign of farming systems, not just tinkering at the margins. A farmer needs the capacity to predict outbreaks of pests or disease; all aspects of farm management must take pest control into consideration; all of which requires the farmer to develop a better understanding of pest ecology and pest population dynamics. The farmer also has to make judgements about when the farm is sustaining 'economic damage', and therefore when to use the last resort of chemical controls. The redesign of the farming system is within an entirely new framework of thinking. Whereas previously farmers have, under the influence of industrial science, tried to reduce diversity, create uniformity, keep nature at bay, they are now being asked to promote agro-eco-system diversity! There will be tendencies to bolt on new technologies too: the demand for biological predator controls is now enormous; they are often simply expected to substitute for chemicals.

Sustainable agriculture as a radical alternative

In the now extensive literature there is a range of meanings given to sustainable development. The main focus of these is on the need to satisfy the needs of present generations but avoid compromising the interests of future generations by degrading the resource base (WCED, 1987). Sustainable agriculture is also frequently defined more broadly: ecologically sound; economically viable; socially just; humane and adaptable (Reijntjes *et al.*, 1992: 2) – a set of ideals which may well conflict with each other, or be adopted in different ways by each interested party. While this is not a helpful extension of the word 'sustainable', its frequency indicates that thinking about sustainability cannot easily be contained within a narrow definition. Nevertheless, it is argued here that the concept needs to be narrowly defined, so that it can be operational and contribute to real change.

In the southern hemisphere there is a wider spread of concerns about sustainable agriculture than in the north due to the geographically more limited use of Green Revolution methods. Converting chemically and energy intensive farms (the main issue in the north) is a subject which has received little attention outside the large-scale commercial sector, where there is some production for the international organic market. Of much wider interest has been the protecting and developing of indigenous systems which remain ecologically sound, and linking these with markets in the south which recognise the quality of their products, as well as with such markets in the north.

There are three broad sets of principles emerging to guide the technical search for sustainable agriculture solutions. First, is the rejection of industrial production methods and the search for effective, productive and economic low external input systems. These systems may not be low input in totality, as a very high level of input may be produced on the farm. Farms with large labour inputs and/or well-integrated farming systems might well use a low level of external input, but be high internal input and (hopefully) high output systems. Second, is the greater involvement of farmers themselves and the cherishing and understanding of indigenous knowledge about agriculture and natural resource management. This knowledge is the basis on which development occurs. If it has been degraded through history, it will have to be recovered before progress can be made. This would include knowledge of genetic varieties and technologies which may have been lost. And third, is the incorporation of active resource conservation (even resource enhancement) firmly into a production framework. Each of these will be briefly considered in turn.

Low external inputs

Natural ecological systems and traditional peasant farming are both characterised by internal recycling of energy and nutrients and a high degree of self-sufficiency by comparison with industrial farming. There is a search for complementarities and diversity and synergy among the elements of a farming system, so that stability and productivity can be enhanced. There is thus a rejection of much modern, compartmentalised scientific research, and a preference for holistically derived knowledge, which can be generated by science as well as practitioners.

In practical terms this means a focus on the soil, and getting the right conditions for plants to grow and animals to thrive, through the management of organic matter and tillage, by limiting nutrient losses from erosion, leaching, removal of wastes, etc.; by capturing and managing nutrients, and supplementing them where necessary. Farmers manage microclimates, controlling temperature and sun, managing water flows and preventing erosion. They minimise losses due to pests and diseases, with an emphasis on prevention and exploiting disease tolerance. Combinations of crops, combinations of livestock, crops and livestock, crops with wild plants and animals (predators), and trees are used to maximise synergy and complementarity (Reijntjes *et al.*, 1992).

Indigenous knowledge and management by farmers

Time and again it has been shown that farmers deliberately accumulate knowledge through experimentation and borrowing ideas. Peasant farmers have also often inherited a rich variety of indigenous technical know-how. Certain aspects of this knowledge – the genetic resources developed by farmers and herders over millenia – have long been recognised by commercially motivated scientists and made use of for profit. Only recently, however, has indigenous technical knowledge and scientific method been more widely recognised by development academics and then agencies, and efforts made to incorporate it into some programmes. Women are often considerable knowledge resources, and their knowledge tends to complement that of men as there is often a gender-based division of labour. There is a vast diversity of indigenous knowledge: for example, in the use of wild plants in pest control (Pretty, 1995: 102), or veterinary medicine. It may be that the process of 'development' has eroded this knowledge, in which case it should be recaptured as far as possible by whatever methods are available. This is further elaborated in Chapter 3.

Integrating conservation

Whereas conventional agriculture has until recently focused almost exclusively on soil and water conservation, often using inappropriate industrial approaches to achieving conservation objectives, sustainable agriculture incorporates a much wider range of resource-conserving and enhancing technologies and processes. These include genetic conservation and bio-diversity, the conservation of soil life, and wildlife conservation. The new approaches to soil and water conservation which rely on on-farm vegetative measures and cultivation practices are much more compatible with this wider notion of resource enhancement than the conventional mechanical or engineering approaches. Conventional agriculture treated conservation as a bolt-on activity. In sustainable agriculture it is integral. The reason for this is that if resources are lost to the farm, in a low external input system, it is very difficult to recover them. Within the wider ecological perspective which informs sustainable agriculture, conserving bio-diversity is an objective in its own right.

From these three 'technical' principles flow certain institutional principles, which will be the subject of subsequent chapters – participatory technology development, local institutional development in the control of natural and other resources, and interdisciplinary approaches to development work. Here one only will be emphasised. While many aspects of agricultural development do concern the farm as a unit (business or subsistence, or more usually a hybrid), we have seen that many aspects also concern groups of farmers, farmers and farm workers together, consumers and other interest groups. Given the centrality of food – to nutrition and health, economic growth, income distribution – it is logical that these interests should, wherever necessary, be allowed (encouraged) to organise themselves around common tasks and interests and to participate in public debate. While the principle of subsidiarity (decisions being taken at the lowest possible level) should be applied wherever possible, the conventional approach to agricultural development has tended to put decisions only in one of three boxes: the individual enterprise, the state, and the formal co-operative, usually supported by the state. This is to miss the many levels at which decisions can and ought to be taken, so that externalities are recognised and opportunities for joint action are not neglected. A discussion of collective decision-making is the theme of Chapter 3.

The search for purity

It will become increasingly difficult to disentangle sustainable agriculture from mainstream agricultural thinking and practice as the latter takes on elements of the former. From one point of view this is clearly a good thing: it indicates that sustainable agriculture ideas have penetrated deep into the agricultural establishment. But there are dangers too. Conventional ideas can easily masquerade as sustainable agriculture. Hence there is a search for purity and consistency within the sustainable agriculture movement. This has given rise to regulation of production through certification schemes so that the consumer has confidence in what is being produced. In Europe and North America, and increasingly elsewhere, certification schemes and definitions of 'organic', 'biological', 'natural' farming have been enshrined in law, with farmers having to belong to organisations which inspect and certify their produce. This makes it imperative for countries wishing to take advantage of their non-Green Revolution farming systems to export organic produce to engage themselves in the regulation of production. This would be better done by the NGOs promoting organic farming in those countries, keeping in mind the points made below about the need for regulatory frameworks well adapted to the situations in the producing areas.

Given the marginally livelier international trade which will arise as a result of the GATT negotiations, this trend is likely to continue, so that environmentally aware farmers in agriculturally exporting and developing countries can take advantage of export opportunities, as well as produce chemical-free food for the small but growing and influential section of the local population which is concerned. The criticism of this narrow concept of sustainable agriculture is that the countries of the south cannot afford environmental protection, and protection against the health risks of polluted food, since the concerns of most people are simply to fill their stomachs. It is argued here, however, that sustainable agriculture has many advantages for food security, income and employment as well as health and environment, and should at the very least be compared with the advantages and disadvantages of the more conventional approaches to agricultural development.

An assessment of sustainable agriculture

The Green Revolution and conventional agricultural modernisation strategies have come under enormous critical scrutiny during the last twenty-five years. The promotion of sustainable agriculture is new on any scale. It is too soon to assess it in the same way. However, some deductions and inferences from limited evidence can be made.

Inequality and employment

A critical issue which does not feature strongly in debates in the north's sustainable agriculture movement is the social implications of promoting a regulatory approach to the development of sustainable forms of agriculture. Thus the movement risks making the same error committed by advocates of the Green Revolution. Under this scenario, sustainable agriculture will be first adopted by the far-sighted wealthy, in some cases the same families as first adopted the miracle varieties thirty years ago. If there are economic benefits to be gained, these will go to people who least need them. There is therefore an argument for development agencies promoting sustainable agriculture to focus on small farms.

On the other hand, it may be argued that the adoption of sustainable agriculture will create more employment (UNDP, 1994) and should therefore be promoted irrespective of farm size or characteristics. The evidence from 21 case studies on this issue was positive: all increased the demand for labour and spread labour better through the year. Increased demand for labour of a more permanent nature should, other things being equal, lead to improved incomes for labourers. In situations where sustainable agriculture increases the return to labour (more farm output or income per unit of labour employed) as well as the demand for labour, farm labourers' wages will improve. However, where agriculture is very chemically intensive and farm output or income already high, there is likely to be a period of reduced output and income before a more sustainable system can compete with the previous high chemical input system in terms of economic returns. Where this is the case, there will be a conversion period during which the new system takes hold; farmers can convert their farms parcel by parcel to reduce the loss of income; subsidies could be offered at this point to help farmers over that conversion period, as is now the practice in most of Europe. In two cases studied by UNDP, returns to labour in agriculture could not compete with tourism or logging, and the availability of labour at a price farmers could afford was therefore a constraint. Where this is the case, mechanisation and the development of high-value farm enterprises would be an appropriate response.

Some of the major adopting farms are estates belonging to multinational corporations or large local businesses. The benefits to workers should include not only more employment (hours of work, extra labour employed), but also less risky and unhealthy working conditions, as the use of chemicals diminishes. However, given that these workers are often very poorly paid, and a significant proportion are migrant labourers, casually employed at peak seasons of demand for labour, and that big farms have often become quite capital-intensive over the years, the overall effect on labour-demand, and wage levels, is likely to be limited.

The alternative, more difficult course of action for the movement is to commit itself to a social analysis in poor countries, which it has failed so far to do in the wealthy countries where demand for organically produced food is most advanced. The case for this has been put by the Brazilian biological agriculture movement as seen in this extract from one of its sets of regulations (Box 2.1).

This is a more difficult strategy because small farmers are hard to reach; the agencies which have historically worked with them are often still committed to conventional approaches, and would thus require a long and painful adjustment process. In practice it means that the northern sustainable agriculture organisations promoting trade in sustainably produced commodities (which are of course far more plentiful in poor countries than in rich) need to work alongside development agencies who can guide them in social analysis.

On the other hand, there is some hope that because small farms typically (but not always) have more labour at their disposal per

---

BOX 2.1

Extract from Brazilian biodynamic regulations

Human aspects
2.4 – The concept 'ecological' includes necessarily the *human* aspects. Organic or biodinamic products should be in accordance with the criteria defined by IFOAM-LA: 'ecologically sustainable, economically viable, socially fair'.

Therefore, in order to be recognised as organic or biodynamic, an enterprise must have as its central goal not merely the fulfilment of economic objectives, but rather *to answer society's needs*, in at least these three levels: i) to offer the needed products; ii) to care for the earth (the environment); iii) the work itself within the enterprise should represent an opportunity (not a constraint!) of *human development* for all persons involved.

Appropriate scale
2.5 – Regarding the *production scale*: small and medium units (organisms) are by their own nature nearer to ecological standards. This does not exclude the possibility of larger units to get their recognition, as long as they accomplish all conditions of these Guidelines, also in the social sense.

Diversity and plurality
2.5.1 – Also on the human level, *respect for diversity or plurality* is the ecological virtue par excellence. This implies the possibility of harmonic convivium between different models and scales of organisation. It is not considered suitable for an organic or biodynamic professional to take part in organisations or activities that aim at preventing or suppressing different ways of organisation. The defence of a space for the existence of a given organisational model may be justified – but never its imposition to society as the only and excludent model.

Source: Harkaly (1991: 77).

hectare and sustainable agriculture is by nature more labour-intensive, and because they have less capacity to operate Green Revolution (GR) technology without negative side effects, they will be the 'natural home' for sustainable agriculture. But this potential will only be realised if the big commercial producers with an eye for the market do not steal the show from the start.

There have been so few studies of this subject as yet that important issues like the impact of sustainable agriculture practices on labour generally or women in particular have hardly been raised. It would undoubtedly be foolish to generalise any expectation. However, women in small farmer households are often knowledgeable about the farming and eco-system: the value of this knowledge will be enhanced. Additional labour may be required to substitute for external inputs: this may hit women hard if they are expected to provide the bulk of it. There is likely to be even more need than usual to make studies of women's time allocation, and to research tools and practices which can reduce their work burden.

Food security

The major lesson of twenty years' study of food security is that it does not depend on food production alone – at household, region or country level. It depends to a greater extent on people's ability to command the resources to acquire the food they need – whether that be through production, farm production of cash crops, other income-earning activities, employment, or remittances. It also depends on the degree to which there are effective local, national and even international institutions and political systems capable of monitoring and providing for scarcities.

In terms of the share of income accruing to labour, sustainable agriculture in principle offers higher returns since external inputs are less. And, especially in marginal areas where industrial methods have not yet penetrated, the type of intensification represented by sustainable agriculture will increase overall production significantly, and with more stability than GR techniques (Maninfeld, 1989; UNDP, 1994). In no way does this deny the need for improved moisture control through irrigation in drought-prone areas, or the value of increasing farmers' choice of seed variety to plant, provided the crops or varieties are suitable for low external input conditions. The major problems for sustainable agriculture lie in the GR areas themselves, where farmers use high levels of chemicals and have reduced the diversity of their cropping systems, taken livestock out of the system, and controlled nature to a high degree. Here there is an issue of conversion, which needs to be organised in such a way that overall income is reduced as little as possible, even if production levels suffer a little.

It was argued above that large quantities of low-grade basic staple food may be a liability for poor countries as much as for rich, and that structural adjustment programmes are making a case for reducing the public procurement functions of food security systems, and for the elimination of the subsidies which have supported GR agriculture since its inception. This will create a fairer basis on which sustainable agriculture will have a greater chance of flourishing. One would expect to see a greater diversity of farming system emerging in GR areas, as farmers look for higher value outputs and reduce their dependence on increasingly expensive chemicals. If subsidies are removed from mechanisation (e.g. on fuel, machinery) and water use, beneficial innovation is to be expected in these fields too.

The analysis of peasant production current in the sustainable agriculture movement is an idealistic ecologism – that sustainable agriculture should focus on developing production firstly for consumption by the peasant family, secondly for very local markets, and preferably not for export, because export agriculture is naively understood to be against the interests of rural peoples' food security. There may be many arguments in favour of developing subsistence production and local markets: these should undoubtedly be explored in the context of food security, income distribution, and environmental costs and benefits, but export agriculture should not, at this current juncture, be ruled out. It may indeed be a key to the development of more sustainable forms of agriculture if it provides a market for sustainably produced products which would not otherwise exist. In fact export and food crop production tends to increase together in a farming system, becoming more productive as a whole, so there may be no contradiction. We have already seen that it is exported crops which often require greater use of agro-chemicals in their production and storage; changing this will deliver major benefits to those working the farms as well as to consumers.

Given historically unfavourable trends in terms of trade for agricultural and other primary produce, any reliance on exports, however compelling the logic from a national economic point of view, carries great pitfalls for producers. Government marketing policies which effectively tax producers can be modified: structural adjustment programmes seek to do this. Beyond this, there are still tariff barriers against exports of processed or semi-processed raw materials into the European Union and other wealthy trading blocs. These prevent primary producers from participating in the potential value-added aspect of the final product. Sustainable agriculture can equally be affected by these forces: hence the need to link efforts with fair trading systems wherever possible.

There is a growing move to link sustainable agriculture with fair trade initiatives (Michaud, 1995). This is sensible, and can help to overcome prejudices against international trade, if it is seen to be conducted on as fair a basis as possible. The developmental principles embodied in fair trading practices nicely complement the ecological principles of sustainable agriculture. The strong emphasis of sustainable agriculture proponents on local markets and maximising on-farm and local value-added is consistent with attempting to even out the availability of employment, and thus wage rates between regions. In general, increasing the proportion of farm product value going to labour – whether family or hired – must be a good thing for food security. Nevertheless it would be unreasonable to expect that sustainable agriculture will solve the economic problems of marginal regions – though it may have much to offer (Maninfeld, 1989). In extreme cases such regions may require other sources of income – tourism, hunting, industry – or investment in appropriate education to enable out-migration with skills.

The impact of sustainable agriculture on overall production and prices – key aspects of food security in any society – is likely to be varied. Where production is labour- but not land-intensive, there may well be scope for increasing production, thus keeping prices down, and increasing the share of farm income going to labour. This would be the sort of result expected from areas like Machakos in Kenya (Tiffen *et al.*, 1994). Even where production is highly land- and relatively chemical-intensive, as in China, there is frequently still scope for further intensification and increased production through non-chemical means (Zhaoqian, 1992).

The availability of labour can of course present an enormous constraint on many innovations. Generally, intensification of agriculture – the foundation of much of what is currently thought of as sustainable agriculture – occurs partly as a result of population growth (Boserup, 1965; Tiffen *et al.*, 1994). Where population is very sparse, where family labour is stretched over competing activities and people looking for work typically migrate to other areas, intensification may not be viable as a strategy for increasing production and incomes. This is the point at which the sustainable agriculture movement is perhaps weakest, not for intrinsic reasons, but because little work has been done on the issue. Dryland areas can benefit from sustainable agriculture approaches, as argued by Maninfeld (1989) for Botswana. While the difficulties of crop production may be greater, the advantage to be gained from developing improvements is often substantial. Farmers in such areas commonly aim for greater security rather than high yields anyway, so conservation of soil and moisture will form the basis of sustainable farming. However, by themselves, physical conservation methods are not enough without improvements in on-farm fertility from the low levels to which it has often sunk in degraded systems. Mixed farming, the use of organic manures, appropriate land preparation methods, inter- and multi-cropping, rotations, composting, mulching, agro-forestry and many more techniques are available to improve soils and enhance the security of production (Maninfeld, 1989).

Nevertheless, there are preconditions which make it worthwhile and possible for people to invest additional labour. The Machakos study referred to earlier suggests that market conditions must be right, infrastructure (mainly roads for marketing) in place, the knowledge available to stimulate innovation, and the social organisation to enable the investment of labour. In the Machakos district of Kenya these factors were all present; other semi-arid districts have fared less well. In any case, much of the production increase in Machakos happened in the higher-potential areas where the cost–benefit ratio for investment of labour was better.

Where the preconditions do not exist, farming system analysis (Chapter 6) may still produce potential improvements which can enhance both sustainability and production, but non-farm (or other farm) activities and social security systems are likely to be of greater importance. Even in the increasingly unusual case where agriculture is largely subsistence oriented, low external input farming practices are attractive, as they can increase food self-sufficiency without expenditure of much cash.

Health and environment

Since sustainable agriculture has developed as a result of health and environmental concerns, it would be ironic if there were not evident benefits in these fields. As we have seen, the health impact of the Green Revolution has been very little studied; comparative studies are not surprisingly a very new field, and so far confined to industrial countries. For example, in Denmark it was found that male sperm counts were twice as high in consumers of organic produce compared with the rest of the population – and declining sperm counts is a feature of industrial society. This has now been replicated in the UK.

Environmentally, research has shown that species diversity is greater on organic than on non-organic farms in the north. Birdlife, insect and plant diversity is all significantly greater: not surprisingly since the organic farmer attempts to live with nature rather than control it to a greater extent than the conventional farmer. However, the health and environmental benefits of non-Green Revolution agriculture would be much easier to substantiate in the south where careful comparisons can be made between regions where chemicals are widely used and those where their use is insignificant. This is a key area in which research needs to be funded.

Sustainable agriculture and the wider development paradigm

In some respects the move to sustainable agriculture is helped by shifts in international economic policy; in other ways it contradicts them. We have noted that reduction in subsidies on agro-chemicals has persuaded many small (and other) farmers to use less, or to stop using them altogether, and has improved the economics of alternative fertility and pest control measures. Likewise, reduction in subsidies on fuel will assist labour-intensive agricultural strategies. However, freer trade may give advantages to primary producers who are still supported by subsidies or protected in other ways, and undermine local markets in other countries. In general, the new paradigm would support primacy in policy for local markets in a hierarchy of local—international exchanges, because the development of local markets has greater spinoffs for the poor and vulnerable in primary producer countries, and because a close link between producers and consumers is a desirable characteristic of any well-functioning market. This may only be able to function when the negative externalities of free trade are internalised by the enterprises producing them, or when trade is taxed in order to contain these externalities.

A significant externality is the pollution from heavy goods transport on the roads or by air. Little progress has been made in charging polluters for the damage, nor in improving the planet's capacity as a sink for pollutants. An environmentally sustainable free trade policy would have to recognise this by promoting carbon taxes or other pollution-reducing measures. The GATT negotiations signally failed to take account of such issues. This highlights the fact that the sustainable agriculture movement has to have an active political front: it is not merely a matter of technology development. It challenges the international consensus over trade, international institutions (like the FAO and the international research centres), and the economic principles underlying the international economy.

The case for sustainable agriculture should not be seen as an argument for zero economic growth. It is rather about the quality of growth. Increasing populations have to be fed, and raising nutritional standards is a very important objective for most poor countries. The economic case for sustainable agriculture is that it permits a pattern of savings, investment and distribution of income which will help alleviate poverty and generate higher returns to labour at less cost to the environment and human health than available alternatives. It contributes to an enhanced quality of growth. If macro-economic measures are needed to protect that quality of growth, that is an issue which the international community should be persuaded to take on board.

3

Common Goods

Rural development is clearly about improving the life chances and well-being of individuals and households, particularly the mass of rural poor who have been left behind in the process of economic growth. The dominant western strategy has always involved a focus on individuals and households, and assumptions that they exist in a context of well-functioning markets. Where markets do not function ('market failure'), strategists resort to the state to provide and control.

However, all of these individuals and households depend quite directly on non-marketed common property resources for their livelihood. This is obviously true for marginalised societies such as pastoralists, landless and quasi-landless households, and, within peasant households, for women, who often have a strong role in taking animals to graze, collecting firewood out of common forests, and collecting water from common supplies. In many peasant societies all households rely on common sources of drinking and irrigation water, common forests and pastures. The well-being of these societies depends substantially on the availability, quality, and sustainability of these resources. Access to them is critical for survival; their construction and maintenance are important tasks which must be accomplished, usually on a collective basis.

Common goods (sometimes called common pool resources) are a special type of public good. There is an important distinction between common and public goods. Public goods are those from which no one can be excluded: protection against air or water pollution generally benefits everyone. It would be impossible to charge air users, but it is possible to fine or tax air polluters. Water users can generally be charged: this makes water a 'toll' good. Roads are the classic toll good. These are public goods for which a charge can be levied. If people are excluded from benefiting – those who do not pay, or who do not live in a certain area, or are not members of a certain organisation or kinship group – and if benefits are positively allocated to a restricted membership, then we can speak about common goods, or common pool resources. Common goods therefore overlap with toll goods, but are not necessarily toll goods: membership may be by ascription, or residence. The term is generally used to refer to cases where members identify with the good in question and perceive it as common to themselves. It often refers to local resources.

Just as there are common goods, so there are common bads. Floods, or forest fires, events which generally affect the residents of certain areas and from which those residents require protection, are examples. Protection can be assured and organised locally, in which case it will only stretch so far and no further. Some mechanism of local governance is required to enable the achievement of this common good. Sometimes hazards are so widespread that protection against them takes on the character of a public good. Similarly common goods are often regarded in law as public goods: there is often much confusion. Sometimes this is deliberate: nationalisation of a resource may be designed to facilitate transfer of access from one social group to another.

Rural development and common goods

Governments and rural development efforts have a bad record of substituting public for what should be common goods. Many of the above resources have been nationalised in many countries – usually over the heads of people who think of the resources as, collectively, 'theirs'. The tendency of state-led rural development in support of private enterprise has been to take over the provision and maintenance of naturally or previously collectively supplied goods. Then, having committed themselves in this way many states have not had the resources to honour their commitments, leaving substantial areas of provision unmet or subject to poor quality and low levels of maintenance. Centralised, competitive political processes have at the same time contributed to the decline of local institutions and leadership patterns which could have taken up the unmet commitments. In some cases centralised states have actively prevented local communities or groups developing collective, locally appropriate provisions. In customary law there are often complex layers of rights to use common pool resources, which are completely disregarded by legislated nationalisations or privatisation. It is important that rural development workers criticise these acts of disenfranchisement, fight them in the courts where relevant, and strengthen commoners' claims over common pool resources.

There are new (or newly conceptualised) commons as well as old – genetic resources, for example. And there is scope for creating new commons in particular from resources previously under state control, but also from privately owned resources where ownership rights are becoming increasingly conditional. The new rural development agenda involves moving from a defensive to an aggressive position on commons: exploiting opportunities to create new ones, and recreate old ones, as well as defending existing commons.

Paradoxically, while states were busy taking over functions to which they could not do justice, they also naively promoted 'community development'. In many cases this turned out to mean the development of a village elite favourable to the central power, and allowing a trickle of funds to enable them to patronise supporters in the village. Among other things, village elites used their influence to privatise village common land which was an important part of the survival kit of the rural poor (Jodha, 1991).

State-controlled co-operative movements were another tool used in the same way. In fact the left-liberal or statist strain of rural development has consistently sought to develop new – and perfect – common institutions, community spirit and co-operative enterprise, and mistakenly frowned on individual enterprise and archaic (imperfect) institutions. These institutions usually led to the development of the few and the exclusion of the many. Typically, the poor, women, and minority groups were excluded, or benefited significantly less. These 'perfect' institutions were often too complex for ordinary members to understand, and assisted with external resources to grow too rapidly. The generation of internal resources was neglected, and external sponsors (usually governments) used the institutions to legitimate themselves (and sometimes to enrich themselves).

A later generation of development programmes promoted 'self-help' and 'self-sufficiency' as a method of spreading the benefits of development more rapidly to a larger group of people. In the 1970s, prompted by the criticisms of the 'development equals growth' school of thought, a strong concern emerged for the participation of the poor in both state-led development and self-help efforts. This did not rely so much on the notion of a village as a community, characterised by equality and solidarity, and therefore good at working together for mutual benefit, as on the idea of groups with sufficient common interest to support each other in enterprises or common services. This represented progress conceptually, but practice often lagged behind, stuck with idealistic notions of community self-help.

Community development and self-help efforts relied heavily on idealism and altruism among participants if they were to work effectively in managing common resources or providing common services. Sociological analyses, such as those conducted for the United Nations Research Institute on Social Development (UN-RISD) (e.g. Inayatullah, 1972) and the International Labour Organisation (ILO) (e.g. Curtis *et al.*, 1979) in the 1970s and early 1980s, shed some light on why certain collectivities succeeded while others failed. These studies situated particular collective initiatives in a wider analysis of the social structure and process of particular societies. Some generalisations were possible on the basis of comparative study – for example, that co-operatives whose members were relatively homogeneous in socio-economic terms were more likely to succeed than those with sharply differentiated memberships (Inayatullah, 1972). There also emerged a more general pessimism about the prospects for collective action, since there seemed to be few success stories which were not highly context-specific. This was reflected in the virtual demise of collectivist solutions in the 1980s.

A more rigorous theoretical approach to the understanding of collective action has awaited the development of the new economics of institutional rational choice by economists and political scientists working on common property problems as policy issues. In enabling professionals and policy-makers to understand what the options for collective action might be in particular contexts, these writers have made it possible to be much less idealistic and wishy-washy about co-operation and much less pessimistic about the possibilities for well-managed common property in the modern world. They have begun to make it conceptually possible to think of renewing and creating common properties, as a better option than privatising or resorting to state control. This means working with people who are struggling to manage common property.

Reintroducing the notion of common property as central to the new rural development paradigm has other advantages too: it does not presume any kind of community of interest among the members of natural 'communities' (i.e. villages, administrative areas, etc.). Community of interest has to be discovered, and conflict among common property users is seen as the norm: the work of development agencies, in co-operation with users, is to evolve solutions to conflict of interest which advance the cause of the poor, of women, and of oppressed minorities. This may involve legal and institutional changes which have to be lobbied for.

The new institutional economics and common property

Until the 1980s, models of how common property resources are managed have been very crude. They have generally been dismissive of the possibility that groups of people with different and often competing interests can use and manage a resource in common. The phrase 'tragedy of the commons' says it all: policy prescriptions resulting from these crude models have tended to conclude that commons should be privatised or that 'the government' should regulate their use. Institutional economics applies economic concepts of rationality, and the calculation of costs and benefits to the analysis of institutions for the common good. 'The government' becomes one (or several) actor(s) in these models; but the most important actors are the users and managers. This economics is useful to analyse situations where commons users struggle to operate their common (be it land, water, forest, a fishery, or a computer network) through the development of operating strategies, rules and constitutions. Rather than government, it is better here to speak about the process of governance. This may be carried out by a government (village, local or central), or by an organisation of civil society.

The economist's basic strategy is

> to identify those aspects of the physical, cultural and institutional setting that are likely to affect the determination of who is to be involved in a situation, the actions they can take and the costs of those actions, the outcomes that can be achieved, how actions are linked to outcomes, what information is to be available, how much control individuals can exercise, and what payoffs are to be assigned to particular combinations of actions and outcomes. Once one has all the needed information, one can then abstract from the richness of the empirical situation to devise a playable

game that will capture the essence of the problems individuals are facing. (Ostrom, 1990: 55)

The key concepts for the analysis of common property resources (CPRs) are:

1. the *resource system,* which produces
2. a flow of *resource units,* which can be used by
3. *appropriators,* who may or may not be the same people as the
4. *providers,* who create or maintain the resource system.

- Appropriators learn about the impact of their actions on themselves and others through *trial and error* over a period of time.
- Their decisions are affected by their time horizon: usually local appropriators expect their children and grandchildren to make use of the resource system, so they will have a low *discounting rate* for future benefits.
- The behaviour of all parties is affected by *values* of right and wrong and the degree of *opportunism* expected of other parties, and the degree of *trust* and *sense of community.*

In most CPRs, resource units are *subtractable* – one appropriator's use affects that of others. This distinguishes CPRs from public goods, where 'appropriation problems do not exist because resource units are not subtractable' (Ostrom, 1990: 49).

Decisions to co-operate depend on expected benefits, expected costs, internal norms and discount rates, in the context of an external world which affects all of these. These decisions are complex and involve weighing many uncertainties. (i) A successful working arrangement be based on rules which can be agreed. (ii) It must generate continued widespread commitment to those rules. (iii) It must engage in mutual monitoring to support individuals' commitment to the rules and to the process of rule-making. (iv) Appropriators need to be assured that the (marginal) benefits of appropriation are greater than the (marginal) costs. Open-access CPRs are likely to fail in this, as users have no incentive to leave resource units for other users. In a limited-access CPR used by a well-defined group, 'the incentives facing the appropriators will depend on the rules governing the quantity, timing, location and technology of appropriation, and how these are monitored and enforced' (Ostrom, 1990: 48). (v) Investment in the resource itself must be adequate to maintain or improve it, and appropriators' current use must not be at the expense of future use.

Decisions about CPR management occur at different levels: the *operational* level (where well-known rules govern appropriation, provision, monitoring and enforcement), the *collective or management* level (where policies are made and disputes resolved), and the *constitutional* level (where eligibility to make rules and manage is decided). People involved in commons move between these different levels of decision, and all are important in determining whether a CPR is well managed.

For common property resources to be managed sustainably in environmental and equity terms the rules may need to change. Successful change, whoever proposes it, requires support from interested parties. Economics holds that individuals assess alternative rules and the costs and benefits of making changes rationally (Ostrom, 1990: 194). However, the data to model individual behaviour adequately rarely exists, so that the analyst must be familiar with the situation as different parties experience it, and identify the 'situational variables' which will affect individuals' judgments about the benefits and costs of changing the rules. These would include: the type of rule change proposed; the skills and assets of leaders; the degree of autonomy available in changing rules; the heterogeneity of interests involved, and so on (Ostrom, 1990: 194–207).

Setting new rules is extremely difficult: it is often impossible to calculate the effects of the new rules with any accuracy. People will weigh likely costs and benefits in a biased way (losses are weighed more heavily than gains; recent experience figures more prominently in people's minds than the more remote past; small changes are less opposed than big, etc.). Different groups of appropriators may have quite conflicting interests and derive very different levels of benefit from existing or proposed arrangements. It will be easier to agree new rules where:

1. Most appropriators share a common judgment that they will be harmed if they do not adopt an alternative rule.
2. Most appropriators will be affected in similar ways by the proposed rule changes.
3. Most appropriators highly value the continuation activities from this CPR; in other words, they have low discount rates.

4. Appropriators face relatively low information, [rule] transformation and enforcement costs.
5. Most appropriators share generalised norms of reciprocity and trust that can be used as initial social capital.
6. The group appropriating from the CPR is relatively small and stable. (Ostrom, 1990: 211)

These conclusions are similar to those of the UNRISD studies mentioned above, and are from common sense. Where such conditions do not apply, CPR management may be enhanced (or simply made possible) by external intervention. However, in the interest of strengthening the institution managing the CPR, governments or other external agencies should not intervene without acquiring a great deal of understanding of the situation, and the different interests involved; they would act in support of local, sustainable institutional solutions rather than taking over the rule-making and other management tasks. Social scientists working on these problems should be able to address their ideas as much to the users as to the agency which has employed them to give advice. Government provides the legal and institutional framework – the courts, policy fora in local government, wider policy formulation. But it should be wary of providing and managing the solution.

Critical issues in the application of the new economics

In its support for local and popular institutions, and in its recognition of the limits to government or external action, the new economics is progressive. Like all economic theorising and modelling, however, there remain strongly mechanistic notions at the heart of institutional economics. It assumes a material rationality, and relegates many important issues to the realm of values or norms. It needs to be complemented by social analysis, which would stress the importance of informal relationships and networks, cross-cutting ties and sources of motivation, the importance of politics, and the existence of altruism based on personal or social philosophies which reject or qualify materialism. A social analysis would also investigate the worldview and knowledge system upon which particular management strategies are based: economics assumes the disembedded (detached), contextless (universal) system of knowledge of modern industrial society; but many societies operate with knowledge systems which are firmly embedded in a complex of thought and practice, and applied in a local context.

In any particular case the range of variables may be so complex as to defy easy analysis. People's perceptions of a situation also frequently vary from an 'objective' (external) analysis of their interests because of the social, political and philosophical complexities involved. Model building can be done in a participatory way, however, such that interested parties are involved, share in the information which is generated, and are then in a stronger position to retain decision-making powers in a local arena.

The remainder of this chapter examines the salient issues for rural development of common property resource creation and management, and the development of common services and infrastructure. It begins with an examination of two currently highly controversial fields of activities – genetic resources and forests – and argues that there is scope for new common goods. This argument is carried forward with an examination of irrigation water, where the best examples of indigenous CPRs exist. The second part of the chapter applies a similar range of ideas to common services, with health as the major example.

Genetic resources

Genetic resources of importance in agriculture (and medicine, but this section will focus on agriculture) are increasingly considered to be public goods. However, plants and animals have in fact been selected over millenia by farmers and herders, and the stock of plant and animal genetic material we have today is a product of a myriad selection processes. In the more agrarian societies this process of selection is still going on today in a very significant way, whereas it has given way to scientific or industrial research in richer countries. The process of selection happens among farmers skilled at the job; it is a community process, in the sense that farmers share seeds and animal genes on a local and regional basis, either through market mechanisms or mutual exchange. In this sense, genetic resources have been common property.

With the advent of biotechnology and the concentration of ownership of the international seed business in the hands of a few transnational corporations (TNCs), seeds and animal genetics have become big business. This has given new momentum to bio-diversity conservation, but has also introduced new international laws enabling TNCs and public sector plant-breeding organisations, mostly based in the north, to patent genetic material developed out of original material collected mostly in the south. The TNCs are seeking to convert common into private property. The concept of breeders' rights (to the genetic material they create) is now being counterposed with farmers' rights. Giving recognition to, valuing and making real these rights is an exciting and new area in rural development. Like many rights issues it requires linking local and international, development and advocacy work.

The expansion of human settlement from Africa through the other continents has led to huge loss of habitat, much more so in the new continents than in Africa itself. The resulting loss of species has been accompanied by the encroachment of a smaller number of species which flourish in the world human beings create. In recent history we know we have lost '0.15% of plants since 1600, 1.2% of birds, and 2% of mammals . . . 10% of mammals and birds are under a significant degree of threat, along with over 7% of plants' (Tolba *et al.*, 1992: 193–4). Most of these losses have been in the last 100 years. The rate of loss has accelerated with industrialisation and twentieth-century economic development.

There is no comprehensive information available about the impact of genetic erosion. It would be sensible to adopt the 'precautionary principle' and avoid reducing diversity further. However, the current methods of economic evaluation and resulting incentives in the market do not recognise the services which nature provides; nor do they attempt to differentiate the perspectives which different interest groups may have about the value of particular resources.

The breeding undertaken by farmers and herders over the centuries promotes genetic diversity, through adapting plants and animals to particular ecological niches. The breeding undertaken by scientific/industrial methods reduces diversity and creates monocultures. The Green Revolution has led to enormous erosion of varieties of rice, wheat and maize, as regions and countries have encouraged their farmers to grow few high-response varieties. Awareness of these losses, and the coming of biotechnology as an industry, have changed perceptions about the significance of genetic erosion. Common property genetic resources are now seen as a public good which must be made available for exploitation, 'for the good of humanity'.

Mooney (1983) has clearly demonstrated how agro-chemical TNCs have gained a substantial hold over seeds and other genetic resources by buying up substantial proportions of the largely family-owned seed companies in Europe and North America. This is a dangerous trend for several reasons. Firstly, private ownership of genetic resources erodes what has often been a valuable common property. Secondly, TNCs have used their wide distribution systems developed for the sale of agro-chemicals to market their seeds, and with the help of aid programmes and government subsidies have captured sizeable shares of many markets. This has led to genetic erosion – the loss of valuable genetic resources. Some have been preserved in seed/gene banks; but many have been irredeemably lost. Thirdly, the connection between seeds and agro-chemicals marketing means that the development of new seeds is heavily biased towards those which promote the use of agro-chemicals. This has been especially prominent in the recent development of biotechnology, where so many genetically engineered varieties are developed to enable greater use of herbicides in particular.

The TNCs, through their host country governments, have dominated the development of international law and resource flows in plant genetics. The International Board of Plant Genetic Resources (IBPGR) was created by rich countries (through the Ford and Rockefeller Foundations) to ensure access to the world's (which meant in most cases the southern countries) plant genetic resources, through collection and preservation in germplasm banks of those seeds which have immediate use or are threatened with erosion. 'IBPGR priorities in the collection of genetic resources do not necessarily correspond to those of the Third World' (Querol, 1993: 71). IBPGR has mainly supported conservation in industrial countries of species originally from the south. It is not accountable to any UN body.

As a result of this situation, FAO set up its Commission on Plant Genetic Resources, which attempted to include all types of plants, including breeders' lines and modern varieties among the plant genetic resources to be freely exchanged. This was not accepted by a number of industrial countries.

The international Convention on Bio-Diversity signed by the world's governments, with the exception of the USA, at the Rio Conference on Environment and Development in 1992, went to the opposite extreme by legitimising the process of patenting genetic material and at the same time limiting the convention to material collected in future. By refusing to include clear stipulations about the ownership of and rights to existing collections in gene banks or botanical gardens, 'there is thus to be no internationally binding obligation on these gene banks or botanical gardens to pay the countries of origin of the genetic resources, or to share equitably with them the benefits of the use of the materials and the technology' (Shiva and Ramprasad, 1993: 155). 'Much of these materials had been collected from developing countries by international agricultural research institutes, and two-thirds of all seeds collected in gene banks are in industrial countries or are stored in international research centres controlled by northern countries and the World Bank' (Shiva and Ramprasad, 1993: 154).

Genetic resource programmes will be a growth area in rural development in the decades to come. The technical mechanisms for such programmes are not complicated (Querol, 1993). The issue of ownership of knowledge and genetic material will remain controversial, however. Most programmes centralise knowledge and material in public sector institutions. *In situ* conservation – maintaining genetic resources by continually growing the plants – is ethically desirable (since control remains in the hands of the creators) and cheaper. But there are difficulties: even in 'biosphere reserves' there may be intrusion from modern varieties, and land colonisation at the frontier. *In situ* storage in controlled conditions is difficult in many rural areas (Querol, 1993: 147–9). Centralisation and state control is the obvious alternative.

Running gene banks may indeed be a function of the public sector in poor countries in the twentyfirst century, though no doubt the world's leading financial institutions will try to persuade governments to contract this function out to the large-scale (i.e. TNC) private sector. However, farmers and their organisations are increasingly taking matters into their own hands, supported by environmentalists.

In Ethiopia, one of the world's richest sources of plant genetic material, farmers have complex market-based systems for seed exchange, and certain areas specialise in the maintenance of elite and distinct landraces of many crops. It is particularly the more marginal, drought-prone areas where traditional seed material is especially valued; and it is women farmers who frequently know most and are relied on in seed conservation work. Development programmes are taking advantage of such processes to involve farmers in the establishment of 'field genebanks', in this case growing drought-resistant landraces for distribution in or after a drought year. Farmers are involved not only in growing the crops, but in evaluating the resulting seed material (Worede and Mekbib, 1993: 83–4).

Ethiopia is a country where modern varieties have not yet swept away farmers' varieties. Zimbabwe is an ex-settler economy where the modern varieties all but dominate. Only in the marginal, drought-prone 'communal' areas do small farmers still select and cultivate small grains (millet and sorghum). ENDA-Zimbabwe is an environmental NGO working with farmer seed committees to research and assist farmers' seed selection and conservation systems (Mushita, 1993: 85 ff). These efforts have been successful compared with the low success rates of official research, with its emphasis on high response. In a country like Zimbabwe where the official system has denigrated indigenous farming for so long, a conscious effort is needed to rehabilitate it, give it a new image, and build up farmers' confidence.

For these reasons many researchers now advocate participatory research programmes, in which farmers are consulted in the initial selection of germplasm, and their selection criteria are used in breeding on research stations. During breeding there is frequent feedback to farmers. There is then early release of a number of varieties for evaluation and selection under farmer-managed conditions. Finally the scientists co-ordinate farmers' evaluations, and use farmer selected material in further trials. Some of the many efforts to build links between farmers and scientists are covered in de Boef *et al.* (1993).

But this process still leaves researchers in command, and ownership of genetic material unresolved. There is a substantial unrealised development opportunity here: much of the world's remaining untapped agricultural (and medical) genetic resources lie in marginal, drought or flood prone areas, areas of male out-migration where they are often maintained by women farmers. Developing and patenting these genetic resources, using local (but evolving) methods of selection and storage, and local institutions represents a challenge for NGOs and governments. Only a degree of organisation and investment will enable farmers' rights to compete with breeders' rights in the markets of the future.

There are models in developed countries, particularly in the field of livestock. Breed societies date back well into the nineteenth century in many parts of Europe. Formed to develop the characteristics of particular genetic lines, they have been run by farmers, for farmers. Breeders have always sought to benefit financially from keeping breeding lines distinct, but have themselves created the markets for their breeds. In many cases European breeds of cattle, sheep, and pig have been exported all around the world – sometimes to the cost of local breeds. There are still livestock breeds being discovered in Europe today, and there are active rare breed conservation programmes. Similar opportunities exist throughout the world.

Identifying and developing new types of common pool resource will lead rural development organisations into new roles and new fields of activities. Not only are lobbying and advocacy of importance, but so are market development and the creation of institutional networks which will appreciate farmers' conservation and genetic development activities, value them and pay for them. Market development is an especially important aspect: the market is a big one, substantially unregulated as yet, and poorly understood by public agencies. This is a major creative activity which needs to be brought firmly into the rural development agenda through action research projects. Development agencies should at the same time take care that they are not helping to wipe out the genetic basis for such programmes in future, by thoughtlessly introducing hybrids or exotics and seeking to replace local breeds and varieties.

Forestry

Tropical forests have become a hot international issue, most recently with the failure of the 1992 UNCED (United Nations Commission on Environment and Development) Conference at Rio to produce agreement between north and south about their management and the degree of northern assistance required for their conservation. In the north the arguments are familiar to all, including schoolchildren. Forests generally and tropical forests in particular play a crucial role in regulating climate and determining the health of the atmosphere. They act as a sink absorbing pollution and their destruction by fire contributes to the 'greenhouse effect' – the heating of the earth's surface due to loss of ozone in the upper atmosphere. Conservationists also point to the tropical forests as the last great reserves of genetic variety.

In the south, different arguments are familiar. Forests and in particular timber trees are still a major source of foreign exchange and an attraction for international investment. Large numbers of workers are employed, infrastructure can be constructed on the basis of the financial returns to forest exploitation, and deforestation makes land available for agriculture, in particular for the production of cheap food for the growing cities and for export.

But these arguments, conducted at a political level, are all very simplistic. Tropical forests are inhabited by 240 million of the most marginalised people on earth, who by and large have subsisted from a sustainable exploitation of the forests' wealth. These people are often in conflict with the developers, and governments until now have generally been on the developers' side. Forest peoples usually have a sophisticated understanding of forest ecology and of what they can take out. They understand that particular trees have particular uses, and that they can select tree species to dominate; they cut trees allowing them to survive or reproduce, they reserve areas and rotate their harvests, they manage individual trees through lopping, pruning, pollarding and coppicing, and above all they frequently survive by exploiting the by-products of the trees (fruit, nuts, rubber, etc.) and 'minor forest products' (honey, rattan, spices, etc). In many countries the value of minor forest products is approaching or exceeding the value of timber exported.

Environmental concerns have joined forces with movements of indigenous forest people and their international humanitarian supporters to demand radical changes in the laws governing forest management. In Latin America it is the establishment of 'extractive reserves' which give use rights over wide tracts of forest to indigenous groups, and on paper at least prohibit logging and deforestation to create ranches. These legal documents are very difficult to police in remote isolated areas; conflict and violence are often close to the surface and the forest dwellers often have to take their security into their own hands. The story of Chico Mendes and his forest workers' union is a dramatic illustration of this (Hecht and Cockburn, 1989).

Logging has often been carried out with scant regard for sustainable exploitation though this is now changing a bit, and will continue to evolve as the scarcity value of timber increases. Many countries have developed logging guidelines for tropical moist forest. These have been based on European systems. The problem has been to enforce good practice. One negative experience which has been documented is the Papua New Guinea Gogol Valley

Project. In 1986, after 13 years of operation this woodchip mill and sawmill sited in an accessible forest of 63,000 hectares had begun to lead to the permanent disappearance of forest from well-drained valley areas and gentle slopes, which was not compensated by serious replanting, nor characterised by proper environmental safeguards (e.g. streamside buffer strips). Nor had the expected benefits accrued to the forest communities (Lamb, 1990).

Understanding of tropical forest ecology and human impact on it has increased greatly as a result of concerns about deforestation. One of the findings to emerge from much research is that tropical forest canopies can regenerate, perhaps not with an exact copy of tree species, but with a very similar range, in periods varying from 30 years upwards. Greater understanding of regeneration processes has led to experimental projects to try different harvesting techniques.

Over time there has been a great shift in perception of the problem of deforestation in tropical forests. Firstly, given the right conditions tropical forests do regenerate, and furthermore their structures are often not 'natural' in the first place, but are the product of selective harvesting activities over the years by forest dwellers. Secondly, the indigenous inhabitants who were often blamed for irrational and destructive use of the forest are in fact rarely the cause of deforestation: deforestation is the product of logging, conversion of forest into farming land usually by commercial farmers or migrants who come in the wake of logging activities, and fires.

In Asia, India and Thailand, facing shortages and mounting protests from forest dwellers, have drastically curtailed export and even industrial use of indigenous forest timber, preferring to rely on farm forestry and imports from elsewhere in Asia. In India, any logging was banned in the Himalayas for ten years as a result of the Chipko movement's protests against commercial exploitation. This has given a breathing space in which foresters have reassessed the ecological and social role of the Himalayan forests. The problem with such a radical measure is that forests benefit from management which includes taking out trees on a selective basis: having once banned logging, it is now very difficult to move back to a sensible management system.

There is a visible drift away from state ownership of forests, towards an exploration of alternatives. Many states have realised that they cannot control what goes on in the forests, and that control has to be decentralised to forest users themselves. Several countries have been allocating conditional usufruct and sometimes ownership rights to indigenous groups and to individuals in the search for mechanisms to reduce deforestation. The basic assumption here is that if you give a family or an organised community the right to exploit a forested territory they will not exploit it beyond its sustainable limits. Until now most experiments have been on a community basis, and with heavy state supervision.

In principle, sustainable systems of forest use need to be built up on the basis of indigenous knowledge and practice. It may be that indigenous management structures have decayed and are no longer capable of regulating forest use. In this case, joint management agreements between local organisations and state forest bodies provide a way forward. But it may also be that state forest authorities are reluctant to give up direct control immediately – because they are not convinced communities can manage forests as common properties, or because they have vested interests in maintaining the forests in public management. Sometimes (e.g. Thailand) this involves the massive leasing of public forests to private companies, originally for logging, but after the 1989 ban for tourist development, golf courses, etc.

Joint management

Joint management agreements, where a state forest authority makes an agreement with a community or its representative body to divide the benefits from and management tasks of sustaining a forest between them, have become commonplace in South and South East Asia. This recognises that people will defy forest regulations in order to survive, and is a tacit recognition of forest dwellers' rights in the forest. It represents a sea change from the traditional governmental custodial ideology which stressed that forest dwellers had no or only very limited rights in an ecology which the state had to protect from them. Not surprisingly this often created huge tensions and sometimes open conflict between governments and forest dwellers. At the same time forest policies are shifting from custodial but extractive to being concerned chiefly with ecological balance. In India, for example, the 1988 Forest Act not only maintained that the search for economic benefit was less important than this primary concern, but that forest dwellers' basic needs of fuel, fodder and building materials should also be a prime charge on the forest. This means that the entire silvicultural system has had to be changed to accommodate these prime needs. The idea of joint management also allocates a share of the sale of any final timber product to local people.

Joint management involves institutional development among the forest dwellers. Heterogeneous communities find this more difficult than more homogeneous communities: tribal villages in India, for example, are widely believed to be better able to sustain the forest protection committees established under the Joint Forest Management policy than caste villages in the plains. Where communities are economically differentiated, joint management will be more conflictual as villagers will have varied interests. Institutional development is a painstaking process, and cannot be imposed as part of a blueprint. So it has worked better as a 'pilot' scheme than when widely replicated. Frequently the institutions established are dominated by men; women, who are often the major users, are largely absent from decision-making fora. A very sustained, gender-sensitive process of institutional development is thus needed.

All this assumes that state forest agencies can be transformed from the western style regulatory and production oriented organisations established by colonial governments anxious to extract timber and to have untrammelled access to the forests, to agencies which can learn from indigenous forest users and can work with them in a genuine partnership, change their working methods and be willing to deal with non-forestry aspects of development. The Philippines has probably gone further in this direction than any country with tropical forests. Its Bureau of Forest Management has been reoriented and restructured by the use of 'working groups' comprising foresters, social scientists and others, in a pattern made famous by the National Irrigation Administration (Korten and Siy, 1988; and see Chapter 9). Without reorientation and the many reversals of attitude and practice entailed, the good work done on pilot schemes fades away when it come to replication.

Joint forest management is only the first hesitant step towards creating new commons out of state forests. Where introduced genuinely, and supported by strong citizens' groups and an environmental movement which can lobby and criticise, it will create the space for local forest management institutions to develop, which can later take on greater management roles. Women are often prime forest users – collectors of firewood, fodder, and other forest produce – but may be excluded from effective management roles in such arrangements, because foresters do not see them as managers, or because public positions in their communities are typically occupied by men. Likewise, the relatively poor in any community may also be excluded despite often being major forest users. These social dimensions of joint arrangements are critical for long-term sustainability of the arrangements themselves. Forest authorities will need the capacity to work on these issues as well as the appropriate technical expertise to include people's ideas and priorities into forest designs. Ultimately, states will develop the confidence to turn over forests to forest dwellers for management, with the state forest service retaining a technical, advisory role.

Water for irrigation

Water is increasingly seen as common property rather than a public good. It has private uses (domestic, industrial, agricultural); it helps dispose of waste; it has recreation and aesthetic benefits; and is the habitat of fish and other wildlife. Multiple uses means that there are often conflicting interests in water; the achievement of both private and public benefits depends on successful management of conflicting interests in what is a common resource.

In the fields of both water for irrigation and water for domestic and livestock use, rural development interventions have typically created free or subsidised goods which have been managed, but not cost-effectively, or sustainably by the public sector. This remains the dominant strategy in both fields. The problems in this strategy have become more and more evident in recent years: problems of institutional sustainability, and environmental impact.

Structural adjustment programmes call for a greater reliance on markets, competition, and phase-out subsidies. They promote the idea that water is a good in limited supply and therefore an economic (or toll) good, no longer a free good, to which everybody has a right. This is a difficult idea for many to swallow; nevertheless, millions of the very poorest people in shanty towns and dry rural areas have always had to pay exorbitant prices for water; it is arguable that if all consumers paid something like the cost, systems would be able to expand and serve those currently not – or poorly – served.

The market undoubtedly has a place in ensuring that supply and demand remain in balance, and that water supplying agencies have the means to maintain and invest. However, the market is no panacea for environmental and institutional problems. Water as a good is characterised by (1) externalities (users imposing costs on others – polluters, or upstream irrigators on downstream), (2) difficulties of excluding non-paying beneficiaries, and (3) natural monopolies. And investments in water often have social objectives – increasing welfare through drinking-water and food supplies.

In irrigation the policy alternative to existing strategies, even when adjusted by market-oriented reforms, is clear: rely on small/ medium-scale irrigation schemes which imitate successful traditional schemes; and encourage user communities to structure water distribution systems so that use and wastage are minimised. In drinking-water, the alternative has yet to be fully conceptualised. The basic elements of a reconceptualisation will be drawn out below.

Three-quarters of the world's irrigated area is in developing countries; 45 per cent in China, India and Pakistan. The rate of expansion has slowed down to around 1 per cent per year since 1975, lower than population growth. Among the reasons, according to FAO (1993a: 285): 'increasing construction costs, falling real prices for wheat and rice, a growing awareness of the environmental and social costs and poor irrigation performance at the farm and project levels.' If all the costs of irrigation were properly accounted for it is unlikely that many new irrigation schemes would be built. Modernising old irrigation schemes is also increasingly expensive, and lower crop prices make it harder to justify. About 30 million hectares (out of the 237 million) have severely saline soils, and waterlogging is common. The drains to remove waterlogging may cost five times as much to maintain as the delivery of water; on big schemes farmers rarely pay the full cost even of water delivery. Management of water by farmers and the authorities on big schemes is a huge problem, which will only improve once the scarcity value of water increases substantially.

Rural development professionals have increasingly found themselves lobbying against big dams, and the support for big dams in particular is waning: partly due to mounting and increasingly strident criticism, but also to growth in understanding of the destructive impacts. The World Bank, a leading investor, has attempted to make its dam projects more environmentally friendly by requiring more detailed impact assessments and a concentration of investments in certain rivers to leave others in a more natural state. It also recognises types of landscape which should be preserved in principle, including tropical forests and wetlands, but if there is no alternative but to develop them then mitigating and compensatory investments must be made (Petts and Cosgrove, 1990: 199).

Irrigation remains the largest user (at 70 per cent) of stored fresh water. Water use on big irrigation schemes is only about 30 per cent efficient. But the scope for improvement is said not to be very great. Pressures for increased agricultural production contribute to the dam-building dynamic. Environmentalists have sought either to oppose big dams outright, or to mitigate their negative impacts, and use them constructively for environmental improvement. 'The current vision has concern for the quality of life, focuses on investment in the environment, and is expressed by symbols of social advancement: restored landscapes and protected wilderness areas. . . An improved approach would be to develop water resources while simultaneously restoring or enhancing degraded or denuded landscapes, as well as preserving special ones', since irrigation permits intensification of agriculture and avoids the need to spread into marginal areas and wildlife habitats (Petts and Cosgrove, 1990: 205).

In the Indian Punjab, celebrated first for its Green Revolution, but later for its civil (secessionist) war, large-scale irrigation has led not only to large and unresolved ecological problems, but has also contributed to conflict. Large-scale canal irrigation has led to widespread waterlogging and salinity. This is very difficult for farmers to manage through drainage, given the large inputs of finance and organisation required (Shiva, 1991a: 139). Crisis has only been averted by the development of deep tubewells for additional irrigation since the 1960s, which has helped reduce water tables, and soil salinity. However, this has been so successful that there is now a serious risk that groundwater levels will descend rapidly such that exploitation becomes uneconomic, or the quality of water is no longer good enough for irrigation (Dhawan, 1993). Because electricity prices for pumping deep tubewell water out are far less than the cost of producing the electricity in rural Punjab, farmers have no reason to conserve water.

The supply of irrigation water from the rivers of Punjab to neighbouring states has progressively been controlled by the central government, whereas, constitutionally, irrigation is a state matter. This fact, and the inter-state conflicts over water between Punjab, Haryana and Rajasthan, played a big role in the Punjab secessionist civil war. Punjab's riparian rights – rights to the water deriving from the length of rivers flowing through the state – have been denied in favour of the rights of other states to water-intensive Green Revolution agriculture (Shiva, 1991a). Permanently constituted conflict resolution mechanisms are needed in such situations.

Alternatives

The radical alternatives offered by rural development are: (i) the increasing appreciation that farmers and local communities are able to organise their own irrigation systems as common properties – and have done so successfully in some cases for long periods of time; and (ii) that new common property rights in water may achieve much greater efficiency of water use and greater equity in society, even in large-scale irrigation schemes.

Indigenous irrigation hardly appears in FAO's review of water policies and agriculture (1993a). Coward's review of traditional systems in Asia (1980: 203–18) came up with several management principles which characterise these systems: the division of even small schemes into 'mini-units' each with its own local leadership, i.e. a very labour-intensive pattern of organisation; the correspondence between these mini-units and common physical features – sharing a canal, groups of field neighbours. Sometimes these groups are the same as the village, sometimes not. The difficulties created by having co-irrigators living in different villages are dealt with by differentiated membership: members living together or close at hand contribute labour for maintenance, members living further away contribute cash, for example.

Coward points out several dangers of outside intervention that sets out ostensibly to improve indigenous systems. One is dependence – changing a locally controlled technology into one dependent on outside expertise or imported materials. Another is that of setting standard rules that must be adhered to if indigenous systems want help – rules about how irrigators should organise themselves; rules about construction and maintenance. Intervention should make maximum use of existing structures, both physical and organisational. This should also apply when small, indigenous systems are incorporated into larger governmentally managed schemes.

The principles guiding indigenous systems can also be used by development agencies involved in building new small-scale systems and in deciding on the structures for large-scale irrigation schemes. Here there is a new orthodoxy that water users' associations should be included in the management structure of a large scheme. At first this was restricted to water users managing tertiary canals and in-field structures; in several countries there have been moves to involve associations in the management of secondary canals. Ulti-mately, and with the benefits of modern information technology, it should be possible to envisage the development and management of entire large-scale irrigation schemes by the users, as is practised in the USA and Taiwan. This is of course easier where the sources of water are relatively dispersed, as in Taiwan. Irrigators' associations there employ their own staff to manage irrigation, as well as provide agricultural advice. These principles are increasingly incorporated into the management of large-scale irrigation (ODI, 1995).

Creating new rights in water

Effectively, decentralisation within large irrigation schemes and the development of new small schemes entails the creation of new sets of property rights for farmers. Perhaps the most interesting and significant example of new rights in water has occurred in Bangla-desh where irrigation water is being sold by the landless under a now famous scheme promoted by an NGO, Proshika, and replicated widely in Bangladesh (Wood and Palmer-Jones, 1991; FAO, 1993a: 279).

In a situation of extreme and rising landlessness, with the landless facing dismal alternative employment prospects, resulting in low overall rural purchasing power and therefore sluggish demand for food and other commodities, the development of new small-scale irrigation sources provided an opportunity for the creation of new rights to a common good – water. The idea has been that groups of landless labourers have acquired, usually on credit, the technology (deep or shallow tubewells, or low lift pumps) to produce irrigation water for a group of farmers' fields. Sales of water to the farmers enable repayment of the loan and the generation of an income for the group's members. The resulting programme has proved not only a tool for redistribution of property rights and income, but has also increased irrigation efficiency, as it is easier for farmers with scattered small plots of land to buy water for those plots from an outside source rather than co-operate among themselves to produce the water. In a situation where small-scale irrigation has been haphazard and uncontrolled, the acquifers are in danger of over-exploitation. A network of groups controlling irrigation water but without an interest in land or crop production has a vested interest in the long-term availability of water, and therefore in conservation and in setting water prices at a level which gives farmers incentives to conserve.

What the programme has achieved is to demonstrate that agrarian reform is a wider concept than land reform: that there are sets of property rights other than those in land which may be redistributed. In Bangladesh this would be true of 'repair workshops, input supply, ploughing operations, processing of agricultural products or marketing' (Wood and Palmer-Jones, 1991: xxvii). Similar opportunities exist in other countries. Perhaps the most widespread may be in trade, for example, where a new crop is being produced. Whatever the new rights created, credit and training are likely to be significant components of the creation of successful individual or commonly owned businesses (see Chapter 4).

Reducing water requirements

Dryland development through minimal supplementary irrigation is a technological alternative to full-scale irrigation which is beginning to attract a lot of attention. Relying on rainfall, combined with water harvesting, and efficient 'Israeli-style' drip irrigation systems on-farm, dryland development has great potential. Similarly, even where irrigation water is available, field level practices (choice of crop, and cropping sequence, planting system, etc.) determine how much water is actually needed.

In Japan, an internationally famous ecological thinker and farmer, Fukuoka, developed a barley–rice rotation which minimised the use of irrigation water, arguing that when the rice was not flooded the plants could develop stronger roots and become more disease and pest resistant as a result. Water was used to drown weeds, but he was careful not to kill the clover, which would regenerate after flooding and form a mulch to hold moisture in the soil. Fukuoka had grown rice for twenty years in this way with high yields and extremely good effects on the soils (Fukuoka, 1992: 53–7). In India, scientists have discovered that paddy yields are only marginally affected by allowing the ponded water to subside for a day or two, while 20–40 per cent of water can be saved. However, farmers have not widely adopted the strategy because they have no reason to conserve water: electricity to operate pumps costs the farmer far less than it costs to produce; and canal irrigation water is still highly subsidised.

Common services

In development theory, certain key services are intimately linked with overall human development. In particular: (i) education enabling useful participation in the global economy, and women's education enabling their employment, empowerment, fertility reduction and improved health; (ii) peace and security enabling investment and growth; and (iii) health care, especially public health and the development of physical infrastructure (water, sanitation, etc.), enabling greater child survival and reducing or eliminating the incidence of diseases of poverty. States have generally been under powerful popular pressure to provide free education and medical care systems. Popular pressure for curative health care has generally been much greater than for preventive or public health measures, which are much more cost-effective in improving health. The pressures have been for a thin spread of access to all these services across the population. Public resources have rarely been anywhere near enough to satisfy demand; even when propped up by aid budgets in the poorest countries they have been inadequate. The pressures of structural adjustment programmes have added to the inadequacy, but should lead to innovative solutions.

Rural areas have often suffered the worst from these inadequacies. Poor rural people have often found themselves supplying major parts of the resources required to provide even the most basic services – primary education, primary medical care, and simple drinking-water systems. They have paid teachers and health workers in cash or kind, and have provided books, chalks and blackboards. They buy their drugs in the market or contribute to revolving funds for community purchase. They fuel and maintain their publicly provided water systems, and supply labour and often other resources for construction of new wells, schools and medical centres. Frequently they provide their own security service, as the regular police and legal system hardly reaches into at least the remoter areas. And yet they remain, nominally, public services. In most poor adjusting economies this is a charade. In fact, the services are common services, provided for the most part with community resources, though with residual inputs from the state: trained teachers, engineers or medical workers, with pay and career structures of a sort; public standards–curricula; guidelines for disease diagnosis, drug prescriptions and referral; and standard models for water and sanitation systems. These publicly provided inputs, though they are becoming fewer and less valuable, nevertheless contain a sting in the tail: they determine to a great extent what service will be provided, to what standard. This is the power of technical expertise. It is still rarely challenged by common service users.

In fact, since communities are often putting up a (or *the*) major share of the resources required to provide common services, they should be entitled to the major share of decision-making about their provision. This entitlement is not only ethical and logical, but also likely to lead to the most efficient outcome. This is not to suggest that there are no longer public objectives beyond the community level: given the statements made above about the linkages between wider development issues and the provision of key services, there clearly are. Certain public goods are just that, and can only be provided by the state: protection against measles through immunisation is only effective if a high proportion of the population is immunised. It can be argued that a basic level of literacy is a *sine qua non* of many aspects of development, and therefore a public good. Aspects of security remain a public good: there are categories of conflict, crime and criminal organisation which communities cannot deal with on their own. However, where there is no adequately resourced and legitimate state to take on these public functions, sustaining them requires at least the association of local institutions with state efforts.

If rural communities are to have a greater say in the provision and management of their own services, what are the technological and organisational principles on which community provision can be based? Should technologies for service provision be: appropriate? intermediate? indigenous? Technologies for publicly provided services have generally been selected as a matter of national policy. In this form they are the means of ensuring that laid-down minimum standards apply. Despite two decades of discussions about people's participation and indigenous knowledge in technology choice, this is still rare in practice. Formalising common (as opposed to public) service provision entails giving responsibility for service provision to user groups and coalitions of user groups, such that technical experts are advisers but not standard-setters. Technical experts need to be trained in analysing the options together with user groups, in redressing the imbalances between western and indigenous technologies, between male and female perceptions and interests, and other social divisions. They need to help user groups adopt a holistic analysis, seeing the effects of actions on different interest groups, including unborn generations. Newly humble technical experts need to acknowledge not only the expertise of users, but also the expertise of other technical experts. Users are rarely only interested in one particular service; their interests stretch across other activities which may be affected by the particular service.

In terms of organisation there is always a variety of institutions which can provide: a public service, indigenous institutions, a local government (quarter, village, set of villages, district etc.), a special purpose co-operative/users' body, one or several private firms. No general rule can be established across all rural development situations, but the trend should be towards special common purpose organisations, local government and (local) private sector. Indigenous institutions may provide a conceptual foundation for an appropriate organisation, but not always be the provider. In general, it is unlikely that indigenous organisations will be able to adapt themselves to new tasks, as new stakes and interests will evolve around the new task. This will require a new structure.

The stress on common services organised by and for the users means that services will increasingly be provided by many institutions. Fewer will be provided by the government or by a multi-purpose local authority. The educated elite will increasingly work in small organisations, directly accountable to users, based on small areas, but networked. One implication of having many organisations providing services is that co-ordination and conflict resolution mechanisms are needed. As Ostrom and Wynne point out (1993: 192ff), such mechanisms must be low cost and accessible – customary courts would be one example; Sudanese tribal conferences another. The existence of significant externalities would also indicate the need for appropriately wide jurisdiction for a service provider. Not everything can be devolved to the village or user group.

Health

Ill-health remains devastatingly common, especially among the poorest sections of the population, and women and children more generally. Infant mortality rates (IMR) vary from China's low of 30 per thousand births to 114 in Bangladesh, and three times as high in countries like Afghanistan or Mozambique subject to chronic conflict (MacDonald, 1993), compared with 4 to 12 per thousand births in developed countries. Poverty (as measured by GNP) accounts for a large proportion of the variation; but there are poor countries (China, Sri Lanka) where IMR is low relative to GNP. These are countries with well-developed public health and education systems where women in particular have relatively good access to these services. The answer would seem, then, to lie in policy and the allocation of national resources.

This must be true, as even the limited package of public health measures proposed as essential by the 1993 *World Development Report* (WDR) on Health would cost much more than many countries currently spend on health services (World Bank, 1993: 66). (Immunisation; school health programmes; tobacco and alcohol control; health, nutrition and family planning information; vector control; sexually transmitted disease prevention; monitoring and surveillance – cost $4–7. Tuberculosis treatment; management of sick children; prenatal and delivery care; family planning; STD (sexually transmitted disease) treatment; treatment of infection and minor trauma; assessment, advice and minor pain alleviation – cost another $8–15). A major problem, perceived for two decades by advocates of primary health care, and reflected in this report, is that countries have spread their resources too thinly and concentrated on the prestigious hospital sector at the expense of primary and especially public health. The *WDR* offers a health agenda in tune with the structural adjustment agenda of pruning the state: privatising tertiary care, contracting out ancillary services to the private sector, and focusing the public service on the limited package of activities. If implemented, this approach would undoubtedly produce major benefits in rural areas. However, although it might deal with the gross under-resourcing of rural health, it would not address the lack of choice accorded rural communities within the health care system – choice about strategies for improving health, about diseases and problems to focus on, and options in dealing with them.

It has often been said that primary health care (PHC), a broad concept addressing the many causes and facets of people's health, has been neutered into primary medical care, focusing on low-level curative care only. The links to nutrition and therefore food and incomes, to preventive public health measures and health education, have always been weak in PHC systems. It is usually reckoned that this is a function of demand as well as the dominance of (curatively oriented) doctors in most health systems. This is a strong conjunction of pressures which can probably be changed only marginally by reforms. But primary medical care is a clear example of a potential common service: it serves a defined group of people with benefits from which others can by and large be excluded. The *WDR* recognises that individuals and communities already put significant resources into medical care, and sees increased community control and financing as a means of capturing these resources in the public system, as the Bamako Initiative is encouraging (World Bank, 1993: 159–60) through establishing revolving drug funds and community-managed health centres (see Chapter 7).

Community management, coupled with financial contributions, carries with it not only the possibility of sustainable service provision but also the potential for increased diversity and appropriateness of service to particular local circumstances. In turn this would require a loosening of centralised control in the health field, allowing local priorities to be met through locally approved methods. This would include traditional practitioners as well as allopathically trained health workers. Wealthier communities would be able to employ doctors, possibly serving a number of networked primary medical centres. These in turn could share access to specialists and district hospitals.

A principle of community management is that people must be allowed to assess what is effective. Health workers, including doctors, too, will need to be trained in the art of working with socially differentiated communities; in eliciting priorities and resolving differences. They will need an openness to the benefits which can be gained from different traditions of treatment, as well as a knowledge of basic management and accounting techniques.

The arguments for accepting a broad spectrum of medical practice, if that is the community's wish, are several. In many rural areas traditional practitioners are well established and respected; above all their services are often widely used and paid for. It may even be that they will treat poor patients for less, or for nothing, thus ensuring equity. The costs of treatment and consultation are often within reach of local people. Treatments, or the mode of diagnosis, may also be linked in with other aspects of a local culture or worldview. Allopathic medicine may be neutral or even contradictory with respect to the local worldview. Finally, people make use of these services because they are judged to be effective. Of course, quacks and charlatans may also convince people that their remedies are effective too. Judgment is always required: the question is – should it be the judgment of ordinary people, or should it be regulated by some regulatory authority? This debate is raging in Europe (BMA, 1993) and throughout the world. Countries like China or India, which have developed independent policies on non-allopathic medicine over long periods of time, have worked on two basic principles: that all practitioners need to know about each other's systems, in order to develop mutual respect and then co-operation, and that alternative traditions of medical practice need to be codified, their training systems formalised and their associations registered. Regulation can then be self-regulation within the professions (Last and Chavundukwa, 1986).

Health is produced through the interactions between individual action and behaviour and environmental factors. In poor societies the latter exert a strong influence. There would remain a strong case for primary medical workers also playing a role in public and preventive health. Most of these programmes would remain publicly funded aspects of the work of a local health centre. Public funds could be biased towards poorer communities. Even where public health measures are involved, local adaptations may be required to ensure effectiveness or sustainability. For example, in child immunisation there is enormous scope for creating appropriate systems of cold chain (refrigeration) and vaccine transport using local transport systems (camels, buses, etc.) and local resources of altruism or revenues (e.g. a small cess on the drugs bill).

Water and sanitation

Improved water and sanitation are critical to general well-being, especially for women, and critical for health, especially for children: but poor rural societies are littered with pumps which are not maintained, have worn out or have never worked, and latrines which have never been used. Often this is yet another symptom of an overcommitted but failing public sector unable to maintain what it has built. It may also be a symptom of running before you can walk – introducing innovations which are too far from current practice: public latrines almost always, and private latrines sometimes, fall into this category. It may be a result of a lack of involvement of the users in design of the technology: frequently programmes offer users no choice about siting, or equipment, or construction materials. For example, there was a vigorous promotion of handpumps during the 1980s – they provide small amounts of clean water at convenient locations – and though many organisations have tried to involve women in users' committees and in handpump maintenance, rarely were women users consulted about designs, so many handpumps proved to be unmaintainable by women – parts were too heavy, etc. The more flexible programmes have shopped around for more women-friendly handpumps. Finally, after many problems, the users have entered the picture. They should invariably be involved in design issues; never should a programme choose its technology before a process of consultation; and consultation should continue as the programme goes ahead.

Problems also occur because village-level institutions set up to operate and maintain water systems fail. Perhaps the village is divided socially, and its constituent parts cannot work together. Perhaps the incidence of incentives is inadequate to compensate leaders for contributing time and other resources for the common good. Perhaps the sanctions available to deal with free-riders are inadequate, and the contributors get fed up. Programmes frequently install the technology in a hurry (because they have ambitious targets to meet), then set up an organisation to manage it. This is the wrong way round. Any programme needs to identify a users' organisation which is (or can easily become) capable of managing and maintaining the asset to be created. It needs to move at the pace the users are able to move at. Deficiencies and difficulties in the programme and the users' organisations need to be confronted at the beginning of the interaction, and a process of bilateral organisational development begun. For example, women might be the users but men probably run the organisation. Or, in the programme organisation, there is a desire to work with women user committees, but the organisation employs no women in spite of recognising that access to village women is difficult if not prohibited for male outsiders. Organisational development is called for in both instances.

In most rural societies water is a free good at source, unless its production costs money, as in the case of an electric or diesel-engined pump. In this case consumers may have to pay the cost of fuel and lubrication. It is frequently the case that water vendors deliver water from a distant source to houses: here there is a strong vested interest in a water source which would make the core of a users' group. Likewise small groups of consumers may own a water source and charge non-members for water. Charges would not be with a view to accumulation, but to servicing the water source. These arrangements may be much more feasible and practical than community ownership. There is no reason to discourage them, where such arrangements are socially acceptable.

Private ownership of water supplies is likely to be unacceptable in the absence of an exceptional level of trust. However, private management of a public or community owned resource may be workable, and indeed, if incentives are well structured, may represent a means of preventing the free-rider problem from assuming such proportions that it undermines the service.

Seeing water and sanitation as a part of health development raises again the issue of where the public interest, as opposed to individual or group interest, lies in health. Most benefits in health (i.e. from public health measures, or medical work) can be appropriated by individuals, small groups or localities. Few will directly affect the wider society. Exceptions lie in communicable diseases; however, even many of these are communicated within relatively small geographical areas. Whereas in the recent past the public interest has been very widely defined, and common interest not really in the picture, the realisation that the public interest has been stretched too widely and the concomitant realisation that groups, communities and regions can also have an interest divisible from the public interest, means that health development can be liberated from the limited choice between the medical care of individuals and public health measures which have universal benefit. In between there is a whole range of household, group, and community-based possibilities for action.

Women's health

Action around a common interest and public action are not necessarily alternatives: indeed the first may catalyse the second. For example, the health of women is clearly a major public good, as it is related to the health of the whole society. However, many aspects of women's health have been severely neglected by public health services and public policy generally. As a result, women have taken these aspects into their own hands. Women's groups have set up centres to help the victims of violence. 'Most shelters offer not only a place to stay for women and their children, but counselling, material support, and sometimes legal help. Most importantly, the woman in crisis feels the solidarity of other women who have had similar experiences. It helps her gain the confidence she needs to decide about her future' (Smyke, 1991: 56).

Women's health is increasingly recognised to be intimately linked to women's status in society. Why do women die in childbirth? The immediate reasons are:

> they received no pre-natal care; they have too many children; they were afraid to go to the hospital; they could not afford transportation; they did not know their condition was dangerous but could be treated; they were afraid to use contraception; they were malnourished as little girls; there is no blood available at the health facility; the untrained traditional birth attendant thought she could handle the complication; they live too far from a hospital which can provide emergency care; they seek illicit abortions to end unwanted pregnancies. (ibid: 63)

The causes of this situation lie in the way society treats women: the access it gives women to education, health services, family planning, financial resources and food. Decisions about the allocation of such resources are taken by public bodies as well as by households. There is a huge opportunity here for rural women and the organisations which work with them to join together in common organisations and begin to act on some of these issues, combining the provision of service with the awakening of awareness.

Summary and conclusion

This agenda for the development of common goods is in line with the general approach taken by proponents of structural adjustment: that the state withdraws from activities it cannot afford to engage in. But in rural areas the private sector will often not magically step in to fill the gap, since the opportunities for profit are often low or at least lower than elsewhere in the economy. Reliance on naive notions of the 'community' to fill the gap, prevalent in primary health care and water and sanitation, among others, will be appropriate where communities are small and their interests relatively homogeneous with respect to the service in question. However, where communities are more stratified and diverse in their interests, the interests of the poor, or women, or marginalised groups may be better served by separate services and institutions. Indeed, as in the case of the water-sellers in Bangladesh, it may be possible to facilitate the acquisition of rights in service provision for groups among the poor. Rural development workers need to be familiar with a wide range of options for organising services. One model rarely suits different communities. Each community may have to experiment for a period with different arrangements before satisfactory institutions are developed. These will also change over time as people's needs and concepts change.

Common goods and their development provides a wide field in which rural development can make a distinctive impact on development practice and thinking. Many of the world's big development issues revolve around competition over common pool resources – the oceans, the atmosphere, the forests, genetic resources, even computer networks. It is the definition of these resources as public that lies behind their degradation. Privatising them concentrates power and excludes people (especially the less well resourced) unacceptably. The development of common goods provides an alternative conceptual framework for the creation of sustainable and equitable resource use systems.

4

Poverty Alleviation

Rural incomes are very low in most poor countries. Economic growth is thus an essential ingredient of rural development. Market-led economic growth has relied on benefits to 'trickle down' to the rural poor, but this has only happened under very specific circumstances among countries coming 'late' to the development process. As a result, thinking – at least in the international development agencies – has moved towards a new paradigm of poverty alleviation (Jazairy *et al.*, 1992) – the IMF's 'high quality growth', which should be equitable, give attention to the poor and vulnerable, and protect the environment; the World Bank's 'poverty reducing growth' (1990), generating income-earning opportunities and improved access to services for the poor. Increasingly it is the positive participation of the poor in the development process which is seen to reduce poverty. This strategy is much cheaper than supporting growth biased to the rich since the poor will supply much of the overall cost of investment, through labour and even savings. By contrast, the rich typically require more expensive support in the form of capital. It may be cheaper, but it is institutionally complex.

Increased rural incomes generates greater demand, which in turn is the key to balanced and sustainable rural economic growth and food security, because it will promote a diversity of local services, trade and production, with impacts locally perceived and manageable. In agriculture diversification of farm and off-farm activities, including CPR-based ones (livestock, fishing, forestry, bee-keeping, wildlife management), has become a major thrust.

In the field of non-farm activities, the key components of the paradigm shift are as follows.

1. There has been a change during the last decade and a half of structural adjustment programmes from heavy direct promotion of enterprise involving subsidy, generally on capital investment, to the creation of an appropriate policy and market environment. This involves removing obstacles and creating equal opportunity for competition: usually removing discrimination in favour of large, urban-based enterprise and external investors. The move is away from 'industrialisation at all costs' – costs not only to the state but also to rural communities – pollution, unhealthy working conditions/sweated labour, child labour.

2. From providing subsidised bank credit for capital investment to creditworthy entrepreneurs, development efforts have increasingly turned to collateral-free group-based lending with a savings base, often supporting self-constituted groups of women, who would be considered uncreditworthy by normal banking standards. These efforts swing between developing entrepreneurial skills among the very poor, to providing critical injections of working capital into existing artisan enterprises to enable a better chance of survival. This implies moving from a belief in modern industry to an understanding that traditional occupations may have a lot to offer provided there is good demand for their products.

3. There has also been a shift away from bureaucratically managed credit back to community/locally controlled rotating or accumulating savings and credit associations which function not only as financial intermediaries but often also as 'safety nets' providing insurance and consumption loans to members. There is a debate about whether development agencies should intervene in such organisations, which are otherwise independent.

4. Poverty alleviation is also about social security. It is clear that savings and credit schemes cannot reach all the poor: the poorest are usually very hard to reach. What they need is a wage; and help in sending their children to school. Many development agencies and governments now offer wage guarantee schemes when the local labour market is slack. Then there is a small proportion among the poor who cannot hold down a job and depend on charity. Most poor countries have yet to provide effectively for these groups, who may be disabled, chronically sick or mentally ill. There is still very great scope for innovation in the field of social security provision.

Poverty and vulnerability

Poverty is a multi-dimensional phenomenon. This was captured by Chambers (1983) and more recently by Jazairy *et al.* (1992: 56 ff). Aspects include: material deprivation, isolation, dependence and subordination (over land ownership, sharecropping, and the poor bargaining position of assetless labourers in labour-rich economies), absence from organisations, lack of assets, vulnerability to natural disaster, and insecurity (the latter sometimes a result of development). Jazairy *et al.* distinguish four types of poverty: (i) interstitial (pockets of) poverty, surrounded by wealth; (ii) material deprivation combined with isolation and alienation found in marginal areas, and labelled peripheral poverty; (iii) overcrowding poverty in areas of population pressure; and (iv) traumatic or sporadic poverty, perhaps better described by Illiffe (1987) as conjunctural poverty (temporary poverty into which the non-poor may be thrown by crisis). In Africa, while structural poverty (i–iii) has remained, conjunctural poverty has increased dramatically as a result of war, drought, famine, and the failure of states to substitute effectively for traditional or pre-colonial institutions.

Poverty is measured multi-dimensionally too. Frequently used indicators are: GNP per capita; a headcount of those below a given poverty line (always an arbitrary income level); various integrated indices which usually combine a measure of incomes distributed below the poverty line with GNP growth; a food security index; and a basic needs index. Generally poverty, as measured by these indices, is correlated with per capita GNP growth. However, the food security index does not correlate well – it relates more to food production and import capacity. And there are several countries which have managed to reduce poverty and insecurity dramatically despite low growth and low GNP, China and Sri Lanka being the oft-quoted examples. There the emphasis was for a long time on containing inequality through redistributive policies and an effective welfare state, and this was instrumental in reducing absolute poverty.

Explanations of poverty are equally varied, ranging from historical, through economic and natural resource-centred to socio-political. Historical explanations usually focus on the impact of colonial and post-colonial political economy. Thus colonial (and post-colonial) capitalist farmers, land settlers, forest reservations and urban development have often marginalised rural populations, and removed resources from their control. Some groups, such as pastoralists and minority ethnic groups, have been especially vulnerable to such processes. Economic explanations focus on trade and the domination of primary product markets by global corporations and cartels. In some countries primary product producers have been cushioned by government price stabilisation and subsidies, and surplus labour has until recently been absorbed outside agriculture, but this has not been possible in many poor countries. Economists have particularly focused on capital and technology as barriers to increased farm productivity: however, this model, derived from rich-country situations where farms are seen as businesses maximising profits, is inappropriate for the majority of peasant farming circumstances. Emphasis on capital and technology serves the interests of bigger farmers and helps smaller farms to disappear: this is not appropriate in situations where the labour market offers few alternatives.

There are explanations focusing on natural resources: the quality of the natural resource endowment is said to determine the degree of poverty. However, human beings have a remarkable ability to transform their environments through investment of labour, knowledge and technology. Thus land which 50 years ago was seen as eroded and overstocked in Machakos, Kenya today supports five times the population at higher per capita production levels, and with greater food security (Tiffen *et al.*, 1994). Once high population densities are reached the non-agricultural economy assumes very great importance, as agriculture is tied up in very small parcels of land. The poor look to the labour market, common property resources and non-farm enterprise. If the rural non-farm economy is stagnant, more and more labour is invested in farming, substituting for capital and reducing returns to labour. This occurs under peasant systems of ownership, where farms employ family members, but under capitalist ownership systems owners often choose to use machinery as it is easier to manage and produces better results on a large scale. A stagnant rural non-farm economy then leads to unemployment, out-migration (often only of men), the urbanisation of poverty and the breakup of families.

Socio-political explanations of poverty centre on the enormous growth of wealth and the middle classes in post-colonial societies. Wealth has frequently been accumulated by people with access to the state, which has provided cheap land, credit, technology and protection for big business. Some states have been 'predatory' on the poor, and have organised the alienation of land on a large scale in favour of urban elites, sometimes using military force. Some of this movement is captured in notions like urban bias, core and periphery, and social class. Urban bias suggests that the development process and policy is biased against rural people through investment allocation, the uneven distribution of technical skills and administration, and price twists (subsidised urban prices and market rural prices), among other mechanisms (Lipton, 1977). Alternatively, there may be certain core regions which are able to grow economically faster than others because of similar biases (Moore and Harris, 1984). Structural adjustment programmes have begun to eliminate the subsidies which have worked largely to the benefit of the already better off, but the other biases generally remain.

In explaining the rise of conjunctural poverty, caused most frequently in the 1990s by war, analysts have highlighted the decline of institutions and the nation-state in particular, the growth of the international weapons trade and of political economies of war with interests which benefit from war and prevent the peace. Armed conflict is most frequently related to the uneven geographical and social spread of development inherent in modernisation approaches, development which channels public resources extremely unequally, usually reinforcing inequities of natural resource endowments and history.

Potential for raising incomes varies greatly from one place and time to another. Opportunities are often greater in more developed areas closer to towns and cities. In marginal areas people have usually identified most of the possible sources of income; even then there can be new demands, especially for natural-resource-based products, like medicinal plants and plants which can have uses in genetic engineering and may be relatively abundant in sparsely settled, undeveloped areas. These sources of improvement may be much less easy to develop, as markets may not be organised.

Both sustainable agriculture, through its greater share of income accruing to labour and its greater labour intensity, and the affirmation and development of common property and services, with equity considerations as part of the equation, will alleviate poverty. Few societies have substantially reduced poverty exclusively relying on agriculture and services. (New Zealand is perhaps an exception.) Rural wealth, even agricultural wealth, is often connected in one way or another with non-agricultural economic development. Urban migrants remit a proportion of their salaries, which is then invested in farming, as among the wealthier small farm households in Zimbabwe (Jackson and Collier, 1991: 37). Richer farmers are often involved in trade: in a very dynamic rural economy such as that of southern Thailand, even smaller farmers sometimes possess the means (a pickup truck) to sell their produce advantageously in well-organised privately run export markets. A beneficial development cycle occurs when increasing non-agricultural wages begin to push up agricultural wages. This effect is enhanced when non-agricultural development occurs in the countryside or small towns, rather than in the big cities. If it is concentrated in the cities, men's wages will be affected since it is often they who migrate alone; if it is more evenly spread, women are more likely to be able to go out to work and to experience increased wage levels.

Thus diversity of economic activity within a local area is an important principle of rural development, mirroring the diversity of a farm run according to sustainable agriculture principles. A healthy local economy will produce and trade many of the things people consume in the area, will have some capacity to substitute for 'imports' (in the sense of what comes into the area), and will process products coming off the farms. It will also make use of indigenous knowledge and skills acquired through formal education. Plenty of 'backwards and forwards linkages' in the economist's jargon.

Diversification is also a sound strategy at household level. In rural Zimbabwe, for example, 'a household is more secure the more its income is derived from a range of independent sources' (Jackson and Collier, 1991: 62). The same authors identified 64 mixes of activities prevalent in rural Zimbabwe with 15 paths among them involving household economic diversification. Income level was also associated with diversification. However, the study omitted to investigate whether security was equally distributed within the household, especially between men and women. Male diversification, for example, through migration, may not convert easily into greater household security if the benefits are not passed to the women who stay behind to run the household.

Income generation: off-farm natural resource-based strategies

Increasing farm production and adding value to farm products are opportunities which have usually been applied to landed households. However, just as roles and functions in common property resource use can be divided among different parties, so can land-based activities. We have already seen an example of this in the sale of irrigation water to farmers by landless groups in Bangladesh (Chapter 3). Farm products are often inputs into industrial/craft production. Mixed farming systems may be divisible among different households. There are 'traditional' systems of symbiosis between arable farmers and transhumant livestock producers, the livestock consuming crop residues and water and returning dung and urine to the fields (Mortimore and Turner, 1993; Powell and Williams, 1993). In pre-White Revolution South Asia, milking buffaloes were kept in cities by specialised social groups; their dung was transported out to the farms usually in exchange for fodder.

White revolutions

The 'White Revolution' in India aimed not only to increase milk production for consumption in its rapidly growing urban areas, but also to increase the incomes of small farmers and the landless. This was to be done through the development of marketing and processing co-operatives which would buy milk from village dairy-cattle owners and supply veterinary and quality control services. Local *zebu* cattle were to be upgraded to cross-breeds by artificial insemination with Jersey or Holstein/Friesian semen. There were a number of reasons why this programme, 'Operation Flood' (OF), was considered to be potentially beneficial to the poor, unlike the early experience of the Green Revolution in India: it was thought that milk production was 'scale neutral or even biased in favour of small holders and landless rural households', that poorer households would have a greater stake in dairying because it supplements their meagre income from wage labour and crop cultivation in a significant way, and that the Anand dairy co-operatives in Gujarat had already shown that benefits could be passed to the rural poor (Doornbos *et al.*, 1990: 171). However, it was found that the larger benefits went to wealthier farmers; logically, the introduction of high yielding crossbred cows would give a competitive advantage to any farmer who could produce home-grown fodder for them. Poorer households would have to rely on common pastures or buy fodder, making their net income, in all probability, lower (ibid: 172–3). Sometimes they added a headload of fodder to their demand for wages. It was also found that the net returns from dairying diminished over time (ibid: 280–1): so, as in the Green Revolution, those (mostly bigger farmers) who got in first reaped the biggest rewards. The net returns from dairying were judged to be low overall, and especially low for the poor and landless who took loans to purchase a cow or two (ibid: 282). The few studies which look specifically at the impact of OF on women, who do most of the work in dairying in much of India, are inconclusive (ibid: 284–5). However, it is clear that where women previously processed milk into ghee for sale, leaving buttermilk for home consumption, now whole milk is sold, and it is often the man of the house who is the co-operative member and, legally at least, controls the proceeds. There is a fundamental question over the intra-household distribution of benefits, which, as so often is the case, links up with the shift of processing and adding value away from the household and to a bigger institution. Poor women were able to benefit much less than men. This was due to co-operative membership being vested in male heads of households. Training was usually provided to the men too, even if the women were more involved in production processes (World Bank, 1991).

The objective conditions (a large urban market, good infrastructure, irrigation for green fodder) for the development of the White Revolution are not present in large parts – often the poorest parts – of India. The crossbred cow strategy requires diverting land from other crops to fodder, and in the long term may undermine (at least will not strengthen) the genetic stock for animal draught power, which will remain very important in India for a long time to come. A more regionally differentiated livestock development strategy, which would also probably produce more income for the poor, would be based on avoiding competition between crops and fodder, would optimise the use of crop residues, and preserve, even improve, the draught power stock. This would entail following actual practice in most villages (Doornbos, 1991: 281): focusing on moderate and balanced improvement of stock, spreading available fodder over a larger number of animals, which would include sheep and goats, easier for the poor to manage. Buffaloes, the traditional milking animal in much of India, would have a central place in this. Selective breeding of indigenous races would produce animals which perform better as dual purpose breeds (ibid: 316–17).

Linked with the lack of balance in the production strategy is an exclusive focus on supplying large-scale, western-style urban dairy plants with bulk milk from fairly remote producing areas. This has displaced the more natural peri-urban and private supply systems, and much local processing and distribution. A strong case for the development of these systems was made by George (1985). An alternative, more balanced (but less dramatic, and 'modern') strategy would be the development of smaller dairies, producing affordable, unsubsidised dairy products in demand in both urban and rural areas. These could even be based on household production (Doornbos, 317–18).

A highly successful example of expanded household-level dairy production was fostered by a UNICEF-funded Women's Development Programme in Kordofan, Sudan (Shepherd, 1992: 15–16). This was a cheese-making extension programme for nomad cattle-owning women, to enable women to process surplus milk into a light cheese wherever they might be, and store the cheese in brine till it could be marketed. The programme started with a small number of simple wooden prototype cheese-making sets which could be carried on a bull – the Baggara mode of transport – and with a few groups of women to whom cheese-making techniques were extended. The demand for equipment and knowledge expanded dramatically as the market was ready and it fitted perfectly into the livelihood system of these nomad women. The cheese had previously been made by government and merchants' cheese factories, the former for sale at subsidised prices largely to civil servants in town. While the government was happy to transfer production to the women it held on to marketing the cheese they produced because each Ministry was rewarded in the annual budget round for revenue it raised, and this was a source of revenue. Ultimately production was too big for the Ministry to market, and the women began to find their own outlets in the market which gave them as good or better returns.

Women's incomes

Where a welfare increase for poor households is the objective, it has often proved valuable to enhance the asset position of the women in the house, as they are more likely to spend their increased incomes on household welfare. However, increasing women's incomes is not straightforward: there are complex intra-household dynamics which often mean that women have difficulty controlling cash they earn; and they have so many other obligations – child care, care of the elderly and sick, housework, fetching and carrying, and so on – that time for earning income is squeezed from many sides. 'Women's income generating projects require a holistic approach to tackle their many needs. For example, community-based health care and child care and appropriate labour saving technology are often crucial to enable women to utilise income generating opportunities.' In some cases, children may get only extra unpaid or low-paid work and few developmental benefits from women's involvement in income generation.

Rural women often do not have the social status to engage in independent enterprise. Group formation, whether among kin (as in the Sudanese dairy example) or among fellow villagers (as in India) helps to give women the confidence, legitimacy and mutual support to overcome status inferiority. This is discused further in the context of savings groups below.

Common property resources are often of critical importance in the generation of new sources of income. In the dairy programmes described above these were neglected; in India, fodder has been a major constraint for landless or very small farmer livestock owners. Common grazing areas remain degraded and marginal through much of India despite the technical possibilities for their rehabilitation. Creative development work, however, combined with a sympathetic legal environment has been able to develop common pastures.

Campfire

A potentially brilliant example of the role of CPR in new income sources is the Campfire programme in Zimbabwe, which involves local communities in the management of wildlife for tourist and hunting purposes. Community involvement in official or NGO schemes to manage wildlife is becoming increasingly common as top-down schemes are recognised as unsustainable or in conflict with the development and survival of local people (IIED, 1994).

Campfire is a scheme run by the Zimbabwe National Parks Administration to promote people's involvement in wildlife management where that can be a competitive activity from an economic point of view. It is not a conservation project, but a development project with conservation spinoffs. It has been successful where ownership and control has been passed to a sufficiently local level – in practice, the village or ward council. Where control was vested in district councils (there were 55 in Zimbabwe's communal areas), inadequate benefits flowed to the local people who were actually managing the wildlife, because district councils faced declining revenues from central government grants and increasing demands on their revenues. As a result the Campfire programme has been rejected, wildlife are not tolerated, and councils are mistrusted. This illustrates the importance of vesting control with the actual resource managers, as well as the dangers of remote, large local government units.

Non-farm income generation

The non-farm rural economy is heterogeneous. Its diversity defies easy categorisation. Students of small-scale enterprise (SSE) have tended in any case to wear rather urban, formal sector spectacles when analysing the rural economy, and have missed much as a result. Firstly, they miss the importance of diversity and flexibility for household income and security strategies, because they are typically concerned with the fortunes of firms not households. Secondly, they tend to lump together very diverse rural enterprises into large categories, either based on arbitrary quantitative definitions (e.g. 'less than 10 employees') or on qualitative characteristics (e.g. 'owner/managers also work on the shop floor', or degree of entrepreneurship–growth orientation, and strategic business awareness). Thirdly, they tend to have a strong bias to manufacturing industry, when it is often services and trade which are much more significant in terms of employment and incomes.

More complex models are definitely needed. This can be achieved by focusing on particular trades or sectors. It may also be assisted by a participatory approach: what categories of enterprise do people talk about, and how do they evaluate them? The more formal the analytical approach the more likely it is that women's enterprises will not be observed, because of their other, household commitments which mean that they look for work which is complementary to those commitments. This work is often less identifiable for the outsider as an enterprise.

Co-operation among enterprises, either producing the same product or service, or linked in a chain of specialisation, is a feature of SSEs. This has until recently been neglected in favour of promoting formal industrial or marketing co-operative societies, which rarely succeed as autonomous businesses. Their common problems are continued dependency on promoting public sector agencies, binding them into never-ending patronage, corruption and lack of decision-making autonomy; poor management and absence of strategy (de Luisa, 1995). The few successes illustrate that it can be done, but usually under special socio-political circumstances.

Co-operation often manifests itself in 'industrial districts' – areas with a concentration of particular occupations. These may be virtually the same for example, weavers, blacksmiths, carpenters; or complementary – for example, blacksmiths, welders and mechanics. Co-operation occurs over procuring inputs, passing on orders to neighbours when order books are full, providing services to neighbouring enterprises, and producing complementary products (e.g. processed foods which can be added together to make a meal). Small-scale traders, too, often co-operate as much as compete.

Slater (1991) has presented the success of north Italian small firms as an instance where a developed economy has retained a growing and dynamic small firm sector. This has partly been achieved through co-operation among small firms in powerful associations which have been able to provide the services and backup required in order to compete with larger companies. These include credit, legal services, and business administration (ibid: 190). Concentration of small businesses in 'industrial districts' was one of the factors encouraging co-operation and inter-firm links enabling a fragmentation of the production process to occur with each firm producing one component of the final product. This is seen as an alternative to the Japanese sub-contracting system.

Given heterogeneity and co-operation as the major characteristics of non-farm enterprises, and given diversity of income sources as a common household or individual objective, what are the policy and programme implications? Programmes abound; policy is a rare commodity in this field in both developed and developing countries.

Programmes

Programmes have tended to be either highly selective, focusing on one or two critical 'missing ingredients', or integrated, where a number of interventions go side by side. Evaluations indicate that the latter are inefficient, costly and rarely succeed in meeting the diverse needs of large numbers of clients (de Luisa, 1995). Single interventions, while potentially more successful, need to differentiate between different types of clients. So Harper identified three types of training and advice activities: those enabling clients to move into the 'modern sector'; those aiming to improve existing very small enterprise performance; and those trying to create something which could be recognised as an enterprise in the first place (1989: 182). For rural enterprises, even this may not be sufficiently differentiated to be relevant for large numbers of small businesses. For example, enterprise problems may have to do with the depletion of a common property resource: what is needed may be legal or organisational advice and training. If household and individual security of income is the perceived problem, then training and advice may be needed to help people maximise their flexibility, understand where to look for opportunities, and work out how to mix and match different activities without one undermining the other.

Incomes from small enterprises depend fundamentally on demand for their services and products; but also secondarily on enterprise productivity. Increasing productivity through investment in assets has generally been the focus of most programmes, whether single intervention or integrated. This remains a valid objective where enterprises have a more fixed, permanent character, and where labour is employed whose productivity could be increased, in the interest of higher profit and subsequent reinvestment. However, where individuals and poor households are trying to increase their security and survival chances, it is the return to labour of the individual or small group which matters most. This may indeed be best served through investment in equipment, but is more likely to be increased through improved access to working capital, critical raw materials, and markets.

Advocates of modernisation have promoted entrepreneurship as the critical ingredient for the transformation of rural economies. However, this has normally been conceived within a framework of technological and institutional modernisation too: 'entrepreneurs' have taken credit from banks, studied western technical processes in training institutions, and produced with modern technology on purpose-built industrial estates. In the 1970s this strategy was roundly criticised on the grounds that the creation of more productive units usurped the markets of less 'entrepreneurial' artisans working with more traditional skills, tools and institutions. The strategy led to greater socio-economic differentiation. Frequently the introduction of modern ways ousted women from productive, income-generating processes.

This critique has led to a radicalisation of the school of thought promoting entrepreneurship. Schemes in the 1980s have increasingly penetrated the lower orders of the 'informal' economy, looking for opportunities for very small, often women's businesses, using small quantities of collateral-free credit disbursed by a variety of new institutions (savings and credit societies, and Grameen Bank clones – see below). What is significant about these moves is the return of concepts of common service and association, local holistic sustainable resource development, and backward linkages to agriculture and natural resources. It is rarely possible to alleviate poverty without strong collective energies, whether this is expressed in bargaining over wages, or in mutual support through savings and credit.

Credit

There are few SSE programmes which do not include an element of credit. This is despite the fact that there is rarely an association between credit and business success (Sowa *et al.*, 1992: 46), and that small businesses often identify problems other than credit as their central difficulties (e.g. Curtis, 1981). However, credit is easy to manage and easy to disburse to a target, therefore making it easy for a development agency to claim success. Low repayment performances, however, often tie large numbers of SSEs and programmes in knots. Low repayment characterises credit disbursed to SSEs by non-specialised banks; some specialised SSE support agencies have better records, since they are usually structured to give particular attention to the problems of their SSE clients, whereas banks have little time for them.

By the end of the 1980s it was clear that many subsidised formal credit programmes had largely failed to reach the poor, and that the development banks and other institutions established in the 1960s and 1970s were unviable, with little prospect of becoming viable. Subsidies were rarely accessible to the rural poor, though some extremely large-scale programmes like India's integrated rural development programme (IRDP) have had some success in reaching the poor (Kurian, 1987; Slater and Watson, 1990; Bernstein *et al.*, 1992: 254–57). Formal commercial credit, requiring a borrower to provide the lender with collateral, usually property, or a personal guarantor, by definition excludes the majority of poor people, and often a majority of rural people. This is an example of market failure and justifies non-market interventions, such as land registration programmes. However, the latter are complex and fraught with difficulties, and in any case do not benefit the increasing proportions of the poor who are landless.

Economists have tried to make the case for intervention on grounds of market failure, in other words that the market was failing to deliver a socially desirable outcome due to shortcomings in the structure and functioning of the market. Market failure could be due to the existence of imperfect information about borrowers, so that the risks of lending cannot be quantified, for example. Imperfect information is often a function of a bank's lack of competence in appraising investments which might well be profitable. It is also a result of the segmentation of rural credit markets – information about borrowers circulates in a relatively small geographical area. There are other reasons for market failure too: the scarcity of acceptable collateral, the lack of insurance schemes to cover problems of income uncertainty, and the likelihood that income failure will affect many people simultaneously, due to natural hazards – drought, pests or disease.

However, on closer inspection, these arguments turn out to be rather ambiguous and weak (Besley, 1995). The major argument for intervention therefore remains a redistributionist one: that economic growth can as well be promoted by credit for very small enterprises as for larger businesses. The fact is also that the poor can make good use of credit, and in fact are often good risks as borrowers, sometimes better risks than less poor people, as judged by loan repayment records. However, credit for the poor needs to be carefully structured so that they can take advantage of it.

There are now a number of comparative surveys of different credit programmes with poverty alleviation objectives. An early survey was Remenyi's, which suggested that the best-known credit schemes have developed a range of different approaches. Savings-linked models were generally superior, allowing discrimination between potential clients, creating a basis for institutional independence from donors, and giving poor savers a real rate of return on their savings. Programmes aimed at the very poor – survival businesses – also benefit from the discipline of being group-based, so that borrowers are open to peer and community pressure (Remenyi, 1991: 111).

The management of the credit programme was often enhanced if a board with representatives elected by the borrowers and savers was accountable for performance. Apparently this works particularly well where programme beneficiaries are existing businesses which are expanding, presumably because the success of the model is sensitive to the quality of board members who scrutinise applications. Bangladesh's Grameen Bank is also run by a board, composed largely of women, who are the Bank's biggest client group (ibid: 78–9). External accountability may be an alternative mechanism to inject an element of discipline into lending operations. This was the case in the Garu Rural Bank in northern Ghana, where the Bank of Ghana's periodic visits helped to keep it afloat when other rural banks were going under in turbulent economic waters (Buturo, Personnel Communication).

Linking credit with training was found to be useful only above the survival level, where record keeping, cash management and personnel skills became more important as businesses grew. The most effective training was often provided informally, on-the-job, and by group colleagues (Remenyi, 1991: 112–15). However, some organisations, the Grameen Bank included, put a lot of emphasis on training of group members (e.g. a 7-day course at the foundation of a group), as well as intensive contact between extension workers and groups.

The Grameen Bank

The Grameen Bank approach, originating with a Bangladesh NGO which became a bank, but spread to Malaysia (Gibbons and Kassim, 1990) and elsewhere, relies on extension workers to get closely supervised small amounts of credit out to where it is needed on a regular basis; and small group formation among borrowers for mutual support, creating the saving habit and peer pressure to repay loans. The important features of the Grameen Bank are: the 'group within a group' structure, where six cells of five members, all of whom have to agree each other's loans, are linked together in weekly meetings; only the poor can join and women are preferred; loans are only to individuals with a low maximum loan size; weekly repayments are made over a year; and all operations occur in the village to reduce transaction costs for borrowers. This combination has led to a high repayment performance, success in reaching the poor (though the absolutely landless are less well served than others among the poor), and a bank which is profitable, though reliant on the interest from concessionary deposited IFAD (International Fund for Agricultural Development) loans.

A key feature of the Grameen Bank is the combination of centralised strategic management and decentralised operational management. At operational level, the procedures are very standardised, detailed but quite simple and include a standardised ethical code (the 'Sixteen Decisions'). Much emphasis is placed on the regular meetings of groups, and initially group members are intensively trained at meetings. A number of groups come together to form 'centres' which also meet regularly, and where the main financial transactions take place in the open. Groups elect their leaders, and leadership rotates. All this institution-building requires intensive nurturing by local bank workers. They have considerable autonomy in doing so. In this respect the organisation is very different from the general culture of organisation in Bangladesh, which is hierarchical and centralised. The Grameen Bank is only centralised in its strategic direction: deciding where to experiment, for example (Holcombe, 1995).

The bank's impact has been substantial. By 1988 bank members had significantly higher incomes than non-members, and credit had led to new production activities and employment. Bank-sponsored businesses experienced rapid growth in working capital. After three years borrowers typically diversified their borrowing into social expenditure on housing, sanitation and education. Bank members were found to be more protected against the losses caused by floods, and there was anecdotal evidence that wages increased in areas where there was high NGO activity. The benefits were particularly striking for women, with substantial increases in employment measured by number of days in each month in work, and higher increases in working capital than men (Hossain, 1988).

The Grameen Bank has been the leader of a host of NGO and NGO combined with public sector bank poverty-oriented credit programmes in poverty-stricken Bangladesh. In a country where landowning, wealth and incomes are highly skewed, if fairly stable, and where the political opportunities for redistribution of land are small, off-farm incomes are absolutely critical in poverty alleviation. Without a massive institutional development in this direction, with supportive national policies, there is little chance of substantial progress. All the well-known credit programmes in Bangladesh emphasise group organisation (group size varying from 5 to 20) for savings and credit, and increasingly commercial interest rates, with confidence that the poor can pay these, and thus help to make poverty banking sustainable. Many public sector bank branches have resisted the idea, despite the existence of an NGO, Swanirvar Bangladesh, as an organising agent for the banks.

Hulme and Turner (1990) reckoned that the basic features of Grameen Bank's approach were quite transferable, so long as the transfer was done as an action research project, learning from the particular context and adapting the transferred institution. A limitation was that expansion required capital injections, which could not easily be generated from within the Bank.

In Malaysia, Projek Ikhtiar tried to copy Grameen Bank in the context of a wealthier society, with better infrastructure and better managed public sector rural development programmes. But its pilot phase produced a huge problem of accumulating arrears in many of its groups and centres. It was rescued by its women borrowers who repaid 95 per cent of outstanding loans, while the overall rate was 78 per cent; and by a toughening up of its procedures so that group members had greater incentives to attend, and groups and local centres greater incentives to chase up defaulters.

In Latin America, poverty banking has moved forward rapidly. A most exciting example is the transformation of a Bolivian NGO, PRODEM, established unusually by a group of businessmen, into Bancosol, a bank targeted at poor borrowers. This was accomplished over a 4-year period (1988–92) through the application of very businesslike principles to the objective of serving the poor. Highly commercial interest rates were charged, despite political opposition, in a high-inflation economy: this was necessary to encourage and protect the savings on which the bank was to depend. The bank had to reach the capital threshold required of banks: this it did not only by raising savings, but also by attracting a variety of international donor investors and grant givers. Like Grameen and other poverty banks, Bancosol made use of peer groups (of around 4–5) to ensure that loans were repaid. By 1993, subsidy dependence was coming down substantially. Many poorer borrowers had increased their incomes significantly. Competition from Bancosol had reduced interest rates charged by local moneylenders, and increased their willingness to lend without collateral (Mosely, 1995).

A recent comparative survey was done for the United States Agency for International Development (USAID), which has been strongly promoting micro-enterprise development (Christen *et al.*, 1995). This concluded that success in reaching poor borrowers depended on the scale of an organisation's operations, and not on exclusively targeting the poor in the ways described above: that organisations which lent money to poor and non-poor were also perfectly capable of reaching the poor provided their lending activities had sufficient spread. This study also concluded that lending organisations could become operationally efficient over a reasonable number of years if they charged commercial rates of interest and also did not inflate their salary bills. Organisations which followed these practices were able to free themselves from the need to resort to concessional finance from donor organisations. Five out of the eleven organisations studied had done so.

These studies would indicate that the future for micro-enterprise credit is bright: it is certainly a rapid growth area both for NGOs and official donors. It may yet become a growth area for commercial finance houses. This would constitute a very dramatic and significant step out of the realm of subsidised rural development. The World Bank set up a $200 million fund in 1995 to finance a 'Consultative Group to Assist the Poorest' with micro-finance to encourage NGOs into the banking field.

Credit has its limits. For example, in the programmes reviewed by Remenyi, most of the agencies tried to act as brokers with the existing financial institutions, so that their clients would in the medium to long term become accepted bank clients as they outgrew the NGO's lending capacity. 'Not one . . . programme was encountered where the track record established at the bank resulted in a flow of bank loans from the bank to . . . programme depositors' (Remenyi, 1991: 117). In fact commercial banks take deposits from NGO-run credit programmes and invest them elsewhere – in the urban economy. This implies that NGO-sponsored credit for the poor remains in the field of welfare; that bankers remain unwilling to enter the small loans sector, despite the demonstration effect of many successful projects.

Without getting the poor into the mainstream, scaling up these NGO efforts will be very difficult. Scaling up of course is especially significant in countries like Bangladesh where absolute poverty is very extensive, and may have less importance in countries like Malaysia, where one institution may be able to reach a large proportion of the absolutely poor. On the other hand, if the credit-giving institution can become financially independent, and cease to depend on concessional finance, it will act as a redistributor of capital from the formal or commercial financial sector to the poor.

Savings and credit associations

The Grameen Bank approach remains institutionally focused. In effect it has become a channel for outside aid or investment. The alternative is an approach based on supporting existing village-level savings and credit associations. Advocates of savings and credit associations tend to bemoan the spread of subsidised and co-operative banking, when rotating or accumulating savings and credit associations (ROSCAs and ASCRAs) and their hybrids are so widespread and effective around the developing world. These associations are independent, run by members for their own benefit, and therefore have lots of advantages over more formal credit systems. As Bouman (1995) has indicated, they are often very dynamic organisations, and there are a large number of innovations taking place in this informal financial sector. In many cases, associations are beginning to compete with the formal banking system, especially for savings. In rural areas there is often no competition as banks are not accessible, and if they are, credit is hard to get without collateral. In countries affected by economic collapse the banking system is ineffective. The characteristics of ROSCAs and ASCRAs are shown in Table 4.1.

Simple ROSCAs have weak points: there is always a last person in the rotation to benefit from the fund, and this person could have saved as an individual with the same result. Similarly, people who take their turn toward the end of the rotation have been saving all along, but do not receive any interest. Early winners get interest-free loans; late winners can borrow an amount which is almost always worth less than earlier loans. This may not matter much if the period over which money is saved is short – a matter of days or weeks – but does matter if it is longer and inflation is high. Another drawback is that each member only gets one loan per cycle: if a loan is needed urgently, a simple ROSCA cannot help. Many modifications are possible to rectify these shortcomings. Interest rates can be charged; earlier receivers pay more for their loans; or late receivers are compensated with higher bonus payments. Last receivers may become first receivers in the next round.

TABLE 4.1

ROSCAs and ASCRAs

ROSCA	ASCRA
1. Fund rotates immediately after formation: its liquidation is automatic: length of cycle seldom exceeds one year	Fund accumulates and is redistributed according to members' discretion; sometimes not liquidated at all
2. Only one loan per member, unless holder of more than one share. Loan is automatic, often by prearranged order, emergency cases enjoy priority	Multiple loans per member possible. Loan decision is needed; emergency cases enjoy priority
3. Periodic and equal contributions per participant require a regular income flow	Contributions may be disproportionate and irregular; no regular income flow required
4. Membership small and homogeneous; poor and rich usually have separate clubs	Membership larger and more heterogeneous, poor and rich often participate together
5. No safekeeping of funds; precludes embezzlement	Safekeeping facilities needed; funds are often deposited with bank
6. Balanced reciprocity in input and outtake of money	More generalised reciprocity in input and outtake; large loan possible on humble savings
7. Loans of (very) short duration; proceedings less affected by inflation	Short and long-term loans possible; inflation may affect proceedings
8. In principle no interest on loans. Exceptions: auction, mutual agreement	High loan interest; makes fund grow fast, allows handsome rewards to savers
9. Main function is financial intermediation for individual welfare	Multifunctional; serving the common interests of group and/or community
10. Few officeholders; no supervision required	Proliferation of supervising and administrative officeholders
11. Simple, usually unwritten constitution and procedures	Written, maybe even printed charter, rules and procedures
12. Little, if any, administration and records	Records and bookkeeping are normal; audit optional
13. Obligatory contributions	Contributions not obligatory
14. Price discounts possible in commodity ROSCA	Less relevant
15. Members pay few other costs than those of food and drinks at meetings	Costs of staff, administration, stationery
16. Member's right to fund is transferable	Not relevant

Source: Bouman (1995).

Auctions are widely held, so that those who need a loan urgently may bid for it, with the successful bid being distributed among those who did not win the bid. 'The most spectacular ROSCA innovation is to use the auction to create "a second fund with auxiliary credit from the bidding gains"' (Bouman, 1995: 380). This gives a ROSCA the features of an ASCRA: the bid goes into a separate loan fund which may be loaned to any borrower(s) according to their requirements. As it is repaid, and further bids for the principal ROSCA fund are made, this secondary fund accumulates dramatically. Increasingly large funds can be accumulated.

Generally, loans from ROSCAs/ASCRAs are flexible: they can be used for whatever purposes individuals want to borrow, though the group will often have priorities: emergencies and consumption usually take precedence over production loans, because they are more urgent. But as a group becomes more secure and individuals more economically ambitious, the trend is towards lending for economic activities.

ROSCAs have their limitations, their own inherent problems:

(a) they have a limited impact since many people in the villages may not participate in such groups, (b) they are not transparent and often have major accounting difficulties, (c) the risk of breakup of the group may be high so that people's money is not secure, (d) they require a lot of time of the participants for monthly meetings, (e) they are not directly linked to the banking system hence they are unlikely to benefit from additional bank loans since they are not organised as a legal entity, (f) the cost of credit through auction-ROSCAs may be too high to allow productive investments, and (g) they do not result in the permanent accumulation of wealth through a single institution since money continuously changes hands. (Jazayeri, 1995: 15–16)

The very poor

Most studies have concluded that it is extremely difficult to reach the very poor with formal credit. The not-so-poor among the poor find bankable activities easier to identify, and group organisation with the obligations which this brings easier to manage. Savings and credit societies are probably easier for the very poor to manage; some will even give them special terms for membership, which makes their participation easier. However, even savings and credit are ultimately no substitute for social security, to which rural development has to date given far too little attention (see below).

Removing barriers to poverty alleviation

For credit-based strategies to work, policy needs to be supportive not only to the credit agency, but also to more general poverty alleviation, income and employment objectives. Credit agencies require autonomy from national political influence and room to expand. Grameen Bank achieved this initially under military rule, where party politics was suppressed. Government, which had been the majority shareholder, also allowed the Bank to become owned by its clients.

Small businesses generally will benefit from policies which remove discrimination against them. Many countries retain legislation severely restricting the freedoms of small businesses. There are often requirements to register, pay taxes and charges which are simply too onerous both in terms of cash and the time required to negotiate them for the poor to manage. There may be zoning laws which prevent businesses operating in particular areas, though this applies more to towns and cities than to rural areas. Organisations seeking to promote income generation among the poor may need to confront some of these discriminatory rules and regulations (Hubbard, 1995: 67).

More significantly, where small enterprise competes with bigger businesses, the latter have often benefited from trade protection, subsidy and overvalued exchange rates because of their wider political and economic significance. Removal of these protections and subsidies is the agenda of structural adjustment programmes: one would therefore expect structural adjustment and liberalisation programmes to have a beneficial influence on small-scale and rural enterprises in particular.

Structural adjustment programmes

A thoroughgoing structural adjustment programme will tend to open spaces for small producers, traders and service providers. Liberalisation of trade and currency devaluation creates a more competitive climate for large-scale, previously protected industry, but has hardly any negative impact on small producers who rely little on imported inputs. In Ghana, 'in facing competition from large-scale producers which are more reliant on imported inputs, the cedi depreciation shifted relative prices in favour of SSEs' (Sowa *et al.*, 1992: 46), and most SSEs experienced increased availability of inputs (ibid: 42).

The retrenchment of workers in the public sector puts a large number of educated people into self-employment. In Ghana the firms which have done best during the structural adjustment era were the older firms owned by people with technical or secondary education qualifications, and located away from the major urban centres where competition with imports was more severe (Sowa *et al.*, 1992: 45–6).

In Kenya the grain milling sector has been the subject of reforms reducing the protection offered to the large millers. It is remarkable that the very numerous small millers have survived and grown in number in a situation where the National Cereals Produce Board, which has monopolised the official trade in cereals until recently, would only assure supplies to the big mills. With deregulation they have greatly increased their share of the market competing effectively with the large-scale mills. Their strong position has been due to the quality of service they offer the customer: each individual consumer is able to have milled exactly what they want, and to take back any byproducts to feed to backyard poultry, etc. (Lewa, 1995).

Jobs and self-employment opportunities can probably be created as much in the trade and services sectors as in manufacturing. Unfair advantages may be given by policy or the actions of state organisations to larger-scale operators in these sectors too. Structural adjustment programmes have been particularly concerned with privatising state trading activities, or allowing traders progressively to take over functions previously monopolised by state organisations. Credit schemes to enable small traders to participate in cereals trade have frequently run into difficulties: the policy framework may not be conducive if traders are subject to arbitrary seizures or price control, or the sudden release of food aid; banks may not see small traders as a commercial proposition; and the crops used as collateral may not be seen as secure by the bank, unless there is a reliable warehousing system (Coulter, 1994: 26). Once again there is a role for NGOs and associations of traders in developing the common services necessary to make a success of small-scale enterprise.

Beyond the crude measures of structural adjustment, growth in the 'poverty economy' will require imaginative and new public (governmental and non-governmental) initiatives. These centre around the facilitation of new forms of organisation (poverty-oriented banks) and the strengthening of existing associations and networks of small businesses, capable of providing the common services and infrastructure needed by small businesses. These strategies will be more successful in the majority of poor countries where strong large-scale, private enterprise hardly exists.

Reaching the very poor

If the very poor cannot easily be involved in development through savings and credit schemes, then rural development needs to take very seriously the available alternatives. These range from the development of food and other social security mechanisms, through employment generation to a concern with wage levels. These issues have generally been seen as central government policy issues. It is a matter of history that social security has been (and still is in many rural areas) ensured by local social systems and arrangements. The extended family, the clan, the patron–client relationship have all been valued by the poor in terms of the security they have provided. State security mechanisms have worked for the rural poor only in rare cases – examples would be the public food distribution systems in Sri Lanka and Kerala state in India. These have succeeded in providing basic rations of staple foods to poor families, when other such schemes have tended to supply urban and better-off rural folk but failed to reach the rural poor. This is explained by the democratic political culture and background of the political systems and regimes in power: they were regimes which depended substantially and directly on the votes of the rural poor, without expecting the rural elite to be political intermediaries. Elsewhere the benefits supposed to go to the rural poor tend to get hijacked by better-off groups with the political muscle to enhance their own food security.

Where state schemes are unlikely to have a positive impact, other approaches are needed. A more combative approach which may work where there are ineffective public distribution schemes in place is the formation of claimants' unions among the poor to claim rights and access to resources which have been denied in practice. Where this is unrealistic, or where the resources are simply absent, it may be possible to develop limited security mechanisms on a more local or voluntaristic basis.

Insurance

Local-level savings to provide insurance schemes are an example of an idea which has great potential, but has rarely been explored in today's poor rural societies. The near universal existence of burial societies indicates that poor people are quite prepared to save for a rainy day, in this case for their own and their relatives' deaths. Insurance schemes protecting against illness, death, and loss of assets could make a great contribution to the security of the rural poor. They may well prefer to save for such benefits rather than to put their money into credit-oriented savings schemes. The opportunity to do so is rare. There is scope for existing insurance companies to put together special low-cost insurance packages for the rural poor but to sell these packages to a wider market, so that the undoubted risks are spread as widely as possible. It is likely that local group organisation would be required to make such packages cost-effective; just as banks wishing to reach the poor have to change their procedures and style of working, so too would insurance companies. If the costs of doing so are too great, new insurance institutions are needed to fill this gap in the market. These could conceivably operate alongside existing savings and credit institutions where these have a good reputation. Otherwise it requires enterprising individuals to start schemes on a local basis. These schemes could eventually federate to increase their financial strength.

There are different types of insurance dealing with physical products which have developed over recent years. Village-level cereal banks are one example. Here, villagers get together, sometimes with the help of a development agency, to place staple grains which they produce into a store, so that they can buy them back at a later date at a reasonable (cost) price. This helps to reduce the impact of the 'hungry season' when food prices are high. These schemes have been particularly widespread in West Africa. Some work well as semi-commercial organisations, selling surplus grain on behalf of members. Seed banks are a similar idea, only here the focus is on saving seed for next year's planting. Where this is done collectively, it prevents families from eating next year's seed requirements rather than taking more drastic measures to ensure survival – for example, migrating to find work.

Perhaps the most common form of insurance in poor rural areas is now in the field of health services. Since ill-health can wipe away the small savings and credit potential of poor households, insurance schemes which share (or 'pool') the risks of ill-health between rich and poor households, and prevent episodes of ill-health from destroying the limited gains of economic development, have much to recommend them. Risk-pooling health insurance has been thought to be less easy to organise in rural areas than in urban, because traditional mechanisms for risk-sharing among kin and between patients and traditional healers or midwives still exist, and because rural incomes are often highly seasonal, so regular payments are difficult to make. However, there is now a number of successful schemes in existence, even in the poorest of rural societies (Shaw and Griffin, 1995: 69–71; Chabot *et al.*, 1991; Arhin, 1991). One of the best known, a prepayment scheme in Zaire's Bwamanda health zone, has enrolled 60 per cent of the population. It has high premium levels and is efficiently run. Most of the population believe that it provides high quality care; hospital user fees are relatively high, so there is an incentive to join the prepayment scheme; the premiums are affordable: linked to the value of 2 kilogrammes of soyabeans; and revenues from the scheme are used to finance local services. In schemes where the quality of care is poor, where fees are low and revenues go into a general pool, there is less likelihood of success (Shaw and Griffin, 1995: 70–1).

Employment schemes

Employment guarantee schemes have proved one of the most effective mechanisms for preventing the erosion of poor people's assets in times of distress, when other sources of wages tend to dry up. These require a flow of cash (or food) and must therefore be mounted by a cash-rich institution. They also require fairly intensive administration capable of rapid responses, both on the ground for the design and supervision of works, and for payment of wages. They have the virtue of being self-targeting: only the really poor or destitute will generally take advantage of them as the work is usually hard manual work.

The absence of competent administration is often a hindrance in mounting labour-intensive works quickly: simple activities (e.g. breaking stones) with the possibility of quick start-ups in an emergency situation may be the best which can be hoped for. Where administration is competent and design skills are present more complex and useful activities can be undertaken: as in India where employment guarantee schemes build dams, canals and undertake other major investments (Hubbard, 1995: 81–2). These interventions can be made by local governments, the central state, or NGOs. In the new paradigm they would increasingly be transferred to local government, or other local organisations. Financing mechanisms would be necessary to ensure a measure of autonomy for the local undertaking.

Wages and employment

Rural households' income and security depends on a diversity of income-earning opportunities. Increasingly, as rural economies become more capitalised, these are in wage employment. This has been so for decades in much of South and East Asia, and South America, with their large populations of rural landless labour. But it is increasingly true even in much of Sub-Saharan Africa. In all cases, while there is rural–urban migration, there is as much or more employment in rural areas themselves.

The availability of employment, and prevailing wage levels, have thus become much more important determinants of poverty and life chances. Given the prevalence of regional underdevelopment these opportunities often involve migration from one rural region to another, where wages are sufficiently high to attract migrants. In Chapter 2 we have already seen how the Green Revolution has tended to provide employment opportunities but in the end to push agricultural wages down even in the Green Revolution areas. There, sustainable agriculture, which often relies more on relatively abundant labour than scarce capital, was proposed as a means of increasing employment, and the steady, year-round demand for labour. A substantial drift to sustainable agriculture would have a positive effect on wage levels as a result, not least because spectacular technical advances would not be so restricted to particular geographical areas as was the case with the Green Revolution.

In the non-farm rural economy, wage levels will depend on a number of factors. Firstly, agricultural wages will determine the prevailing local unskilled wage rate. This will tend to be lower where there is a large pool of landless labour, as in parts of India and Bangladesh. Where most families still have access to some productive land there will be significant opportunity costs of engaging in wage labour, and both farm and non-farm wage levels will tend to rise faster as demand for goods and services rises. In the unusual situation where demand for labour outstrips supply, either because of extraneous demand from industry or from urban areas or abroad, farmers are likely to substitute capital for labour, and wage rates rise across the board.

Secondly, non-farm enterprise wages and the incomes of the self-employed will depend on enterprise productivity levels. It is these which most programmes aim to affect through training, improved technology, better management, credit for working capital and so on. It has been argued that there is a rural transition from low agricultural productivity, through a phase of higher labour investment made possible by population growth, to a stage where higher agricultural productivity eventually leads to rising demand for both agricultural and non-agricultural goods and services. As agriculture mechanises, off-farm activity develops its own dynamic as labour increasingly specialises. So long as demand continues increasing, productivity increases in non-farm enterprise will add to employment and incomes. However, if demand for labour is stagnant, enterprise productivity increases would have the opposite effect.

Thirdly, the organisation of labour may have some effect on wage and employment levels. Rural labour is generally weakly organised; trades unions find it difficult to organise labourers who are geographically spread out, and socially poorly linked. Where labour is abundant the difficulty is the greater. Legislation on minimum wages, terms of employment, and working conditions often remains unimplemented in at least the remoter rural areas. However, we have already seen that such regulations can affect small business development and employment, and need to be carefully evaluated.

Conclusion

Poverty is a complex phenomenon, and we know that economic growth *per se* does not necessarily alleviate it. Poverty has been alleviated by direct measures: development programmes, savings and credit schemes, employment programmes, and social insurance and security measures. Currently attention is focused on making micro-finance widely available. Given that poverty is complex, this smacks of a technical fix: however, well-managed credit is a sufficiently flexible tool to enable poor people to decide for themselves how they will use the resources. This is its attraction over more prescriptive development programmes.

The aspect which is most glaringly missing from most rural development policies is social security. There is a range of approaches to security from employment schemes, through food security measures, to a variety of insurance schemes. Here then is great scope for innovation, in business and local governance. This is particularly important as the very poor rarely benefit from savings and credit.

It has also been argued strongly that rural wages are a critical determinant of poverty, and that development agencies concerned with poverty alleviation cannot ignore the political and economic factors which influence wage levels and terms and conditions of work. Lobbying for improved wages and working conditions has not been in the tradition of rural development, but clearly should be.

5

The Project

Much of the first part of this chapter is written in the past tense: as a historical reflection on the nature of *the project* as the major form within which development work has been carried on. Today the project is being stretched to and beyond its limits; its basic parameters face insurmountable challenges; the search is on for alternative forms, and alternative languages which more effectively represent the work which is being done.

A major proportion of public sector investment in developing countries has taken place through projects. There was a coincidence of interests around the project. Donors felt they could ensure accountability if funds were disbursed to projects rather than put into a common revenue pool. They often insisted on special administrative arrangements to ensure their influence. Recipient governments, on the other hand, preferred using projects to achieve objectives rather than policies. This was for political reasons: Bates (1981: ch. 5) argued that projects allow governments to select more precisely the beneficiaries of their expenditure than would a blanket policy. A project allows selection on a geographical basis, which often neatly corresponds to prevailing divisions in politics. Projects can thus be used to reward supporters or neutralise opposition. Their generally short time frame may also fit in with the politician's need for quick results.

Projects became the universal language of international development by the 1970s: activities were somehow separated or protected from routine administration or management, and given a special status and priority. In the aid business, donors expected recipients to produce projects to be funded; if they could not, or if their projects were not prepared to certain standards, donors were prepared to pay others (consultants, or NGOs) to do the job of project preparation. 'Projects are convenient-size modules that correspond to the structure and resources needed to initiate and implement donor-assisted development activities . . . the project approach has value in its ability to cement relationships between donor and recipient and to remove a modicum of the uncertainty surrounding the development process' (Bates, 1981: 301).

The project concept originated in western industrial society. Large engineering activities were cast in project form, with the following basic elements:

(a) disciplined conceptual disaggregation of complex, or ill-defined problems into discrete tasks for which resources can be mobilised and targeted
(b) specific time boundaries within which projects begin and end according to a funding schedule and work plan
(c) pre-programmed activities in which the resources, contracting, procurement, training and anticipated outcomes are all planned or 'designed'
(d) applied economic and systems analysis used in the appraisal of a project idea to determine whether it is economically viable or rational according to other technical criteria
(e) standardised reporting procedures for monitoring, control, and evaluation. (Morgan, 1983: 330)

The project developed far beyond this original concept. In developing countries it was first used for large capital construction activities, but as the uncertainties and complexities of development have come to be more appreciated, projects have tended to become more and more inclusive ('integrated'?) and multi-sectoral, especially in rural development. During the 1970s many donor agencies, frustrated with the lack of connection between activities managed by separate line ministries, persuaded recipient governments to set up project authorities which would command as many as possible of the resources needed to accomplish project objectives under one roof. In the 1980s, as the problems of separate project authorities were learned, donors turned away from this approach, to the relief of some recipient governments. On the other hand, some governments (for example, India, Indonesia) restructured major parts of their own development investments into projects.

The project became the major means of raising and channelling aid funds, whether in the official or NGO sector. Project documents were critical to the orchestration of funds from different funding sources. The financiers were thus able to exercise extraordinary influence over the process of development, way beyond what a western private financier would generally look for. Project documents became compromises between what their authors knew different funding agencies would appreciate. Each funding agency developed not only preferences for different sorts of project but also sets of procedures which had to be followed at the various stages of a project. The project became an administrative jungle. This was an irony in situations where administrative energy was in very short supply, and where projects were originally justified partly to circumvent tiresome administrative procedures. The term 'projectisation' – turning an administrative process into a project process – often has irksome implications today, of unnecessary procedures, artificial and wasteful competition, and long delays.

Projects nevertheless remained attractive at least to external funding agencies and Ministries of Finance. 'Projects are attractive because bureaucracies in much of the Third World have so little capacity to implement plans and policies by other means' (Morgan, 1983: 308). Moris (1977) identified weaknesses in African administration which undermined policy implementation: personnel recruited through personal and political contacts rather than merit and skill; professional and technical standards not met; suspicion and distrust among civil servants leading to conflicts or inaction. Supervision was weak and the flow of information inadequate. Leadership and top management was also weak and decisions tended to be made through political and social interaction. Morale at the bottom was low, and directives often ignored. Budgeting was an *ad hoc* process and liquidity problems prevented rational planning. Apathy and corruption were widespread, and crisis management was the order of the day. The system reacted slowly to changes in external circumstances.

Projects were attractive by contrast because they offered a precise frame within which action could take place. Resources required to meet objectives could be quantified. The meagre resources of a country could be brought to bear on specific problems. Because of the justification which was required in the project framework they were more convincing to external financiers. The appraisal techniques used in theory encouraged systematic exploration of alternatives. In practice there was often little real exploration of options, and appraisal was used to justify a project which was preferred in any case. Whereas large programmes 'encase errors in concrete'

(Caiden and Wildavsky, 1974: 309), projects were short term and allowed for review and reformulation and learning from experience. This was the theory, but project evaluation has always been the project's Achilles' heel: rarely done, even more rarely publicised so others could learn from the experience. Vested interests have always been against it, or at least not sufficiently for it to make a difference. So learning has been limited.

They were attractive because they allowed for innovation, experiment and special conditions all of which were usually difficult to manage in a routine programme (Rondinelli, 1983). Here, taking a project out of the line civil service and giving it its own organisation reduced the risk of failure for parent departments. This is the theory; practice is that projects have become much more a routine way of doing the business of development, and tend to become routinised in content and procedure rather than being at the thinking or cutting edge of development.

There were certain characteristics of the project as a concept which were fundamental, and fundamentally problematic for the achievement of rural development objectives of strengthening the hand of local, rural people, reaching the poor, alleviating poverty, and improving rural people's environment and health. The project had a control orientation, and an economic core. These derived from the project's engineering origins where control is vital, and from the economists' dominant position in project analysis.

Control orientation

Out of unknown pasts, presents and uncertain futures, projects attempted to carve islands of apparent control and predictability. The feasibility of this is questionable in rural development. In many rural development projects too little was known, too little understood, and because of the interconnected nature of many issues and phenomena in rural economies and societies, reality was too complicated to be easily subjected to neat predictive analysis. So the assumptions and reductions which had to be made to fit into a project framework were truly heroic.

Porter *et al.* (1991) offered a brilliant critique of the control orientation in rural development, drawn out of their case study of the Magarini Settlement Scheme in Kenya. Following a colonial and post-colonial history of intervention in the lives of the Giriama people of the Kenyan coast, characterised by retribution and blundering, the Magarini Project illustrates how good intentions to act on behalf of the Giriama, in their interests, rendered them once again victims of development, despite millions of dollars and 'immense and sincere human effort' (Porter *et al.*, 1991: 3).

A control orientation is 'the belief that current events and various states of land, labour, technology and capital can be manipulated according to causal relations which exist between them, to achieve a desired objective in a controlled and predictable manner . . . in physical and social environments characterised by a great deal of uncertainty, everything must be rigourously controlled . . . such an approach is deeply flawed' (ibid. 1991: 4–5).

In tracing the history of the Magarini Project a central fact about Giriama life and cosmology emerged. This was their search for diversity, choice and options, to minimise risk of failure. Development projects which present no – or a limited – choice of ideas, technologies, and methods of organisation represent the antithesis of this diversity principle, which characterises all vulnerable societies.

Porter *et al.* advocated a pluralist orientation, characterised by methodological anarchism in which 'institutionalised rules and procedures which, rather than ensuring success, give substance and permanence to errors' should be questioned, and attempts to reduce diversity should be viewed with suspicion. Good development practice is about widening, not narrowing choices (ibid: 203–4). Arguing that professionals and decision-makers should be humble about what they can control, and the outcomes they can generate, the authors believe 'we must abandon the ambition to find one "right" answer to every dilemma. . . Even if it exists, by the time we have groped our way towards it, the problem to which we have initially sought an answer, will have changed' (ibid. 1991: 205).

Of course, decisions about investment and resource allocation still have to be taken. A pluralist orientation would recognise that things can go wrong, that people need to be able to protect themselves against that possibility. This can only be brought about by people being empowered with information on what is likely to happen, or on what the options are. This information should be far more in the public domain than it is. Resource-allocators' decisions will then at least be constrained by public knowledge and perhaps debate.

Uncertainty even affects projects which would seem at first glance to be more predictable. The classic example is the dam for irrigation and/or hydro-electric power. There has always been opposition to big dams, so big-dam projects have been under extreme pressure to show a return to society. Engineers have consistently made optimistic assumptions about the life of the dam, the amount of silt deposition in the dam, and the areas irrigated or power produced. Salination affects irrigated command areas in many parts of the world, reducing cropping possibilities and yields: this has often not been anticipated, or the cost of mitigating its effect has been underestimated. Time and again, dam construction has been held up as local opposition has mounted, or as new technical problems have surfaced or new information has been discovered. Delays have led to sometimes huge cost overruns.

The search for certainty and control leads ultimately to the search for authoritative organisation – an organisation which can impose its will. In practice, unless this is backed up with considerable disciplinary powers only available to a relatively strong state, organisations can only be strong because of the resources they command, and through skills in using those resources in negotiation.

The desire for control may be psychologically based on fear of uncertainty and anarchy, but must be based philosophically on the belief that what is best, right or necessary can be defined sufficiently uniformly to constitute a uniform activity. This belief cannot be very strong in anyone who examines the evidence in rural development dispassionately.

In fact the need for control is dictated largely by organisational requirements. To maintain or expand jobs and structures – in governments, donor agencies, NGOs – resources must be acquired, budgets must be presented and argued, objectives and targets agreed, promises of delivery met, and trust maintained. These requirements are especially accentuated for organisations (like aid agencies, or ministries with field offices) spread over long distances, where communication is difficult, and control over field staff, inputs and outputs is by nature very problematic.

A control orientation is antithetic to many common progressive rural development objectives. Despite the rhetoric of participation, strongly proclaimed in many rural development project documents, politicians' speeches and academics' commentaries, a control orientation necessarily limits the influence ordinary people can have. It is therefore very difficult (if not impossible) to reconcile local 'institutional strengthening', or decentralisation, let alone 'empowerment', with control. In fact, all these objectives imply local control exercised by ordinary people.

A control orientation travels with short time-frames (typically 1–5 years for a rural development project), whereas rural development is a long process, as we have seen. There may be phases or aspects of that long process more amenable to a short-time-frame, controlled activity (e.g. the redistribution of land in a land reform process, which has to be accomplished systematically, quickly, and according to standard and agreed rules), but the general process is not amenable.

A control orientation is also related inversely to the specificity of the work undertaken. Very clear, specific work has a lower management requirement than more multi-faceted work. The latter tends to involve more management, which in turn strengthens the perceived need for control (Israel, 1987). There is a very important organisational implication from this observation: that organisations wishing to move away from a control orientation should avoid over-complex work, or be prepared to 'unbundle' activities into separate but related (networked) units, so that management never has a chance to become too powerful (Chapter 8).

Paradoxically, a measure of control or influence from outside may be needed for the achievement of some objectives in certain circumstances. In a highly stratified society, the poor or marginalised will only participate in decisions or benefit from investments if their interests are upheld against the tide of local power by outside forces. However, this issue may be more effectively addressed through policy changes (e.g. on agricultural research to favour employment generation in agriculture – see Chapter 2), wider socio-cultural change, or the establishment and support of institutions to support the interests of the poor (Grameen Banks, for example), or to represent the poor (associations, unions).

The case for external control has been argued (Chapter 3) too with respect to regulating common property resources and environmental management where internal institutions among the parties involved have failed. Too often, however, regulatory frameworks are erected without prior exploration of the scope for internal institutional improvement. Again, this may work, where there is a strong state to buttress regulation, but hardly where the state is weak. Even where the state is strong, regulation often offers the illusion but not the reality of control. Of course, regulation may also be used to further the interests of particular groups or enterprises to the exclusion of others.

The project cycle and project rationality

Rondinelli (1977: ch. 1) outlined the comprehensive project cycle and the activities associated with each phase. There were many phases:

- identification and definition
- formulation, preparation and feasibility
- design
- appraisal
- selection, negotiation and approval
- activation and organisation
- implementation and operation
- completion, termination or output diffusion
- evaluation.

A variety of more or less complicated and systematic methods are associated with each stage, but especially with appraisal. On the other hand, methods for project identification have remained rather informal and inspirational (Birgegård, 1975), and strongly influenced by ideology and politics.

The skills needed to thrive on the project process have not always been easily available especially in the poorer developing countries. The skills to implement even the simpler projects were also often inadequate. There was rarely any idea that activities should be tailored to administrative feasibility. More frequently a case was put to upgrade planning skills, through training. Project skills were often equated with planning and design skills, rather than management and implementation. Actually administrative feasibility should always be a filter through which any project design passes; all too often this does not happen. Greater efforts need to be made to improve operational performance rather than design skills. However, this could probably only happen if implementation improved in status compared with design. This happens once a process approach is adopted. Implementation skills ('getting things done') are generally much more available in the rural areas of developing countries. Rather than separating out planning from implementation, and creating a rural development planning profession, it makes much greater sense to upgrade the existing policy, planning and managerial skills of administrators, politicians, villagers, leaders of local organisations, and others.

Evaluation has always tended to come at the end of a cycle – often too late to influence the project; and has tended to be carried out largely for reasons of accountability to external financiers rather than in order to learn from the experience. Since rural development deals in such high levels of uncertainty and lack of basic knowledge and information, it would be logical to expect evaluation to be central to the process: instead it has been marginalised. A symptom of this is the position that evaluation units typically occupy in rural development organisations – detached from the rest of the organisation, without influence on planning or implementation processes, an 'add-on' component.

The project cycle is an indicator of how linear the process of development is seen to be. It represents a Victorian and heroic notion of progress being achievable within limited space and time, and with more or less limited interventions. But in fact, change is rarely linear. More often, progress of one type is at the expense of good things elsewhere (more productive or effective technology at the expense of local knowledge, natural and genetic resources; capital accumulation at the expense of loss of assets by the poor). Sometimes change is circular; in the 1990s many countries appear to be retrogressing as nation-states break up, and basic frameworks are challenged.

The project cycle is a microcosm of the notion of linear progress. Every activity is in its place. Objectives will be achieved if order and sequence can be maintained. This is very similar to the notion of comprehensive and rational policy analysis informing policy-making, which has been dear to the hearts of especially American students of public policy and administration. However, in the case of policy analysis there has been a long and continuing debate about the extent to which such a high degree of rationality is possible, and even desirable. The opposition 'incrementalist' school argues that policy-makers have no choice but to 'muddle through'. This argument was to some extent resolved in Etzioni's 'mixed scanning' approach. Here the costs and benefits of carrying out analysis at different points in a policy-making process are assessed; and where analysis is going to bring enough more benefits than costs it is pursued. This is refreshingly more thoughtful, creative and practical than slavishly following a pre-set pattern of stages in a cycle, or a required range of disciplinary investigations (economic, social, environmental – see Chapter 6). The mixed scanning approach to policy analysis is well suited to rural development situations in which resources for analysis are very limited.

Policy analysis has also been rather wider in its scope of concern than project analysis. For obvious reasons it has explicitly included political and social factors. It has been more concerned with the views of different stakeholders, and the effects of those views on policy options. In project analysis the objective has been to reach objective conclusions about likely project impact, and this has been achieved by employing professional assessors. The whole process is usually very undemocratic and unparticipatory, and as a result rarely challenges the prejudices which often get dressed up as projects.

The mixed scanning approach to policy analysis argues that there is no such thing as a policy cycle: the activities may seem intrinsically to have a cyclical character, but in fact may occur at any point in a policy process. It actually makes greater sense to centre rural development work around the notion of evaluation, and participatory or democratic evaluation, rather than the currently favoured central ideas of design and appraisal. Because organisational interest focuses on the flow of resources (fund raising, control and allocation of funds, disbursement) naturally the entire project cycle is geared to enhancing and smoothing the path for this flow. Hence the current focus on design and appraisal, and the relegation of other parts of the cycle to a less important category of activity.

This includes implementation: downgraded in the project cycle to an unglamorous status. Implementers are people who execute other people's ideas. But the studies we have of projects (and policies, for that matter) would indicate that implementation is far more important than this. In policy analysis the divergence between the stated policy and what is actually implemented is often so enormous that it can be argued very strongly that a policy is no more and no less than what is implemented. This challenges the notion of policy as something written down, legislated. Likewise, the divergence of actual achievement from objective in many projects is so great that the concept of a rural development project cannot in any way be contained in the project documents.

The logical framework

During the last decade, logical framework analysis (LFA) has often been used to guide donor-funded projects. In brief, this is the delineation of objectives (wider and immediate), outputs and inputs and the relationships between them. In each case project planners or implementers are supposed to think out what indicators will show achievements, how these will be measured, and – most usefully – what assumptions have been made in projecting likely achievements. The great advantage of the logical framework is that all these issues can be presented diagrammatically as a matrix. Sometimes this can be summarised on one page.

The thinking behind the logical framework is not quite as linear as the project cycle it complements. The advance it makes is to focus on the assumptions which are made in calculating what effect inputs or outputs will have. This means that some analysis (evaluation) of past experience is needed if assumptions are to be well grounded in reality, as opposed to dreams. The logical framework is also at root a very simple device which can be used in a village to structure discussion between villagers and an agency. Taken seriously, it can orchestrate a consensus around objectives and activities which is based on analysis as well as values. If used frequently over time it can prompt changes and adjustments in activities as assumptions are challenged and indicators reveal varying levels of performance.

However, LFA is frequently used in a routine way, as a required element of a project document, but with no further significance. Project financiers may use it for monitoring as an instrument of control; in one now popular version it is part of a computerised management information system. In rural development at this point in time, this is bound to lead to accountability upwards – to financiers and controllers.

The financier-economist's project

Historically, development projects were initiated and planned by engineers, and development was almost the same as construction. In fact the construction bias in development while originally a very western phenomenon, spread through the socialist world and is now widespread. Based on a belief in 'linear progress, absolute truths, and rational planning of ideal social orders . . . modernism . . . was imposed by the work of an avant-garde of planners, artists, architects, critics, and other guardians of high taste' (Cosgrove and Petts, 1990: 8) and implemented by engineers. This constructionist focus for development peaked in the west in the 1960s, by which time many of the potential mega-projects had been constructed. From there it transferred to developing countries, in the form of the Aswan and Kariba and other dams.

In the west, in the post-modernist phase there is a tendency to question large-scale development. Part of the reason for this is that economic (and other) evaluations have increasingly shown that the ambitions of the developers are not always met in practice, and that there are uncertainties and ignorance which generate unintended consequences. Economic evaluation has thus been at the heart of western society's ability to question its developers, and to protect itself against the excesses of capitalist development.

In contrast, in developing countries, economists have largely played a subordinate role to policy-makers in governments and the big donor/development banking organisations, producing ex-ante justifications through social cost–benefit analysis of whatever intervention policy-makers have wished to undertake. Whereas economists in the west have been more preoccupied with policy issues and macro-economic management, in developing countries they have been frequently employed at project level. Here they have not occupied the position of independent evaluator, but have been employed by financing agencies or spending ministries, which have been under pressure to disburse money, whether as loans or grants.

Project appraisal and disbursement pressures

Project methodology has been dominated by cost–benefit analysis, used in both appraisal and evaluation. This transforms data into monetary values and derives social welfare functions in order to select the most financially or economically profitable activities. The theory is that by reducing costs and benefits to a common monetary value, the net return on one activity can be compared with that on another, and a rational decision taken to favour the activity with the highest net return. This is a basic measure of economic efficiency.

Cost–benefit analysis (CBA) was first used in the west to select the most economic project in sectors where market prices were not available or an adequate guide to value. In developing countries CBA has been used primarily to analyse activities with marketed output, on the grounds that market prices are heavily distorted and do not therefore give a reasonable idea of social preferences.

In practice, appraisal is rarely used to examine and compare alternatives in a thorough way, since key decisions have often already been made. Appraisal is then designed to justify those decisions. Social and environmental perspectives are rarely allowed to undermine the advocacy nature of the project preparation process: a project is prepared only if someone or some important group wants it badly enough (Morgan, 1983: 332).

A study of the use of economic assessment procedures in the World Bank and other agencies sheds light on the importance and effects of disbursement pressure within an organisation. The World Bank commits itself to a view of the borrowing requirements of developing countries, raises capital from members' subscriptions and in world markets, and then naturally has to demonstrate that its interpretation was broadly correct. 'Given this way of planning, there is a natural internal pressure for the fulfilment of aggregated lending plans. A similar pressure to lend is also built up in most bilateral agencies when they receive their budget allocation as a fixed percentage of GNP. Both are, furthermore, never penalised for unsound lending and bad project performance' (Carlsson *et al.*, 1994: 177). The World Bank's own 1987 evaluation or rural development projects shared these criticisms (1987: xviii).

Agency staff are then judged by their effectiveness in getting projects through the organisation's procedures, massaging them if necessary (Mosley *et al.*, 1991). Incentives are geared to organisational objectives. The result of this is that, even in the World Bank, the major proponent of 'rational' economic analysis, project appraisal is 'continuously being manipulated, because it is subordinated to the individual interests of Project Officers (getting projects to the Board) as well as the organisation's own objectives (meeting the disbursement targets)' (Carlsson *et al.*, 1994: 180)

The pressure to disburse is aided by the way in which social cost–benefit analysis is carried out, and the widespread reliance on the internal rate of return (IRR) measure of project worth. Cost–benefit analysis values the flow of costs and benefits over the life of a project. Benefits received early are preferred to those which come later, so both costs and benefits are discounted over time. This means that benefits (or costs) which occur soon are valued more in the calculation than those which occur later. This clearly involves subjective valuation, and reflects the preferences of people alive today, and the general concern with the near future. The net present value (NPV) is the sum of all the discounted benefits and costs: it measures the value of the project in cash.

The IRR is calculated as follows: it is the discount rate (per cent) which gives an NPV of zero. The IRR is a measure of the return on capital investment. A requirement that a project produce a high IRR, which is typical of development finance organisations, means that the discount rate is generally high. In turn this gives excessive weight to short-term benefits. For further discussion of this highly intricate subject the reader is referred to Gittinger (1982) and Winpenny (1991: 67–72).

It has been argued that the IRR is biased against projects which:

- start slowly
- are implemented in phases
- endure beyond 10–15 years
- involve flexibility. (Tiffen, 1987: 365–7)

The emphasis of the World Bank on the IRR is likely to be related to its concern with disbursement, and its inevitable lack of responsibility for the long-term impact of its usually very substantial investments. Disbursement pressures do not only affect development banks: bilateral donors with legally required proportions of GNP to spend on aid will experience similar pressures.

That the use of economic measures of project worth is highly fallible as a criterion for decision-making is demonstrated by a statistical analysis comparing rates of return of 1,015 World Bank projects before and after completion of project construction (Pohl and Mihaljek, 1992). This showed a wide discrepancy, with estimates at appraisal generally significantly exceeding estimates after construction. Cost overruns and implementation delays seemed to explain a small proportion of the discrepancy; much more important were the policy environment, especially the quality of national economic management, and the strength of national institutions. Overall, what impressed the authors of this study was the high degree of uncertainty surrounding even World Bank projects, with their stress on physical infrastructure and large scale, and their relative avoidance of difficult social and rural development activities. The 1987 World Bank evaluation of its rural development projects also commented on the fact that the resulting stress on 'early production benefits may conflict with those essential institution-building and human resource-creating elements that a long-term, self-sustaining development process requires' (World Bank, 1987: xix)

Project management

In the public sector, organisations tend to be vertically or hierarchically structured. Rural development projects often required integration between several different vertically structured offices. Administrations were restructured into project organisations to accommodate this integrated logic. Projects were thus an opportunity to reduce some of the constraints of working in a bureaucratic system: task-based teams were developed which could work on a collegial and interdisciplinary basis. Some governments have institutionalised the project, the most notable being Indonesia (Fernanda, 1991). Here, capital (and other) expenditure is frequently implemented through a project organisation which operates under local government co-ordination with seconded officials from parent departments who are given financial incentives. While the arrangement gets things done, increases accountability to the Ministry of Finance, and provides public information about public expenditure, it has also led to increased nepotism, inequity in project secondments, and reduced morale of those never seconded.

Donor-funded development projects have rarely been institutionally sustainable. Governments can often not afford the recurrent costs, and there is a classic and unglamorous termination problem, which is rarely adequately planned for: how to reintegrate staff and assets at the close of donor funding. However, this is a minor problem, viewed from the perspective that success in development organisations is at best episodic (Tendler, 1991), and projects may contribute significantly to the creation and maintenance of a critical mass of skilled development professionals.

Are NGO projects different?

The discussion to date has been focused on public sector agencies. The same issues apply to NGOs, though in different ways. In fact some apply with even greater force, since southern NGOs funded by northern NGOs sometimes have no other means of financial support. If they lose the support of one financier they have to search for another, or risk closing down.

The markedly increased flow of aid funds from northern official donors (and some southern governments) to NGOs means that NGOs are succumbing to donor influence on how projects are developed, analysed and documented. The same disbursement pressures are there; donors are worried that NGOs should be accountable to them, and auditors play a growing role in ensuring accountability. These processes risk undermining the comparative advantages of NGOs, which form the rationale for channelling funds to them rather than public sector organisations in the first place: their closeness to beneficiaries and grassroots organisations and movements, their flexibility and capacity to learn, their special levels of inspiration and motivation, and so on (Fowler, 1988). Formalisation of work is likely to inhibit learning and adjusting, innovation, people's participation and institutional development. On the other hand, the proponents of formalisation might argue that it seeks to improve quality of work, for example by insisting that certain issues (e.g. gender, sustainability, cost recovery) be addressed, and that NGOs would often not consider such issues without prompting (Wallace et al., 1997).

NGOs often work in partnership with government, in which case their projects will face similar issues to those discussed above. Even where they work independently they may be finance and target driven, as many NGOs have espoused the goal of financial growth above all other goals; in this case disbursement pressures can be very strong. Disbursement pressure can also help to generate a positive process of organisational change, if the limits to disbursement are largely due to insufficient capacity to execute plans: in this case an option many organisations have adopted is to involve communities and other organisations as partners (or contractors) in getting work done (see Chapter 9).

Project results: success and failure

Of course evaluations show a range of results. It is often stated that projects which involve much activity on the part of ordinary citizens are more difficult to implement than 'hard' technology transfer activities. So building power stations or desalination plants or developing a hybrid-seed-breeding programme are easier activities than farming-systems research or women's development projects, because the uncertainties are fewer and the situation is apparently less complicated. However, the frequency of major unintended consequences, especially environmental ones, has led to a shift in perceptions about hard technology transfer.

The 1980s was a decade for evaluating large-scale, donor-funded rural development projects. The evaluations were quite negative, despite being conducted or commissioned by donor agencies which had set great store by their rural development work. Evaluating USAID-funded Integrated Rural Development Projects, Morss and Gow (1981) found that:

- top-down projects were less successful than participative ones
- information systems developed were too costly and elaborate
- it was difficult to recruit the right professionals
- conflicts between team members were common
- strong leadership and management was required; this was only provided by academic contractors or a management team
- there was a long gap between identification and start-up
- there were frequently staff shortages
- donor and governments frequently had differing agendas
- sustaining benefits in the long term was difficult.

The first finding is perhaps especially significant. The project as a form of administration does not sit easily with participation. It is unlikely to be linked into whatever participative mechanisms exist (councils, parliaments, associations, etc.). Since the very logic of the project is that of insulation of its activities from society or routine government and the by-passing of routine administration, project managers or designers are unlikely to be willing to subject their activities to the influence of the public. The need to situate development work firmly in local institutions is the theme of Chapter 7.

The World Bank was the single most important promoter of integrated rural development (IRD) projects during the 1970s and early 1980s. It evaluated its experience in poverty-focused rural projects from before the publication of the Rural Development Sector Policy Paper (World Bank, 1975) through to 1986. Its main findings were quite negative, and indicated what not to do more than the reverse. Even successful area-based multisectoral projects produced unsustainable benefits, especially when managed by independent units; co-ordination arrangements among government agencies, upon which integration frequently depended, rarely worked as planned; research components produced too little, too late; international staff had difficulty training and handing over to local staff; viable technical packages were often not available, or only of modest use. Many projects took place in inauspicious policy circumstances – especially with respect to farmgate prices and currency exchange rates: policy-based lending was to take this issue up in a big way. Other pointers to a better approach were: that the Bank's own disbursement and appraisal procedures were not appropriate; and there was a need to move from big, lumpy investments to 'a larger number of small, simple and flexible pilot projects and other timely small-scale initiatives, which would help develop appropriate designs for larger projects' (World Bank, 1987: xviii). There is also a need for qualitative monitoring and more flexible management of poorly performing projects; greater use of sociological studies, especially of women's labour time; and a balancing of the short-term bias of the rate of return calculation with long-term commitment to the institution-building and human resource creation required for sustained long-term development. The report also recommended using more self-standing infrastructure projects, especially in Sub-Saharan Africa. This latter recommendation may be the only one which has been seriously implemented by the Bank, for it has otherwise largely switched out of rural development.

More recently, a review of 23 World Bank/Government of Brazil rural development projects in north-east Brazil focused on the lessons which could be learned from their successful parts. The first finding was that success was a characteristic of episodes, not agencies, components or projects. 'Good performance often had less to do with the *inherent capabilities* of an agency itself than with a set of other factors – namely, (1) the ease and difficulty of tasks, (2) the presence of outside pressures, (3) built-in incentives to perform, and (4) the involvement of keenly interested actors and organisations at the local level' (Tendler, 1991: v). Agencies having more successful episodes had tended to narrow down the vision of what was required – down to a governor's signature activity (i.e. what he or she was elected to do), or a project manager's favourite component. Here again we can note the importance of the individual in fostering a process of development. These agencies also tended to take over tasks from organisations set up to carry them out, out of frustration at slow progress and political searching for quick results. After takeover, successful agencies often contracted out the work to public agencies, private firms or NGOs, giving them the power to control operations through the contract, rather than co-ordinate unwilling or demotivated public agencies. Better performers were able to mobilise additional resources, from local communities and especially from municipalities, transforming them into 'a source of healthy outside pressure on state agencies to behave accountably, to get things carried out on time, keep costs down, and use less sophisticated and capital-intensive standards. Bank staff had tried, often to no avail, to accomplish the same thing' (ibid: vii).

Towards a learning process

Rondinelli (1983) argues that the project has so many advantages to the organisations involved, especially to donors and governments, that it will not go away. Indeed, since he wrote, it has not gone away, though some donors at least have indicated their willingness to move away from it.

The main line of improvement 'from within' is to make project analysis increasingly sophisticated and get the plan 'right', in particular by adding social, cultural, political and environmental analysis, moving towards a holistic approach (Chapter 6). This tendency stretches the project to and beyond the limits of its capacity as a concept. The alternative advocated during the 1980s by Rondinelli, Chambers, Korten and others is to view projects as participatory experiments, as learning processes, and to simplify greatly the analytical and planning methods used so that ordinary rural people can be involved (Rondinelli, 1983; Chambers, 1993; Korten, 1980, 1984b, 1987).

This alternative has developed into a strong concern in recent writing and practice on development management with promoting development agencies' learning abilities, and understanding what it is that helps organisations to learn. This has come particularly out of frustrations with blueprint-style projects in the difficult sectors of development – rural and agricultural, urban poverty alleviation, social development. It is a school of thought which argues that development cannot be reduced to expenditure, and that innovation is critical. If an agency is seeking to advance participation of the rural poor, it must develop a capacity to learn from its experience, and from the wider environment in which it operates. Similarly, the rural poor themselves will learn from experience. Outsiders from development agencies frequently perceive that the learning the rural poor have done is negative – they have learned what not to do, because they have had their fingers burnt. Either they have stepped out of line too far and been punished, sometimes violently, in a situation where they had inadequate support or protection; or they have been persuaded into risky, ill-thought-out ventures where they have been the risk-takers, and therefore the losers. It is important that these experiences (as well as other, perhaps more positive ones) be documented as part of a mutual learning process in any development activity. Chambers (Table 5.1) has contrasted the characteristics of these two approaches.

Brinkerhoff and Ingle (1989) have argued for a structured flexibility approach to development management. Previous attempts to increase the flexibility of the blueprint approach were made, for example, in East Africa (Chambers, 1974; Moris, 1981). The basic idea is to run with the conventional project approach, implementing

TABLE 5.1

The blueprint and learning process approaches in rural development contrasted

Idea originates in	capital city	village
First steps	data collection and plan	awareness and action
Design	static, by experts	evolving, people involved
Supporting organisation	existing, or built top-down	built bottom-up with lateral spread
Main resources	central funds and technicians	local people and their assets
Staff training and development	classroom, didactic	field-based learning through action
Implementation	rapid, widespread	gradual, local, at people's pace
Management focus	spending budgets, completing projects on time	sustained improvement and performance
Content of action	standardised	diverse
Communication	vertical: orders down, reports up	lateral: mutual learning and shared experience
Leadership	positional, changing	personal, sustained
Evaluation	external, intermittent	internal, continuous
Error	buried	embraced
Effects	dependency-creating	empowering
Associated with	normal professionalism	new professionalism

Source: Chambers (1993: 12, adapted from David Korten).

activities through the bureaucratic hierarchy, but to structure in a learning process through extensive reconnaissance/analysis of the organisation's environments, and continuous monitoring and feedback, leading to redesign and adaptation. The conditions for implementation of this approach are:

- felt need for change
- commitment to assign resources
- multi-level involvement within the organisation and participation of key beneficiaries
- openness to learning, willingness to innovate and take risks
- continuity of effort and allocated resources.

This represents an important strategy for attempting to marry the top-down, project approach with the notion of learning process. These are not easy bedfellows, however. There are now many public sector organisations as well as NGOs which have made serious attempts to work with participatory approaches in a learning process from within initially conventionally structured organisations sometimes operating with a project cycle. There is a review of some experiences of this in Chapter 9, where the focus is on the changes highly structured organisations need to make to accommodate a process approach. Here it should simply be noted that the changes required are substantial, and that the conditions mentioned above are not easily met. In fact it may be highly idealistic to expect hierarchical organisations to be able to change their *modus operandi* sufficiently to accommodate the new approach.

The centrality of research and evaluation

The blueprint project brought with it a strong emphasis on initial planning activities. Evaluation was necessarily de-emphasised by short-term perspectives, and an input-driven approach. Monitoring was only done to demonstrate achievement in terms of inputs; impact monitoring, even output monitoring, threatened to require inconvenient rethinking of practice, and ultimately to disrupt the flow of finance into the project. Monitoring and evaluation has therefore always been marginalised, despite almost universal, but ritualistic, acknowledgment of its importance, the need to learn from mistakes and so on. Once rural development takes place as a learning process, rather than a project, however, planning can be relatively de-emphasised, and evaluation raised to the status of central thinking activity. Resource allocation needs to be linked to evaluation: what sort of evaluation it could be needs further discussion.

Rural development work almost never writes on a blank sheet – there is always a history of development of some sort. If the view is taken that development is not encapsulated in what agencies do 'to' a society, but that society has its own change processes, of which what an agency does may be a part, then there is always something to assess and evaluate. This ought to be the starting point for any development work, but all too often is not. If rural development is a process, then initial planning can be minimised to that which is necessary to launch a particular activity; what is more important is the assessment and evaluation as the activity proceeds. In many situations local-level participatory planning is an ideal starting point, to which technical parameters can be added as time goes on. This is especially true where each piece of work is essentially small scale. In this situation, lessons can gradually be transferred from one piece of work to another.

In this rendering, the boundary between development work and applied research is increasingly blurred. This recaptures some of the lost essence of projects in rural development: that they are experimental, and suited to situations where not enough is known to make major investments, or where routine implementation capacities are not adequate.

The extent to which an incrementalist approach to decision-making can be realised will depend partly on the nature of the work to be done. The more that work has to hang together technically, the more comprehensive planning work will be required. An example here would be the development of substantial irrigation facilities. Where these might cover many communities it would be necessary to envisage a long process of participatory decision-making, negotiation, and conflict resolution accompanying the exploration of a number of technical alternatives, with the participatory process interacting with the technical process before any plan is drawn up. Even then, it would be realistic to expect that the plan will continue to be altered in the light of new information and new assessments, even as construction proceeds or after construction. Evaluation would play a much more important role than it normally does in such work.

The objection to this sort of approach is that there is not time to permit it. Needs and problems are pressing: people cannot wait for the results of research or evaluation. Part of the solution to this justifiable concern is to speed up the process of evaluation and research, and of the reporting and discussion of results. If participatory research is sufficiently small scale, for example, results can come out quickly. Some results might have wider implications – e.g. the impact of small-scale irrigation development in one village on downstream villages, which will require that action be postponed until relationships between upstream and downstream have been established, and conflicting interests reconciled to a common plan of action. Another objection is that agency staff are often not trained in research or evaluative work, and that training them would be costly and time-consuming, and that in any case they would find it difficult to produce research or evaluation results of quality. It would be important to pick out staff thought capable of this sort of reflective, analytical work, and to recognise that these skills are not taught in many education systems. The personnel, education and training implications of this approach are therefore significant.

Agencies seeking to move to a learning process approach have begun to develop suitable evaluation methods. They cannot wait for the mid-term review or end-of-project external evaluation. They need shorter, quicker, more interim forms of evaluation, both internal and external, to enable lessons to be learnt from experience. Where participatory evaluation can be done this is undoubtedly best (Save the Children Fund, 1994; Feuerstein, 1986; Narayan, 1993; Case, 1990). A process approach implies that work is increasingly shared among partners rather than concentrated in one agency. If participatory evaluation can become participatory self-evaluation (Uphoff, 1986), then much of the work of evaluation can be shared by participating organisations or groups of people.

Strategic management and planning

The revolution in working methods suggested by making evaluation central to the development process is paralleled by a necessary revolution in the organisational context. In the private sector, phrases like 'thriving on chaos' (Peters, 1987) and 're-engineering the corporation' (Hammer and Champy, 1993) indicate how companies have moved to a process approach and developed strategic decision-making capabilities to meet requirements for adaptability and innovation. Evaluation and assessment are at the centre of a process of strategic management involving the different stakeholders in the process. In a participatory approach the very activities themselves are built up, designed, implemented, and evaluated by rural people themselves: they are major stakeholders. Organisational change equivalent to 're-engineering the corporation' may be needed to allow this change to take place. What is indispensable is that evaluation results are fed directly into strategic thinking processes.

Following from the introduction of strategic management and planning in private sector corporations struggling to thrive on the increasingly chaotic world market, many public sector and non-governmental organisations have begun to introduce these processes. Strategies are based on assessment of the agencies' values and objectives, the resources available to it, and the environment within which it operates. The role of top management is to translate policies for organisational survival and growth into operational tasks, and to monitor their execution.

One of the outputs of this process is the production of strategic plans – documents which guide action at different levels or locations within an organisation. Starting again from values and objectives, a strategic plan would explore a wide range of trends in the environment, pick out priority issues which match with organisational values and objectives, and research these in greater depth. This is put alongside information coming out of the available research and evaluative work on the impact of particular development activities. There would then ensue a process of adjusting the organisations' objectives, activities, procedures and culture to the priorities for action which emerge from the wider analysis. Strategic planning can be done at any level – from household through to entire organisation. It could also be undertaken by a consortium of organisations. And it can be done in a participatory way. Long-term rural development projects would be better off with a strategic planning process, combined with evaluation of its own activities, than a detailed blueprint planning process.

Conclusion

Achieving control in rural development is rarely possible, due to the lack of certainty and predictability in the environment. It was argued that the mixed scanning approach to policy analysis has more to offer rural development workers than the project cycle. In particular a much greater role for implementation and evaluation, and a corresponding downgrading of planning and appraisal is required. The project form is not really very helpful to these objectives, though the evolution of process projects is a step in the right direction. NGOs in particular need to find ways of breaking out of the project mode because it is restricting the utilisation of their much advertised comparative advantage. This should be easiest for those NGOs that do not depend on official donor support. Research, evaluation, strategic thinking and management are at the core of the new mode of operation.

Projects have been led by finance. Economists have played a subservient role, justifying whatever investments organisations have wanted to make through cost–benefit analyses. They have rarely challenged the pressures to disburse in aid agencies or multilateral banks, which have made for such a poor overall level of quality in aid. Investment decisions have been taken by professionals, endorsed by politicians, and sanctioned by economists.

Projects still lead to the restructuring of administrations, despite awareness of the substantial problems involved. It could be that in the new mode of public sector reform, project authorities can be commercialised, even privatised, or autonomous bodies formed, which could work under contract to governments. This would reduce the significance of the old probematik of projects in administration.

NGOs are also stuck in the project groove, as a result of their dependence on government or donor funding. Because of their small size this has been even more limiting for them than for public sector organisations: small size often means that projects are conceived as of short duration and focus on material outputs rather than on the policy or legal changes which may be needed to enable a particular development. The project has helped to deradicalise NGOs, to encourage them to take on the mantle of working at the margins of economic growth to ensure that some of it does trickle down to the deserving poor, but not to use projects to challenge the strategies of growth.

Alternatives to the blueprint project include programmes and processes. The latter has become the most important alternative in rural development, and has now permeated many donor agencies. It resonates with recent writing on private sector management stressing adaptation and flexibility in the face of a chaotic international business environment. But in rural development the concern for learning processes has come out of the interaction between bureaucracies and the poor, and the realisation that 'new professionals', with a different set of attitudes, and restructured organisations, with different incentives, were needed to make the interaction fruitful. Both NGOs and public sector organisations are now grappling with these issues.

The key to successful process work is evaluation, research and the development of corresponding strategic thinking and an effective management response to the research and evaluation carried out. This can best be ensured by adapting notions of strategic management and strategic planning for use in rural development.

6

Holistic Approaches

The project has provided a slender framework on which to hang ever more complicated concerns. Financial and economic analysis of project activities is now rarely enough to justify a project; and it is important to assess impact as much in social, environmental and even political terms as in economic terms. Development agencies are also adjusting to the increasing prevalence of conflict in the modern world; it is argued here that this is bringing concerns about political development and human rights back to the forefront of the development agenda. One strategy is therefore to conserve the project cycle and framework, but to improve on the comprehensiveness of the analysis carried out particularly during planning, so that assumptions are more strongly grounded. However, this may be flawed because any practicable degree of comprehensiveness will not remove uncertainty from the picture: what happens in the process of implementation is all-important, and will turn up surprises. Assumptions made at first will have to be validated or the activity adjusted as experience is gained.

What is required, therefore, is a holistic approach to rural development, focused around the livelihoods, social development and environment of the rural poor. This should be sufficiently flexible to take in its stride unforeseen events, and to be able to select for analysis the aspects of the wider picture which are of significance in any particular place, following the policy analysis procedure (Chapter 5). The first part of this chapter describes the ways in which social and environmental analysis have been added to the financial/economic analytical procedures which became conventional. Today development agencies are also struggling to deal with the growth of conflict in the world, and the chapter makes a case for adding political analysis. The chapter finally presents and argues the case for a holistic, systems-based perspective on development which will serve the range of current and likely future concerns in rural development. Examples of appropriate analytical techniques to support this perspective are presented.

Comprehensive approaches to analysis

The economist has long contributed analytical skills to the project process, as we saw in Chapter 5. As other social sciences have matured over the last two decades they have also been asked to contribute, as the primacy of the economic in development has been questioned. Globally, environmental issues have come to the fore, so projects have increasingly had to jump through hoops of environmental analysis too. The resulting project process is beginning to look very different. The introduction of social analysis in particular has created a demand to change the nature of rural development programming from a blueprint to a process approach so that work is done *with* people, at their pace, and to some extent under their direction. The integration of environmental concerns has begun to make a reality of the key idea within project formulation of exploring options – an idea which has had little use in the past.

Social analysis

Social analysis is the development of an understanding of the key social relationships which may have an influence over people's behaviour, attitudes and states of mind. Social analysts develop models of social structure, indicating how social groups are positioned relative to each other, and the critical aspects of life which determine this positioning. The basic concepts which help to differentiate people include status, class, caste, ethnicity, race, gender, and age. Social analysis is usually concerned with difference and the potential for conflict, but may equally be concerned with shared interests and the potential for solidarity and community. Sometimes social analysis is distinguished from cultural analysis, which focuses more on the values or norms, and the ways in which these are transmitted from generation to generation, or circumscribed by social structure (Cochrane, 1979). In reality the two are inseparable, and here I will include cultural analysis as part of social analysis. There are now a number of manuals on the application of social analysis in project work (e.g. ODA, 1995).

Social analysis is seen to be relevant not only to 'social' development projects (i.e. health, education, social welfare, community development), but to most of rural development, and much of urban development. Industrial corporations have long recognised its value: industrial sociology is perhaps the strongest intellectual branch of the social sciences outside economics.

The inclusion of the social in project planning is an attempt to increase the comprehensiveness, and thus rationality, of the process. It assists with problem and goal definition; it helps in listing alternative strategies and courses of action; it improves the prediction of important consequences of action; and it makes the measurement of costs and benefits more accurate. In particular, the inclusion of social dimensions means that society does not have to be treated as uniform and homogeneous. The interaction between a project and the various groups which make up society can be assessed. It does not need to be assumed that all will benefit or contribute equally.

Integrating social considerations into cost–benefit analysis was illustrated by Stewart in a classic article (1975). She showed how projects could be assessed differently from the points of view of different social groups, and how these interests could be incorporated into financial or economic analysis at least in a rudimentary way. Sadly, this is rarely done in practice. For example, projects could be weighted in favour of those which favour the poor, or women.

Historically, social analysts have been preoccupied with equity and justice issues. Thus the critique of the Green Revolution in the 1970s was a social critique, stressing the bias of the new technologies to big farmers, landowners and the rich in alliance with the urban elite. This was based on extensive and time-consuming studies in the field – the hallmark of classical social analysis. More recently, as social analysts have become more involved in practical development work either as managers or commentators, the issues they have worked on have diversified.

Social analysts have had a substantial impact in the approaches to development adopted in certain sectors. Thus agricultural scientists have come to recognise the value of farming-systems research which incorporates systematic investigation of farm situations, perceptions and interests to guide the research process. Systems approaches are discussed later in this chapter.

Social analysis has also repeatedly emphasised the importance of gender in development work. As with the critique of the Green Revolution, this has sprung from a mass of detailed field studies, mostly carried out by women social scientists, exploring relations between men and women in households and publicly in markets and institutions. This literature has not only drawn attention to gender differences in terms of roles and perceptions, but has also produced a constructive critique of the project process.

Gender

More and more development organisations require gender issues to be taken into account when planning and appraising development projects. It is no longer adequate to assume that what will benefit a (usually male) head of household will equally benefit, or will not disadvantage, women members. It is no longer adequate to let men speak for women in the public arena. Women's and men's interests may coincide, but this should not be taken for granted.

Of course the relationships between men and women are at the core of any culture, and development organisations would be foolhardy to rely on any one formula. Their actions must always be adapted to the culture – not necessarily in a conservative way, but in the sense that the norms of the culture need to be recognised. If a challenge is being mounted to those norms it should be done consciously and deliberately, and for good reason.

Many projects have failed because the interests of one gender – usually women – have not been taken into account. (On the other hand, a women's development project may fail because men are not in the picture: women's organisations sometimes face this consequence of a refusal to negotiate with or include men.) The point is that culture assigns roles to both men and women which vary enormously from place to place and which change over time. Projects need to have some understanding of these roles. The World Bank's 1987 evaluation of rural development projects admits the failing: 'Family labour constraints posed frequent difficulties, especially those relating to women in agriculture' (1987: xviii).

It is probably true that the majority of projects are still designed in a 'gender-blind' way. In particular, assumptions are made about household relationships and resource use and ownership which neglect any differences between men and women, and indeed mask the role of women in society or economy. Paying attention to gender issues is a way of bringing women back into the mainstream of development. Gender relationships are deeply personal, however, and many individuals and organisations have great difficulty taking them into account in their professional work. Of all the changes required in the new rural development paradigm this is one of the most difficult to institutionalise, as it is one of the most challenging.

Information about gender issues is often absent. (Information about all social issues may be absent, in which case a wider social assessment may be needed.) With participatory rural appraisal (PRA) methods (see Chapter 7) some of this can now be done quite quickly. A search through the literature on PRA comes up with the following types of information which can usefully be collected while designing/appraising a project to help with assessing the gender implications of a project:

- daily routines of men and women
- seasonal calenders of men and women
- shifts in responsibilities between men and women over time
- preference ranking (of activities, crops, food, problems and opportunities, etc.) by men and women
- sources of information available to men and women.

This list still leaves out critical information. People – men and women, perhaps in separate groups, possibly stratified by age, class, caste, neighbourhood or any other important variable – can also be asked to comment on the likely impact of the interventions proposed in a project. Impact on social structure and social networks will normally be perceived differently by each group. Impact is usually assessed financially (money returns) or absolutely (e.g. clean water available). Additional issues like how any new cash returns will be distributed, whether it is women's or men's incomes and time commitments which will be affected, what it will do to household food supplies and food security, and what it will imply for women's and men's control over resources, take the project into gender analysis.

Gender analysis comprises: information about access to and control over resources (land, labour, capital, services, income) separately for men and women; the division of labour within the household; the impact of current and past technology changes on the division of labour and control over resources; and the participation of men and women in public decision-making and organisations. This sort of information can be an input into decision-making processes at all stages of a development process: through monitoring and evaluation to re-identification of activities.

USAID has led agencies in incorporating gender analysis into its procedures. In a recent formulation (Hubbs *et al.*, 1992) there are two basic steps. Step 1 is to analyse the gender differences in four key factors: the allocation of labour in the household, the different sources of income and expenditure patterns, and access to and control over resources. Other factors relevant to a particular situation should also be determined. Step 2 is to draw conclusions about the 'significant gender differences which should be taken into account in planning or adapting the project under consideration' (Hubbs *et al.*, 1992: 13). This is done by identifying the differences between men's and women's constraints (e.g. time, labour, access to credit, education, etc.) and how these relate to a particular programme. The other side of the coin is to examine the opportunities which the analysis throws up for improvements in the programme or in household or community survival, production or participation processes.

Step 3 is then to incorporate information about important gender differences into the significant organisational procedures, in this case USAID's Country Development Strategy Statement, the Action Plan, the Project Identification Document, and the Project Paper. Any organisation would need to review its important procedures and incorporate a consideration of gender differences.

A simple but critical aspect of gender analysis is the need to consult with women as much as with men. In some societies there are cultural barriers to men interacting with women. Where these cannot be overcome clearly the employment of women development workers is a must. Normally, even in difficult cultural situations the barrier can be adequately overcome, with persistence, a willingness to adapt methods of interaction, and some willingness on the part of male staff and village women to change their attitudes.

There are not only barriers to talking to women. Women and men also experience barriers to particular activities in different ways. For example, in the development of small-scale enterprise women cluster in particular types of enterprise and may be restricted to very small businesses. There are barriers to business diversification and growth. These may be:

- societal norms (what is seen as appropriate for women/men, views of their abilities. . .)
- institutional structures and processes (discrimination in schools, banks, businesses. . .)
- legal (ownership rights)
- economic (access to markets, degree of competition, lack of control over money).
- political (representation, voting norms, norms about who speaks in public. . .)

Assisting women's enterprises may involve lobbying for changes to the law, access to resources, and political culture. Alternatively an agency might decide it was not qualified to tackle these concerns, but could link up with another agency/project which is. This is an example of how the analysis of gender roles will frequently not remain at the level of the household or community.

There are now many guides to gender analysis, and examples of its use in action (see e.g., Rao, 1991; Young, 1994; Moser, 1994), so any rural development agency should have its own procedures to deal with these issues. Developing these will undoubtedly require a process of organisational change: and it could be difficult to change project development procedures without changing other organisational processes, for example the emphasis given in the organisation's internal management to gender equity.

Improvements in project quality through social analysis

A study of *ex post* evaluations of 57 World Bank rural development projects found that 'the thirty projects in which project design was judged to be compatible with traditional cultural and local socio-economic conditions in the targeted area had an average estimated rate of return at audit of 18.3%, compared with 8.6% for the twenty-seven projects in which socio-cultural incompatibilities were identified' (Cernea, 1985: 331). Kottak (in Cernea, 1985) argued that in rural development there are two important social keys to project success: avoiding over-innovation and cultural incompatibility. Projects worked better if they did not try to move too far too quickly in terms of innovation. In general the more substantial the innovation the less likely it was to be accepted or used in the intended way. The more substantial and structural the innovation therefore the more important social analysis became.

Projects should aim for a good 'socio-cultural fit' between project interventions and the way local society is organised. Important elements here would include: the structure of family life (demography, relationships, division of labour, etc.); the labour requirements of meeting basic needs and allocation of labour to non-'basic' activities; values and preferences (e.g. on meeting subsistence needs, security, income generation and expenditure, individuals' roles in public, etc.); concepts of rights; existing forms of co-operation among individuals, households and communities; incentives and returns to activity; accessibility of the project to the target group and its influence over it.

'Facts' about these elements are often assumed in project design, because planners feel they know what the situation is, or because they typecast the situation and transfer assumptions from elsewhere. Where the assumption is critical to the project's success some investigation is usually warranted. In all these aspects it would generally be important to disaggregate by gender, since perceptions, rights, costs and returns to activities so often vary substantially between men and women. The same is true for race, ethnicity, class, caste, age, and religion where these are important facets of social difference.

Rural development work generally relies on people's initiative in terms of investment, institutional development, and knowledge: social analysis is indispensable to an agency seeking to work with and strengthen people's capacities. The more an agency attempts to incorporate grassroots organisation, local knowledge and efforts, the greater the requirement for social assessment, since local organisations are always rooted in social structure and social relationships in particular ways. It is important that the external agency understands how an organisation is placed. Does it include all social groups, or exclude some? What place does it give to women, and is that an important issue? On the other hand, the very fact of incorporating local organisations creates opportunities for participatory social analysis, based on the local organisations' concerns and strengthening their analytic abilities.

All this suggests rather a conservative view of the role of social analysis, in adjusting a project to existing social structure and culture. However, these are dynamic, ever-changing: they should not be seen as something which only constrains development work. They also provide opportunities: analysis of culture and society can suggest work to be done, just as analysis of a farming system or environmental change might do. For example, the understanding that religious worship involves protecting certain sites as shrines, usually in a grove or forest (a natural site), would suggest an exploration of the involvement of religion and religious institutions in forest and land-use management work. An understanding that an increasing proportion of households are headed effectively (if not legally) by women (or even, in AIDS-affected communities, by children) provides opportunities to work directly and acceptably with women, opportunities which might have been restricted in more stable circumstances. Above all, social analysis can help development workers identify and see through the obstacles to working with the poor.

Activities which have social engineering objectives which involve substantial restructuring of people's lives (e.g. resettlement, introduction of co-operatives, major new technologies) are likely to be particularly sensitive to the degree to which project design and implementation takes account of the social dimension. In general, the new rural development paradigm shies away from mega-projects and massive social engineering.

Environmental assessment

A variety of techniques have been evolved to incorporate environmental considerations into planning and decision-making. Of these, Environmental Impact Assessment (EIA) is the best known and most widely used. It is important therefore that rural development workers should know what it is, and be able to adapt it for use in rural development. EIA is a procedure used by development agencies or public decision-making bodies for describing and analysing the major environmental impacts of a proposed activity. It leads to the creation of statements (documents) which report on these impacts as well as proposals to keep negative impacts to a minimum. The best sort of EIA may evaluate several several different options and advise on the best course of action. EIAs frequently examine not only impacts on the physical environment, but also on the human environment, and overlap considerably with social analyses.

The cost of a professionally done EIA puts it out of reach for smaller-scale rural development work. However, as with social analysis there are low-cost, participatory ways of doing it. Like many planning techniques, EIA was developed in the USA, and has only recently begun to be applied in some developing countries.

Before adopting any such technique, careful analysis is needed about its relevance, appropriateness and feasibility under particular conditions.

EIA is most often used as an aid to decision-making at the stage of deciding whether or not to go ahead with a development proposal, and whether the developers need to take action to mitigate (reduce or counter) any adverse environmental effects. In the past it has stressed making good any damage, and has been criticised for this limitation. At least, if the EIA is well done, the environmental costs of a development will be known and the 'polluter pays' principle can be implemented. Today the stress is less on mitigation than prevention of environmental damage. EIA for rural development should thus draw attention to the least adverse options, should emphasise resource conservation, recycling of materials, and the use of residues and wastes wherever possible. In order to do this effectively, EIA should not be left too late in a decision-making process: as with social analysis it is important that environmental considerations figure strongly in identification and design processes.

EIA as developed in the democratic west has some features which rely on democratic processes for their validity. Scoping, the process at the beginning of an EIA which defines the significant impacts of a project which the EIA should study, and on which the Environmental Impact Statement (EIS) should particularly report, can be done participatorily with good effect. People themselves can decide which are the significant impacts that may need further research, and whether a development agency can help them do it, or get it done. This involvement of ordinary people in identifying and appraising impacts is perhaps the most critical contribution EIA can make to many rural development activities. EIA involves scientific study, measurement and evaluation. This may be expensive and complicated. The scoping exercise is critical as it enables any costly scientific study to focus on particular issues of importance.

Once priorities are set, information can be collected – either existing information, or in new baseline surveys. The lack of baseline information is a great constraint on the economical use of EIA in many poor developing countries: much has to be collected from scratch. Great stress is laid on the value of the baseline surveys for monitoring environmental changes over the duration of an activity. Any baseline data collection should be designed with this in mind, and any EIS should make recommendations about how monitoring will be carried out and interested parties kept informed. In the new rural development paradigm, ordinary people will be involved in deciding what is to be monitored and how, and may even carry this out themselves, as a form of participatory research. Carrying out big baseline surveys can easily distract attention from the development of a genuinely participatory approach to work, and absorb large amounts of resources and time. They should therefore be used sparingly.

EIA methods which are so far in widespread use can be divided into simple and complicated. Simple methods are suitable for use in rapid EIAs where resources for study are very limited. These are the *ad hoc* checklists and matrices explained in detail in Biswas and Qu Geping's useful guidelines (1987). These all involve developing lists of environmental impacts, with an assessment of how damaging the impacts are, in terms of how widespread, how significant, how short/long term, and how irreversible they are. Constructing a matrix involves listing the components of an activity, and for each component assessing the likely damage. The objective of these simple methods is to construct a crude but quantitative index of impact: so that the impact of one alternative can be compared with that of another by the decision-makers.

These methods have quite wide application, and do not require a high level of expertise to use. They can be adapted for use by rural communities, and are quite compatible with the PRA methods to be discussed in Chapter 7. However, producing indices (indicators) of impact involves weighting, which is subjective: this is the main limitation of these methods. In a participatory approach weighting could be done by the different social groups in a community or number of communities affected by a particular development. The difficulty is that different people will attach different weights to particular impacts: some will be more concerned with the quality of water for drinking or as fish habitat; others will be more concerned with the availability of jobs, and may discount environmental impacts.

With respect to Asia, where these methods are now frequently used, Htun (1988) remarks on their limitations. They do not bring out the relationships which exist among components of complicated systems. They hardly integrate socio-economic aspects with the physical components which they emphasise. They rely on an inadequate data base which makes objective evaluations of possible changes in environmental quality difficult or impossible. Some of these problems can be corrected by getting the participation of people in local communities who know about the different aspects of 'the system' and how different systems might be related. Thus, participatorily generated information should not stop at the simple indices. Analysis of problems, causes and effects, at least on the micro-level, can also be done participatorily.

The main advantage of index type methods is that they face a decision-maker with an easy decision. 'By scaling and weighting impacts, index methods provide a means for encapsulating impacts in total indices for alternatives. As such methods contain explicit rules for the selection of the 'best' alternative, its identification is easy' (Bisset, 1988). The introduction of such methods may well be the easiest way to get environmental factors included in decision-making.

More complicated, commonly used methods are systems diagrams, networks, and simulation or modelling. These all attempt to portray the interactions between components of a system and to measure the impact of a change in one or more variables on others. This is a valuable move in the direction of systems thinking. Systems diagrams show energy flows between components of a network – energy being a denominator to which much can be reduced in calculation. However, while networks can show nicely the duration and direction of a change or impact, magnitude is more problematic since it depends much on local knowledge. The disadvantage with this method is its expense, and the fact that not all relations or interactions can sensibly be reduced to energy flows (just as not all transactions can sensibly be reduced to money in a cost–benefit analysis). However, the method has been used in a participatory way, as part of investigations of nutrient flows in farming systems. Here farmers draw the flows of energy and other nutrients and estimate where gains and losses occur.

There is sometimes a spurious scientificity about EIA. Scientists are often critical, as the scientific method (hypothesis and testing) is not sufficiently used. There is a move to make EIA more scientifically based (see Bisset, 1988: 59). For rural development purposes, however, it is more important to make it people-based. Scientists can be called on to provide critical detailed information on significant impacts that are of concern to communities and decision-makers.

The costs of an EIA are often substantial (Wathern, 1988: 237). They are highly variable depending on the project, how it is done and who does it. Costs will obviously be kept low by adopting the more rapid techniques, by doing as much 'in-house' as possible, and by avoiding large data-gathering exercises if possible.

Example of an EIA

India's major poverty alleviation programme – the Integrated Rural Development Programme – has commonly distributed dairy cattle to poor households on a subsidised loan basis. The numbers of livestock distributed sometimes become a significant proportion of the local cattle population. When they are distributed in environmentally sensitive areas like mountain slopes their fodder requirements may create pressure on forests or other common grazing areas. It is not difficult to calculate 'fodder balances' for a village eco-system, and work out how much extra fodder is required, and the options for generating it. Clearly there is a need to prevent damage to sensitive areas: alternative sources of fodder may therefore be a condition of distribution of cattle or other stock.

An analysis of inputs and outputs would also be concerned with dung and its management. If the poor beneficiaries were also landless they might produce dung which could be sold as fuel, or composted and sold in the village. This in turn could be a more sustainable source of fertility than the artificial fertilisers relied on by so many farmers. Here the analysis begins to incorporate conservation (the improvement of soils) into project design.

Incorporating environmental considerations into financial analysis

We have already noted how important financial and economic analysis has been in rural development project planning. A large amount of economists' recent effort has been directed at including environmental factors in their analysis. A number of ways of valuing environmental costs and benefits have been developed which can be integrated into financial and economic analysis. Firstly there are those which are relatively easily applicable: measuring the effect on production – determining the physical effects of a development and estimating or modelling their effect on productive activities; the need for preventive expenditure – the expenditure needed to prevent degradation; and necessary replacement costs – the expenditure needed to restore the environment to its original state or provide an alternative environment (Winpenny, 1991: 42–123).

Other techniques are less well used, and require data which is often not easily available. These include measuring the effects projects on: human capital – often by calculating loss of earnings; on property values and wage differentials; travel costs – only really applicable to evaluate tourist projects; and also include contingent valuation, which is basically market research focusing on willingness to pay for conservation (see Winpenny, 1991: 62 for a useful summary of the advantages and disadvantages of all these methods). Whatever the method, data from such calculations can be used to affect the IRR or NPV calculations. These can be combined with a social analysis to disaggregate the costs and benefits by social group.

There has been a lot of writing about the discount rate in cost–benefit analysis, and a tendency to argue that a low discount rate will give greater emphasis to costs and benefits incurred in the future. Given that most people look for gratification in the present before they think about the future, and will risk (or even court) huge problems in the future for present-day benefits and satisfying present-day powerful interests, this argument is understandable as a crude attempt to redress the balance.

Environmentalists have also proposed that the costs and benefits of conservation projects should be discounted at a lower rate compared to other projects, on the grounds that environmentally scarce goods will appreciate in value over time. Economists seem to be against this, as it would create many practical difficulties in defining those projects which can be treated differently, and making the public discount rate different from the private one will have distorting effects in capital markets. However, they are agreed that straight financial or economic calculations need to be set beside calculations which indicate environmental costs and benefits. Many argue that a criterion of 'sustainability' should be built into project assessments, for example by requiring that 'any environmental damage be compensated by projects specifically designed to improve the environment'. Thus 'requiring that no project should contribute to environmental deterioration would be absurd. But it is not absurd to require that the portfolio of projects as a whole should not contribute to environmental deterioration' (Markandya and Pearce, 1991: 150).

Prevention of environmental damage

Prevention has generally been the concern of environmental movements, and often they have sought to stop certain types (if not all) of
development. The negotiations they undertake with developers
sometimes result in the mitigation of some negative environmental
or social impacts.

Our knowledge of the environmental impact of most human
activities is still very slight. Impact prediction is therefore very
difficult. We could adopt a 'precautionary principle' which argues
that where we are only beginning to perceive the range of impacts
which might result from today's developments, but cannot describe
precisely or quantify them, resources should be committed to 'safeguard against the potentially catastrophic future effects of current
activity' (Perrings, 1991: 160). However, in rural development,
where needs are often acute and immediate, it is important not to
be held back unnecessarily. Positive approaches must be found.
Integrating conservation is one: which operates clearly in agriculture
and natural-resource management, and it can be applied more
widely. Development which achieves resource conservation in addition to other goals is clearly the most desirable form. It is one way of
committing resources to safeguard the future. However, the search
for 'sustainable' development has begun only recently on any scale.
The environmentally sustainable alleviation of poverty is the agenda
of rural development for the coming decades.

Prevention of damage and integrating conservation are the
aspects of environmental analysis which challenge the conventional
notion of the project as finite and located investment with a
primarily economic rationale. These concepts require more than a
modification of what project designers would normally do. They
require exploration of a wider range of options and the application
of several criteria of evaluation – environmental, and social as well
as economic. Options can be examined in a participatory way;
criteria for assessment can be ranked (and weighted) by ordinary
people. However, operating in a participatory way does not exon-
erate a development agency from the need for an ethical position –
for example, the commitment to the value of selecting development
activities which contribute to environmental improvement. Operating in a participatory way will also necessarily involve development
agencies in conflict, since not all social groups will share the same
interests and attitudes.

Preventing damage quite possibly means abandoning an idea which will generate damage. It might mean delaying an investment until key uncertainties can be resolved. Integrating conservation means looking at production, construction and other resource-using activities in a new light: focusing on substantially reducing energy inputs, encouraging beneficial energy cycles, recycling, and making use of waste. The project embodies notions of control over nature, the ability to find the quick-fix solution, or the dramatic transformation. Integrating conservation and preventing damage are ideas which move in the opposite direction.

Stretching the project

Social and environmental analysis stretch the project almost to breaking point. Once social or environmental analytical approaches are used – and it is for good reasons that they are used – the nature of the project begins to change. It becomes harder to create and maintain a project framework: too many things are admitted which do not fit. Control becomes difficult to imagine. It is harder to maintain a project cycle, as implementation and continuous evaluation become more central. Options which might classically have been rejected (or not considered) need to be worked up and retained in case they are needed. Unlike economic analysis, social and environmental analyses are likely to affect the substance of any project, either negatively or constructively.

Political analysis and project planning

Political analysis has not generally been part of project planning. Planners have tried to keep projects as insulated as possible from politics. This has meant showing a high level of disinterest in politics and political processes. The closest project designers have got to the political arena is in their recent exploration of social analysis. Otherwise the politics of projects has been hidden, even secret, certainly not public, certainly not debated openly along with economic costs and benefits, and environmental and social impact, and certainly not considered when revising projects to mitigate predicted negative impacts.

The use of the logical framework has sometimes raised political issues to the level of debate, but this usually only takes the shape of a brief proviso in the assumptions column. For example, a cursory review of project frameworks for seven ODA-funded (Overseas Development Administration) process projects in South Asia discovered only the following references to politics in the Assumptions column of the matrix:

Govt of . . processing complete soon
Disabled people accepted as spokespersons
Vested interests can be controlled
Govt of . . continues to support objectives
Local political context conducive
Councillors recognise benefits
Councillors responsive to community pressure
Villages cohere and committees are not dominated by powerful minorities
Govt of . . reintervention in input supply might decrease availability

These were all projects which had undergone a degree of social analysis during their preparation, and to which the ODA's social development advisers were paying some attention. Nevertheless, they illustrate the problem. Some of these assumptions indicate risks which would quite likely undermine the achievement of objectives of reaching the poor or vulnerable. However, the risks are only imprecisely stated. Other risks – that the projects might contribute to inter-group conflict, or conflict within government or between government and people – are not admitted as possibilities.

The assessment of these risks by explicit political analysis as an activity proceeds would enhance the likelihood of objectives being achieved. It might even indicate a need for a change in strategy or objectives, or even demonstrate that the activity was not feasible. Political analysis is rapidly coming to be seen as important. The driving force for change is the greatly increased prevalence of political conflicts within states, and the ways in which many development agencies have got caught up and involved in conflict. The number of ongoing wars in the world has increased from ten in 1960 to fifty today (Duffield, 1994). Most of these are internal conflicts. Projects may contribute to the creation of conflict, unwittingly or wittingly. Lack of political understanding may also mean that opportunities available to projects to prevent conflict are missed. Projects may also simply get caught up in a conflict situation. Personnel need to know what to do.

Even if the link between specific projects and a particular conflict may not always be easy to trace, conflicts are usually determined by patterns of development or underdevelopment, incorporation or exclusion. Many of the internal conflicts in today's world have strong ethnic, religious or racial dimensions; and are driven by the relationships among particular social groups, between certain groups and the state, and by territorial inequalities between 'cores' and 'peripheries'. The object of many conflicts is to reshape the state geographically, or to renegotiate terms of inclusion. Patterns of development typically produce differential benefits for different social groups. Development projects are always caught up in wider patterns of development, either running with or against the tide. An understanding of those wider patterns is essential. If projects are not to contribute to conflict, an understanding of how they relate to political processes is also imperative.

Most models of development assume that development can only happen under conditions of peace and security. Conflict is seen as something temporary, to be resolved before the march of progress can be resumed. Conflict is equated with natural disaster and famine in terms of determining appropriate response. Relief measures are seen as appropriate; these are followed by rehabilitation measures, which finally shade back into development activities. This model increasingly does not fit a reality where in some places conflict is intermittent or continuous over long periods.

The growing involvement of the United Nations in providing security in situations of internal conflict is the major indicator of a further significant broadening of the notion of humanitarian assistance. This has several important implications: the notion of the sovereignty of nation-states is no longer sacred; the difficulty of external agencies remaining neutral in a conflict situation is becoming much greater; and, most importantly for our purposes, the notion of development as linear progress from a state of poverty, insecurity and vulnerability to one of wealth and security is under challenge (Duffield, 1994).

Development agencies are increasingly having to operate in 'turbulence' (ACORD, 1991), even if this does not always reach the stage of a recognised war. This is a function of the reduced legitimacy of many poor nation-states in the post-cold-war era.

Post-colonial states went through a period of stability, inheriting machineries of government which functioned well, and reinforced by aid from supporting superpowers; but that stability declined as terms of trade went against primary producers and states were poorly managed by predatory social groups.

There has also emerged a new critique of development and its relation to conflict, focusing largely on the concerns of environmental movements. This has begun to pinpoint how patterns of 'development' and/or development projects actually create or foster conflict. An example of this was the argument that the Green Revolution in the Indian state of Punjab contributed to the long period of violence in that state during the 1980s – see Chapters 2 and 3 (Shiva, 1991a).

Violent conflict between Sinhalese and Jaffna Tamils in Sri Lanka has been linked to the development of two competing 'core' economically and socially advanced regions around Colombo and Jaffna (Moore and Harris, 1984). The JVP rebellion in south Sri Lanka was widely attributed to the fact that though there are excellent education facilities provided, the economy is too weak to absorb school-leavers.

Perhaps the most common direct links between development work by development agencies and conflict lies in resource use. Dams, deforestation, fisheries and mineral exploitation tend to marginalise groups of resource users, and sometimes lead to large-scale protest based on the particular issue (Shiva, 1991b). Such protest has the potential of being linked to or exploited by wider opposition political movements.

Conflict is widely seen as negative, to be avoided. There are writers who have drawn positive relationships between conflict and development, however. These range from the opportunities for change (e.g. to support local organisations, emphasise gender relations) presented in turbulent situations (ACORD, 1991) to Leninist theories of development which stress the importance of leadership by advanced or progressive classes, which will enable saving, capital accumulation and investment; in short, create the conditions for material progress. Such leadership may only be achieved through conflict, even violence. On a more local level, a development strategy aimed at including groups of poor or landless people, or women, in the benefits of development may run up against the opposition of 'vested interests' which see their own interests threatened as a result. This consequence of development interventions has to be faced, thought through and acted on by the development agency involved. It would usually involve supporting organisations of beneficiaries in their struggles with vested interests by attempting to locate a level of government or organisations of civil society which will actively defend them, or linking them with a popular movement.

What is important for rural development analysts who recognise the importance of conflict is to ask questions about the politically vulnerable: those who do not have political representation or protection. What is the impact of development activities on their political fortunes? Are they enhanced or diminished by the investments or institutional development proposed? Development which is area-based is often located in areas with political influence: the impact of such development on nearby (or even faraway) areas with no influence may be substantial, but ignored. Project proponents naturally take advantage of the artificial boundary given to them by the very idea of the project to avoid looking beyond at potential impacts.

The likelihood of conflict is something recognised by many (including 'traditional') political institutions, and is the stuff of any public administrator's role. Institutions with competence in conflict management and resolution should therefore be involved in any matrix of stakeholders in a rural development activity. It should not be left to such institutions to implement what others have designed: they too should have an input into design.

Bringing conflict into the rural development arena in this way further undermines the notion of the project as a set of self-contained known activities. Conflict itself generates so much uncertainty and instability that endstate planning seems purely speculative; the need for conflict resolution mechanisms and institutions to be built into project processes adds a further dimension, since conflict resolution can throw up needs, aspirations and opportunities (as well as constraints) for development work which cannot easily be anticipated.

Holistic frameworks

So far in this chapter the focus has been on the kinds of analysis needed to accompany rural development work. The framework for analysis has expanded progressively as rural development workers have had to become more effective in a world which we conceptualise in ever more complex ways. The range of analysis is impossible to carry out in a systematic, academic fashion for most rural development work, small in scale and programmatic in character as it often is. The quantity and quality of management required to co-ordinate the analytical efforts of so many different specialists would be prohibitive in most situations. So what is required is a new approach, based on integrative thinking and methods. Participatory development offers half the answer, since ordinary people integrate various disciplines in their practical daily lives; the more so the less people have become westernised and educated in the scientific mode which compartmentalises life. This is the subject of Chapter 7. The other, more philosophical half is derived from systems theory: 'soft' systems methodology and the idea that systems 'co-evolve', or have impacts on each other as they evolve. The two should become closely interwoven in fact; the remainder of this chapter deals with the latter.

Soft systems

Systems thinking now has a long and diverse history, and has had all kinds of practical applications in engineering, biology, organisation, management and planning. Most 'hard' systems thinking is based on the assumption that problems can be clearly formulated in terms of making choices between alternative means of achieving a known and clearly defined end. This was not very successful when applied to human activity systems, though intuitively systems thinking should have something to offer to a world which is recognised as densely interconnected, and changing. Most of the systems applications in rural development have been based on 'hard' systems thinking: that there is a reality which has properties of wholeness, boundaries, subsystems, wider systems, inputs and outputs, transformations, emergent properties and interactiveness with the environment in which it exists (Bawden, 1992:162). Projects have generally tried to mould complex, changing reality into such systems.

'Soft' systems thinking has developed out of 'hard' systems thinking precisely to tackle the ill-structured problems of the real world. It calls for a process- rather than technique-oriented approach to solving problems, and recognises that problems are endemic in human affairs and cannot be solved 'once and for all'. In defining a human activity system there are two vital aspects: one is the *Weltanschauung* (literally, worldview) which makes a description or model meaningful – human activity is always purposeful; and the other is the fact that real world action is always more complex than the structured activity in any model of a human activity system, so a number of models built according to different viewpoints will have to be constructed if the richness of the real situation is to be embraced. The cluster of models can then be used to structure a debate about change. The models are compared with perceptions of real-world action, which suggests new definitions of the problem situation, and new ideas for relevant systems in an iterative process.

The problem-owner, problem-solver, or intervener are all part of the system, which of course has a history. The system is actually the organised process of enquiry, not some part of the real world. It is an abstract concept which can help to make sense of the real world. However, the interveners can become a major part of 'the problem'. In this sense they need to stand back and restrict their role as 'experts' to helping people carry out their own study: soft systems methodology is participative.

'No human activity system is intrinsically relevant to any problem situation, the choice is always subjective' (Checkland and Scholes, 1990: 31). There are 'primary task' systems, based around the work of a particular group of people or a functional division of an organisation (e.g. relief, in a relief and development agency). And there are 'issue-based systems', relevant to mental processes which may not be encapsulated by any real-world arrangements. There is a spectrum between these two extremes. Defining the system, its boundaries and its components is always an issue and change in the definitions an ever-present possibility.

The core of soft systems methodology (SSM) is the idea of a transformation process, taking inputs and producing outputs. In this aspect it is very similar to the prevalent notions of the logical (or project) framework (Chapter 5). The use of SSM will be illustrated with an example of the attempts to bring population pressure and resources into balance in the Himalayan foothills, the focus of several of substantial projects during the last two decades. The specifics of the problem situation, taken from Ives and Messerli (1989: 177–90), are summarised in Figures 6.1 and 6.2.

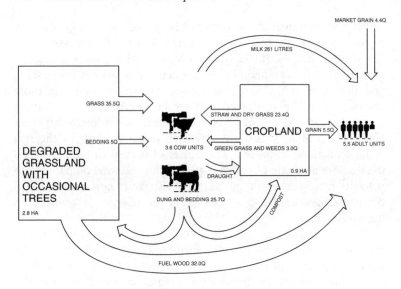

FIGURE 6.1   The situation of an individual fanily holding today in the Dwarahat Block, Almora District, Uttar Pradesh

Source: Ives and Messerli, 1989: Figure 8.6

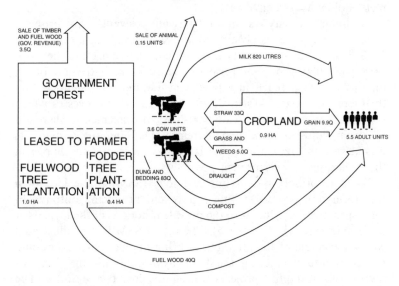

FIGURE 6.2   Idealised representation of plan for rehabilitation of uncultivated land in Dwarahat Block, Almora district, Uttar Pradesh

Source: Ives and Messerli, 1989; Figure 8.7

The transformation process

The change proposed in this transformation process is to focus on the technical and institutional means to improve the degraded grassland so that inputs of dung and fuelwood increase and so that agricultural land becomes sufficient for its users' needs (see Table 6.1).

A 'root definition' of the transformation process links its core purpose with the inputs and outputs, and considers the elements given in Table 6.2.

In the Himalayan example, customers are the farm households. The actors are government officials or NGO workers. The goal is an improved transformation process capable of increasing incomes and self-sufficiency. The *Weltanschauung* is one which stresses community self-sufficiency alongside multiple sources of family income, where a history of government control of forest and grazing has removed the need for community management of those assets. The owners are not only community members (men and women, rich and poor, with separate and different roles and interests) but also

TABLE 6.1   The transformation process: inputs and outputs

Inputs	Outputs
Degraded grassland with occasional trees	Fuelwood
Grazing/cut fodder	Dung for compost
Cropping system, labour, working capital, draught power	Crops for sale/consumption (enough for 2/3 of the year)

TABLE 6.2   The transformation process: definitions

C	Customers	the victims or beneficiaries of T
A	Actors	those who would do T
T	Transformation process	the conversion of input to output
W	Weltanschauung	the worldview(s) which make this T meaningful in context
O	Owner(s)	those who could stop T
E	Environmental constraints	elements outside the system which it takes as given

the Forest and Revenue Departments. Salient environmental constraints include a harsh climate, party politicised village leaderships, and a sceptical Forest Department and profession.

The system is judged by the following criteria: efficacy (does the means work?); efficiency (amount of output divided by amount of resources used); and effectiveness (is T meeting the longer-term aim?)

A simple root definition in the Himalayan example would be: a system in which farm households control the resources required to produce adequate grain, other foodstuffs and income through improving degraded grassland and related livestock management changes. Having established the root definition, models are constructed which are relevant to change in the real world. 'Models are only a means to an end, which is to have a well-structured and coherent debate about a problematical situation in order to decide how to improve it. The debate is structured by using the models based on a range of worldviews to question perceptions of the situation.' (Checkland and Scholes, 1990: 43). An advantage of soft systems methodology over the logical framework is that it encourages consideration of more than one model of the system. These models may include: a model of the activities which the problem-solver(s) hope to turn into actions to solve a real-world problem, which could include participatory activities, dialogue, negotiation, study, and plan formulation; models of the implementation of a change according to several different *Weltanschauungen*.

In our Himalayan example, relevant models would include: (i) different systems for managing and improving degraded grassland, based on the *Weltanschauungen* (plural) of farm households (rich/poor, landed/landless, men/women), professionals (foresters, agriculturalists), and community activists (Chipko movement, local NGOs); (ii) different systems for the participation of outside expertise and development agencies in this process, again derived from the different interests involved; (iii) a specification of the range of organisational and legal actions by communities and official bodies which would facilitate the improved transformation. And so on. These models would generate debates, out of which one or a number of desirable and meaningful changes could be identified.

A second advantage of SSM is that there is a 'stream of cultural enquiry' which accompanies the logical process of model building and comparison with reality. This asks for continued analysis of the intervention, the social system and the political system. These can often best be represented pictorially. Indeed, soft systems methodology lays great value on painting the 'rich picture', pictures being a better means for recording relationships and connections than text. SSM has most often been applied in management problem situations: hence the selection of social and political systems for analysis. These are also extremely important in rural development, as we have seen, but to them we would naturally add economic and environmental systems. This stream of enquiry is not a once-and-for-all activity at the beginning of the work, but a continuing process.

In specifying the focuses of enquiry, SSM shorthand specifies the following: intervention, social and political systems:

- Intervention system: client, would-be problem-solver, problem-owner
- Social (including economic) system: roles, norms, values, structures, relationships, differences
- Political system: how power is expressed, the resources on which power is based

To which we are adding:

- Natural resource system: key nutrient flows, balance enhancers/disrupters

It is important to keep these systems simple, so that they can be adapted to suit particular situations, and so that they do not generate enormous demands for data. It may be that in the course of debate certain issues are identified which require much deeper research or more rigorous data collected over a period of time.

In the Himalayan foothills, social system analysis would drive any would-be problem-solver to discuss their conceptualisation of the problem with the various users, in particular the main users – peasant women – of the hills, compare the way in which degraded grassland is valued and managed, and raise issues of power and control both within and outside the local communities. In the 1980s this would have represented a huge advance over a majority of projects which embarked on their work knowing broadly what their problem was and how they wanted to solve it. The solution (to whatever socio-economic problem) was often to extend Green Revolution technology, which is in fact extremely inappropriate in much of the foothills, where ecologies are varied and uncertainties of weather and natural hazards common. Room for analysis, and participatory reflection, let alone experimentation, was rarely allowed. Only now are these elements beginning to creep into rural development in the hills, through a new generation of participatory projects.

Finally a 'system to make the changes' is pinpointed, whose activities then become action. The changes should be systemically desirable, and culturally meaningful (Checkland and Scholes, 1990: 52). They are systemically desirable if the model(s) constructed is perceived as relevant – a close approximation to reality as perceived by the occupants of the roles listed under intervention above. They are culturally meaningful if they can be understood as useful by the same people. Whereas the project framework with its focus on a limited range of project activities tends to gloss over conflict between interest groups and assume that consensus is possible, SSM allows for the co-existence of several models based on different *Weltanschauungen*. These models are used to generate debate; it is this debate which may produce a (or several, if there is no consensus) final model of a system to make the changes.

In the Himalayas no one model will be adequate to the range of legal, social, environmental and economic situations which exist. Even within small areas SSM can generate a range of models which will be relevant and meaningful. The solutions to the problem of degraded common land will vary from individual leases, to collective management with varying degrees of outside regulation. The degree of actual local control will also vary, as will the distribution of benefits between classes, castes and genders. Changes satisfying the broad aim specified by the root definition will be possible through a number of avenues.

A third advantage of SSM over the logical framework is that the procedure includes reflection by its users on their role in the whole exercise. They too can be part of the problem being researched, and a potential owner of both problem and solution. In any case, any reasonably sophisticated use of the method becomes research on the method itself, with a potential for developing it further.

In the Himalayas, foresters are a key part of both the problem and the solution. In Chapter 3 we saw how foresters have dramatically changed the social and technical parameters within which they work. The change is still in process, however: some foresters have taken some steps towards change; others have not. The foresters' *Weltanschauung* is still in transition: it remains wedded to control exercised by foresters which will limit the range of common or individual property models which can be applied. What may be required is small-scale experiments capable of convincing the sceptics in the longer term.

Co-evolution

Soft systems methodology provides a useful way of thinking about method in rural development. It does not offer a philosophical basis, however. The adoption of a holistic approach needs a philosophical basis too: it cannot rely on a development paradigm which is widely seen as unsuccessful in the sense that either the solutions are not really solutions, or that they create as many problems as they solve. Development has stood for material progress, with or without justice, depending on ideological standpoint. A holistic approach would not be so exclusively concerned with economic progress; if people themselves were more concerned about, say, spiritual development this would be quite legitimate. The protection or enhancement of a culture or a place might be at stake. A holistic approach is also very concerned with the interactions among different systems: in fact, the cutting edge of science is often at the boundaries between disciplines. For example, there is now a widely perceived link between most cancers and diet centering around the consumption of fresh fruit and vegetables as an effective preventative diet. Common sense, yes, but until very recently no medical research was carried out on these links. Dieticians and nutritionists have had a low status among the medical professions. Food of course cannot be patented, so the drug industry had no interest in such research.

Systems are abstractions from reality: mental constructs. Our notion of system needs to be capable of experiencing influence from the outside, or from other systems. The influence of one system on another can lead to important changes. In our Himalayan foothills example, the influence from the transhumant and nomadic livestock rearing systems on the settled agriculturalists' systems is profound, but these interactions are almost never taken into account in practical development work. This is because the system boundaries are implicitly too rigidly defined. The most that is generally done is to see the transhumants as a problem group who should be kept away or settled, without recognising the complementarities which exist between the two systems. In fact, systems co-evolve (Norgaard,

1994). One system influences the evolution of another. As a race, human beings are now very conscious of influencing the environment, generally negatively, in the course of our own development. The environment does not take this 'lying down', however. The use of pesticides has in a remarkably short period of time led to genetic adaptation and pesticide resistance in pests. Every activity which changes the environment selects for species which can best tolerate that changed environment. Those species are then the resources available for further evolution and interaction with other systems. Environment and human culture have co-evolved, through mutual genetic selection, but also through the development of appropriate human cultures which fit the evolving eco-system.

> Through this process the world can be thought of as having become a patchwork quilt of loosely interconnected, coevolving social and ecological systems. . . This worldview is distinctly different from the dominant Western view of a natural world that just is, minds that just perceive and acquire objective knowledge, and societies organised to utilise knowledge rationally to exploit resources, and to correct the environmental catastrophes this view creates. (Norgaard, 1994: 90–1)

Thus there is a co-evolution of indigenous knowledge and culture with western scientific knowledge: as eastern philosophies have become better understood in the west they have started to influence physics in particular; and on a practical level, indigenous knowledge produces for western science many of its base materials – plant and animal varieties, for example.

Can the concept of development, which has become so problematic, be replaced by co-evolution? This may indeed happen in the longer term, but in the short term it is only necessary that development workers understand the profound inter-systemic impacts their work may have and that their work gives recognition to these impacts. Since ordinary people the world over are able to understand and act on some such connections, usually at the micro-level, it is the least we can ask of scientists, social scientists and development professionals. In the meantime co-evolution is the most promising alternative concept available at this juncture.

Norgaard lists six principles of a co-evolutionary cosmos (Norgaard, 1994: ch. 9). (i) As in SSM, we are a part of the system we try to understand: there is no neutral or objective position. In the real world it is not possible to set up laboratory conditions. And the explanations we offer for what we see depend on our social position. (ii) How we think also affects the systems we try to understand. We cannot anticipate the unintended consequences of our thoughts and actions; we cannot foresee a co-evolving cosmos which does not yet exist. Since the system is changing all the time, there is no accumulation of knowledge. There should therefore be no fixed rules about how to manage a system. (iii) We have already come across the need to operate with plural concepts (Chapter 5). Any one pattern of concepts (or model) cannot cope with an entire system: parts get left out. Different disciplines also produce incongruent data and mutually incoherent explanations. Conceptual pluralism needs to be recognised as a fact of life. (iv) Synthesis only happens socially: scientists and the public debate 'until sufficient consensus is acquired to facilitate decision-making'. However, this is rarely conflict-free, and the ideas can only really be tested by history. (v) and (vi) Events are contingent on what has preceded them, and the parts of the system can only be understood in the context of the system in which they are embedded. 'There are no principles by which to predict on the basis of one part or event the nature of the next' (Norgaard, 1994: 100).

The co-evolutionary philosophical framework has consequences for the way in which we should see development.

> If we accept that there is not a comprehensive right way of predicting the future consequences of our choices, we will be more likely to make decisions sequentially in relatively small increments, build monitoring and learning into every program of change, and be adaptive. . . If we hold to the belief that knowledge consists of universal laws with universal applicability, we will apply it accordingly and destroy the diversity in the cultural and ecological systems we are trying to sustain. (Norgaard, 1994: 103)

Agriculture provides the best example of convergent development.

There are fundamental aspects of western thinking which are weak: for example, until the recent interest in common property, community has been a missing concept in economics, which jumps from the individual straight to the nation or the globe. In the dominant western social science it is individuals who make choices. But community and collective choice are very important in non-western societies. Western social science still deals poorly with these issues.

Centralised power does not permit conceptual pluralism, and it increases the transaction costs (the bureaucracy, with its layers of decision-making) of development enormously, so that it can rarely be adaptive to local understanding and choices. A co-evolutionary framework provides the philosophical underpinning for devolution of power, participation and the democratisation of knowledge and progress.

Integrative methodologies

Rural development has always had a tendency to cast its net wide, to resist being restricted to narrow technical specialisms. This can be seen in the repeated attempts to broaden the scope of agricultural programmes, and to incorporate social analysis. This tendency is there for very good reasons, and will not go away, even though large-scale, donor-funded integrated rural development programmes may be out of fashion. The lives of most rural people cannot naturally or easily be compartmentalised; the activities promoted through rural development are usually dependent on other activities, and assumptions about behaviour, policy and institutions. A stake-holder analysis usually demonstrates this nicely (Honadle and Cooper, 1989). This examines the range of interested parties in a development programme, and analyses their degree of influence over the activities which make up the programme. It is usually a sobering experience for a development agency which realises how little it controls directly. The worst effect of this syndrome is that rural development practitioners become imperialistic – they want to take over or dominate the work of a great number of organisations. This can lead to opposition from agencies which feel threatened. Stake-holder analysis, with its emphasis on appreciating and influencing what you cannot control is a healthy corrective. Post-modernism's stress on networking is a useful alternative guide to action (see Chapter 8).

Integrative methodologies are still evolving. In the agricultural field there are methods which incorporate different disciplinary perspectives. Farming Systems Research (FSR) focuses on the interdependencies between the components under the control of the members of a farm household, and how these interact with physical, biological and socio-economic factors not under the household's control. It is a process built around four activities:

- identification of common problems and formulation of 'recommendation domains', comprising areas of common farming and household activity, leading to forming groups based on the principle of maximum variation between them, and minimum variation within them;
- diagnosis through consultation to collect baseline information;
- priorities drawn from the first two activities leading on-farm to trials exploring the interactions of technology and practice;
- evaluation and recommendation, release through the extension system.

FSR was designed to deal with non-Green Revolution situations: the 90 per cent of Africa and 50 per cent of elsewhere with which commodity-based, on-station research could not cope due to their variety, multiplicity and complexity. However, it still assumed that the problems were clearly known, the variables clearly definable, and solutions could be found. In this sense, FSR was still a hard systems approach. The scientist was still the hero in a basically non-participatory framework. Critics have proposed (and in some cases implemented) more participatory approaches to research (see Chapter 7).

Farming Systems Development (FSD) is a method that extension agents can use to understand and help improve peasant farming systems. It relies on identification of farming system 'zones', and within those of farming system groups of farm households with sufficient common characteristics and interests to work together. It focuses on and tries to model the farm household, including all its members, with special attention to avoid excluding women farmers. It stretches out from the farm to understand the relationships between the farm and non-farm enterprises or employment which may be significant for the farm household. It can be complemented by a broader livelihood system analysis. In analysing the farming system, and the operations of groups of farm-households, FSD identifies constraints and opportunities, and applies cause–effect analysis to them. Improvements are sought through participatory on-farm research, creating networks of farmers and information exchange, and through taking well-adapted technologies from research stations.

Its significance lies not only in its holistic character, but also in its institutional 'position'. Developed at FAO it has become the major alternative to 'top-down' and commodity-based extension systems, which are still the conventional wisdom. It is an attempt to bring a holistic approach to farm and rural development down to earth, make it usable. FSD can operate within a framework of soft, co-evolving systems. Based on FSR, and some vague notions of a participatory approach, its first appearance has now been updated to reflect a more participatory, eco- and gender-sensitive approach. It is designed for use by well-trained public, private or NGO extension workers, though it has enormous implications for the nature of the organisation undertaking it.

Other holistic methodologies include the PRA approach and suite of techniques discussed in Chapter 7. There is still plenty of scope for further holistic methodological development.

Conclusion

Uncertainties are great; there are clearly lots of issues to think about in rural development work; large amounts of information might be needed to think about them systematically. All this is too much for the conventional project: what is required is a process, with a strong element of research and evaluation, the adoption of a holistic perspective and methodology, and an awareness of the range of issues which may need to be considered at various points in time. Different knowledge systems – scientific, indigenous – can be called on at appropriate points in this process to offer analysis and suggestions.

7

Participation

In previous chapters frequent reference has been made to the centrality of participation in the new rural development paradigm. This chapter explores the concept and its application, at first in general, and later in two sectors: agriculture and health.

For more than two decades development theorists and practitioners have lectured the world about the need for participation of ordinary people in development. In much of rural development, however, thinking about participation has remained at a very idealistic and ideological level. It has lacked analytical tools, practical methods and an adequate theoretical framework. So it has degenerated into a kind of propaganda – words to convince audiences that agencies, NGOs, and governments have recognised the necessity of involving people in development activities. Sometimes it is the participation of particular categories of people which has to be demonstrated – women, the poorest of the poor, minority groups. But participation is usually asserted, not demonstrated. Few in the audience have time to examine the indicators, which are in any case poorly developed. Indicators of how participation happens, and what its effects are on participants and in the wider society, need to be developed and applied.

It is no longer possible to be naive about participation. So much has been spoken and written which identifies participation with issues of power, not least by United Nations agencies. For example, the United Nations Research Institute for Social Development (UNRISD) defined participation as the organised effort to increase control over resources and regulative institutions by groups and movements of those excluded from such control (Pearse and Stiefel, 1979: 8). This definition recognises that it is potentially conflictual, and that redistribution of power is involved. This means that there will be interests opposing participation, based on political affiliation, class, race, ethnicity, or gender. There are many typologies of participation; a basic distinction is that between a system-maintaining and system-transforming process. Participation, as defined above, would be system-transforming. Used in this way, participation is closely tied up with equity and empowerment.

Rahman (1990: 45–49) identified several dimensions of empowerment which provide a good starting point for developing indicators about participation: (i) organisation of the disadvantaged and underprivileged in structures under their own control; (ii) knowledge of their social environment and its processes developed by the disadvantaged; (iii) self-reliance, an attitudinal quality strengthened by the solidarity, caring and sharing of collective identity; (iv) creativity; (v) institutional development, in particular the management of collective tasks, and mass participation in deliberation and decision-making; (vi) solidarity – the ability to handle conflicts and tension, to care for those in distress, and a consensus that all should advance together; (vii) progress for women in articulating their points of view, and the evolution of gender relations towards equality, as assessed by women themselves. Empowerment would also imply that there were changes going on in the wider society as a result of grassroots changes: the development of human dignity, popular democracy, and cultural diversity.

This type of evaluation is qualitative; is a learning experience for the community of 'beneficiaries' or participants in development; and is a continuous process (rather than a point in a cycle) which accepts that situations unfold and objectives may change.

From the preceding chapters it is possible to develop an argument about participation as a necessity in rural development. We have seen that rural development is an experimental process; by no means all of the answers are known; those which were known yesterday are questioned today. This is true in technical terms as well as in terms of process. Policies and programmes have new contents – low external input and sustainable agriculture, savings- and collateral-free credit, industrial districts and artisans' associations, new common property resources, community and group-based services. All these rely on local people's knowledge, managerial abilities, skills in problem identification and assessment of solutions, and social and economic relationships. These new ideas recognise the importance of context in development: centrally produced, packaged technologies do not work in much of the world. Local contexts are infinitely varied and can be known only by local people. These programmes need to be executed in new ways: programmes replace projects, with a strong degree of local managerial flexibility; activities are increasingly self-funded – even the poor save and contribute to their own bootstraps. Self-funding gives power to the 'shareholders'.

It will be argued in Chapter 10 that development aid as we have known it is coming to an end. While its end will be spread over many years, it has implications which have already begun. The paternalism and welfarist character of much aid-dependent public sector rural development is in decline, either as a result of structural adjustment expenditure cuts or of switching aid to more urgent causes (containing conflict and relieving its victims, trade-based rehabilitation and introduction of markets). Public sector resources are in increasingly short supply in many aid-dependent countries. There is a concentration in western aid now on infrastructure – roads and other transport infrastructure, and dams. Smaller-scale rural development aid tends increasingly to be channelled through NGOs, in diminishing quantities, and the NGO presence means that it comes increasingly tied to particular strategic concerns of the NGOs. In fact, there is a new paternalism here: that NGOs know best, because they are close to the grassroots. NGOs have tried to take the concept of participation as their own, but are often as idealistic and demagogic about it as the previous generation of rural development workers.

With this gloomy scenario for public sector and aid resource flows into rural areas, rural people may nevertheless acquire greater opportunities to come of age politically, to develop movements to counter extraction and exploitation, which can be the basis for enhanced accountability of local and national institutions as well as NGOs. They will be freer to set their own political and policy agendas; they will be more equal in negotiations with development agencies which will become more responsive and less imposing. This strength is based on: individual development and leadership; group activities, which may be networked into associations; political organisation for lobbying to change policies, stop negative development and propose alternatives; local development finance, possibly as a basis for seeking matching funds; institutional development for the management of common resources; and development strategies which respect local knowledge, people and institutions.

While participation has been generally seen by development agencies in terms of collaboration, and as a means to project success, as bringing additional human resources into the project process, participation increasingly is about civil society playing roles which development agencies and governments cannot play, and in particular about the rural poor associating together to defend common interests and challenge structures which keep them in poverty. In this (empowerment) sense it is a much more overtly political concept than it was. The challenge for rural development workers is to recognise and facilitate the process of organisation and representation, and to ensure that development work is consonant with advancing the inclusion of the poor.

'Structures' and 'fora' are necessary for participation to be meaningful (MacDonald, 1993: 97). Based on material in the earlier chapters, and the above definitions, this is not an adequate conceptualisation of the organisational implications of participation. Controlling resources and institutions is not merely a matter of having an opportunity to share ideas and collectively plan action: it is a matter of organisational definition (inclusion and exclusion, rules, etc.), policy and management. Viable, sustainable organisations which can be run by the rural poor and exert an influence in the wider development arena are the mechanisms for participation.

Progress in participation

Whatever the cynics may say, the concept has had a widespread impact. In agriculture, farmer participatory research and farming systems development are gaining respect. In resource conservation, communities are often expected to be capable of developing a longer-term view and management role. In forestry, community forestry has been the vogue for years. In primary health care, rural water supply and sanitation, participation is a by-word. In irrigation, small schemes are widely appreciated for their participatory qualities, and water users' associations have been introduced into many big schemes. User-controlled credit unions and savings and credit groups have come to compete with banks. The roles of farmers' and (less often) rural workers' organisations, women's groups and organisations are widely appreciated, although projects frequently resort to creating their own organisations of beneficiaries (Oakley, 1994: 14–19).

There are lessons to be learned from experience. (i) Participation requires attitude change: understanding, humility, flexibility and patience. (ii) There are facilitatory factors such as: political support, decentralisation, traditions of community organisation, the availability of good leaders and managers, and helpful procedures, technologies which promote autonomy and self-reliance – these factors need assessment before an activity commences, and as it is running. (iii) Governments and NGOs both have roles in promoting participation; the evidence for who is better at it is patchy, but the widespread belief is that NGOs are, but have difficulty 'going to scale' – or broadening their impact. (iv) Projects limit the scope for participation in the sense in which it is being used here. Something else is needed, unless a mechanical approach to it is adopted. (v) Operationally, there are lessons too: work with existing community organisations; get quick results to motivate participation; respond to local initiatives – outsiders take the initiative less often; people should be involved in identifying problems and solutions; the project should be small enough to be understood by local people. Preparatory work (analysis, explanation and dialogue, definition of approaches to be used, assigning responsibilities) is crucial. (vi) Key components in World Bank funded projects which have been participatory include: staff training in participatory methods; a focus on small, socially homogeneous groups of people as 'beneficiaries'; the building up and strengthening of effective people's organisations; and an educational component developing the skills and knowledge of participants (Oakley, 1994: 26–9)

However, the cynics would argue that it is only a minority of projects which work in this way. The majority of big projects into which most aid and public resources go pay only lip-service to notions of participation. Even many small, NGO-led projects impose their ideas, or operate with a restrictive idea of participation – confined to collaboration over narrowly defined project activities. Turning this correct perception on its head would lead back to the argument that the project as a form of development is inimical to participation. It is possible but unlikely that a 'new genre' of projects will be designed, focusing on 'a realignment of power via changes in institutionalised arrangements for resource allocation and which also promote and build upon people's skills and abilities and then integrate these into development practice' (Oakley, 1994: 34). This type of work could probably not be contained within the framework of time, budget and accountability which a project, even a process project (see below), implies. It rather requires more open-ended commitment by governments, donors and partners to objectives which may be pursued in a number of ways: through particular (usually small-scale) activities under the control of local people and institutions; through strengthening the organisations of civil society, and removing the barriers they face; and through helping them to lobby for change, and so on. This pattern of work can still be 'programmed', and indeed can be divided into discrete but connected activity areas, with different organisations involved in each.

The cynic would continue that the legal, technological/professional and bureaucratic structures have rarely changed substantially to facilitate participation. It remains to be seen what aid that is conditional on 'good government', democracy, human rights, etc. will achieve in this direction, and, more important, what impact the growing citizens' movements will have. Perhaps the biggest changes so far have been in the thinking of professionals, especially in agriculture, forestry and natural-resource management, as we have seen in earlier chapters. Chambers's work advocating the development of 'new professionals' (1993) reflects considerable though patchy change in third world professionals. The reform of government which is now increasingly the focus of structural adjustment programmes still represents an opportunity for social movements to press for change which facilitates their role, makes possible common property resource management across a wider field of activities, and retains resources where they are needed. The changes needed will be highlighted in Chapter 8.

Community participation

Participation has all too frequently been limited to 'community' participation. It was argued above (Chapter 6) that community is often missing in western economists' notions of institutional structure, as western society is seen to have moved from its previous base in communities to one in formal associations (*Gemeinschaft* to *Gesellschaft*). However, even economists working in peasant societies are inclined to give the community a significant status. Practical development work has combined the use of communities' institutional structures to propagate modern ideas and technologies, with promoting the idea that the community should identify its problems, agree solutions and then manage and maintain investments. Community participation has been seen as the key to sustaining development investments, identifying the right ones in the first place, and avoiding the need for rural public services to be run by the public sector.

The stress on community is probably a hangover from colonialism, which relied on hand-picked community leaders to keep discipline and make sure that colonial laws were implemented. Colonial governments were unwilling to incur the expense of delving beneath the level of community leaders in their interactions with rural people. In the 1950s and 1960s, the Community Development movement generated community-level development activities under the control of the village leader(s) and elite. The poor, women, and marginal groups were left out. Often projects were used by nascent political parties as a means of consolidating their rural vote. Local leaders had patronage to dispense, in exchange for votes. The critique of community development combined with critiques of the Green Revolution and other aspects of modernisation to form a powerful case for greater social analysis, closer contact between development agencies and the groups they were trying to reach, and less reliance on community leaders to include the excluded. Community leaders often turned out to be faction leaders, and communities split into political, religious or ethnic factions as well as by wealth and gender. Even communication across those lines could be difficult. Reliance on the community leadership, in the name of participation, was a vehicle for exclusion as much as inclusion.

This 'naive' community development has given way to a more sophisticated version, in which agencies work with individuals and groups within the community, attempting to enhance the rights and representation of disadvantaged people, while recognising community leaders for what they are. There is also now a recognition that conflict is a consistent feature of the life of many communities – among members or with neighbouring communities. External agencies can play both a stimulating and a calming role in relation to conflict. More and more NGOs are self-consciously analysing their roles in conflict situations, and recognising the effect that development may have in periods of peace.

If the community is less a vehicle for open, non-exclusive participation than was once believed, what are the alternatives? Two vehicles are popular: the group, and 'institutional development'. Working with smaller groups within the community is an obvious way to get around the problems of working at community level, and to avoid the expense involved in working directly with individuals.

Groups

Working with groups of poor workers and producers has been a theme of rural development since the 1970s. We have seen how they can play strong roles in provision of services, and how their position can be enhanced by control of assets (Chapter 3). A review of practice led to the identification of the following factors conducive to group success (Burkey, 1993: 163). (i) Group membership is voluntary, and groups are homogeneous – have a common interest, and belong to the same socio-economic category. (ii) Small groups allow open and intensive discussion, a higher quality of participation. (iii) Leaders are elected, and leadership rotates. Decisions should be taken by collective deliberation. (iv) Regular meetings, savings and credit funds activities help build unity and cohesion. (v) All decisions (what to do, how to do it, etc.) are taken by the group; external agents should only provide advice when asked. (vi) Among poor people activities are initially directed at improving livelihoods.

There are now numerous manuals giving guidance on group development. These cover, first, the skills which groups need that centre on the group itself – building trust, communicating, getting a balance of roles, structuring leadership so that it enables co-operation and teamwork, and conflict resolution; and second, the skills a group needs to be effective in development – information collection and processing, decision-making, management, participatory monitoring and evaluation. (This list is from Grieshaber, 1994, a manual written for women's clubs in Zimbabwe.) Groups and their actions are often evaluated from the outsider's point of view – for example, how effective are they in helping members to change in some way desirable to the outsider? Insiders' evaluations, using their own criteria of effectiveness, and their own indicators, will be more influential in determining the long-term success of the group. Likewise, the skills needed can be established by the group's members rather than imposed, manual style, from outside.

There are many situations in which groups contain sub-groups which may have different interests or views on particular issues. Much effort in serious working with groups is devoted to identifying differences, learning to respect them, and looking for points of convergence and agreement. This is illustrated by an ActionAid-sponsored HIV (human immunodeficiency virus) prevention and support programme in Uganda, which developed a training method involving breaking the community into peer groups by gender and age to save embarrassment and create solidarity among members. The peer groups would meet to develop group dynamics, share information, fears and hopes and listen to each other; they would develop an understanding of the different behaviour patterns around sex and death, the cultural norms and pressures involved. Peer groups would occasionally interact with each other, and would make requests for behaviour change in the other groups which would be public, and ideally lead to community-wide agreements on behaviour.

This painstaking type of work can have good results. In Uganda it led to a localised uptake in condom use, reduced tension because of improved communication, a public commitment to new norms of behaviour, discussion of previously taboo subjects, greater confidence especially among women to say no, and reduced stigma for HIV-positive people. It combines a process of individual change with group and community change (Welbourne, 1994). It relies on committed individuals as facilitators, trained in the method and able to guide the different peer groups through the process. Training of trainers/facilitators is thus a key to spreading such micro-activities wider. Establishment of groups can be very expensive; much of the training and facilitating/promoting needs to be transferred from expensive researchers or trainers to local people as quickly as possible.

Groups which are effective in development – for themselves, or as contributors to the wider interest – can sometimes remain based on informal relationships, trust and spontaneity. We should not discount altruism either as a motive for action and participation. However, it is human nature to look for a flow of advantages and benefits out of participation in group activity. In the Ugandan example, everybody needs to participate to define and generate the public changes in behaviour appropriate to a situation of high HIV risk. Changed behaviour is ideally a public good in this case. However, if only one or two peer groups participate or change their behaviour, their changed behaviour would become a common good which they would have to defend against other disagreeing groups. This would be difficult in this case. Common goods – with boundaries drawn around a particular beneficiary group, rules followed by that group, and norms of behaviour to ensure the continued viability of the group – are easier to achieve, but often involve a need to protect the achievement. Viable groups tend to develop clear boundaries and rules; however, these do not always need to be formalised. We will examine further examples in the sections below on agriculture and health.

Institutional development

Primary groups can rarely survive for long without a wider framework of support and linkage. There are simply too many powerful cross-cutting issues and networks for most individuals, such that loyalties to groups will be conditional on the group serving the individuals' interests. Small groups are rarely able to support significant services or defend significant common property for sustained periods: hence the need to form wider alliances and associations which can carry the costs, and provide the necessary mutual support. In rural development to date this associative role has sometimes been played by a movement, but more frequently by a development agency. Where this is the case, an agency could either support an association controlled by ordinary people or transform itself into a user-controlled organisation within a limited period, as we saw in the case of the Grameen Bank (Chapter 4): if groups of underprivileged people continue to depend on external agencies over which they have no control, there is little institutional development and therefore no long-run sustainability. The self-aggrandising tendencies of development agencies often get in the way of poor people developing institutions in which they participate.

There are many kinds of associations which have considerable scope to support primary groups or individuals. Some of these will be formally constituted, like the water users' associations on big irrigation schemes, which have developed during the last fifteen years to manage small-scale gravity or groundwater schemes, or local sub-systems within large gravity schemes. Research into indigenous farmer-managed irrigation has helped to identify principles on which water user associations (WUAs) might work. WUAs have developed in large-scale schemes where government irrigation departments have encouraged them. Where associations have been representative of farmers, they have been instrumental in getting decisions about water allocation made equitably, and have supplied more accurate information on water needs to canal managers, which helps improve efficiency. The results include higher incomes to farmers and improved agricultural productivity (Meinzen-Dick *et al.*, 1994).

The advantage of formally constituted associations is that they may employ people and contract to do things for their members. Employees of an association covering a number of primary groups can provide a service to those groups, supervise their activities or provide technical assistance or other facilitation services. Associations can develop to the stage where they are offering a complicated range of services to members, and are also politically influential.

Chipko

There are other associations that are more like movements. Movements are by nature more diffuse and composed of coalitions between groups which associate for particular purposes. They have less structure than an association, and less discipline than a political party. They are frequently composed of different wings. This is illustrated by one of the best-known rural movements – the Chipko movement, in the Indian Himalayan foothills. Chipko is widely known as an environmental movement, associated with the image of women hugging the trees to protect the mountain forests from commercial exploitation, which in turn protect springs, streams, farms and provide fodder and fuel. Guha (1989 and 1993) has interpreted the movement as a peasant movement, with a historical lineage of peasant movements before it, protesting against various aspects of the commercialisation of the hill economy. There have been various agitations, the most famous of which in 1980 led to a 15-year moratorium on the commercial felling of green trees in the region, Uttarakhand. During the last decade the issues for the movement have been: opposition to the liquor trade, led by women fed up with their husbands drinking away household incomes; opposition to dam-building and open-cast mining. The movement has campaigned for the decentralisation of government, which is definitely required to address the serious problems of degradation in the hills (Ashish, 1993; and Chapter 6). The movement has three wings, with different perspectives on ecology and society (Guha, 1993: 102–4). It has spawned numerous NGOs, which tend to work within the ideological framework of the particular wing they are attached to. And it has had an influence on politics and government, with a number of public sector projects developed in response to its concerns, and the recent concession of a separate state for the region.

The Chipko movement has not only raised issues of concern to local people in a region of India to the national agenda which would otherwise have remained dormant; it has fostered a widespread sense that rural people can take their affairs into their own hands and discuss them as equals with members of the elite, professionals, and political parties. In practical terms, apart from successful agitations it has also generated a large volume of environmentally sensitive, and participatory development work.

Social movements of peasants and agricultural workers often depend on: the opportunities offered by a softening of oppressive anti-participatory structures (states are usually representative of other social interests); the availability of interlocutors – who 'advise, guide, direct, help, study or simply exploit the . . . movement' (Stiefel and Wolfe, 1994: 42) and arrange alliances with other social forces; and the degree of threat to livelihoods, and concrete opportunities to gain control over significant resources. They are usually local or regional in scope, but sometimes become national if the state is very weak. While rural social movements usually seek accommodation with other interests, there are plenty of cases where they have become involved in violence.

Social movements

There are many problems arising out of the dependence of movements on interlocutors due to the interlocutors' difficulties in understanding peasant rationality, characteristics, motivations, and the rapidly evolving rural scene (Stiefel and Wolfe, 1994: 43). These difficulties are due to rural social differentiation – peasants are rarely socially homogeneous, and it is difficult for outsiders to understand social difference; peasants' rationality, interests, perceptions of risk and opportunity differ from their urban/literate/educated supporters. Peasants are usually suspicious of interlocutors. Ideally the latter should be self-critical, prepared to interact with mutual respect (though not giving in to sentimental abdication of their own integrity and socio-economic position). However, there are many constraints: persistent ideological preconceptions, institutional constraints, and the shrinking of space within which to develop alternative strategies. Movements generate their own leaders which may conflict with the interlocutors.

Governments' responses to associations and movements have often been repressive, where they are perceived as challenges to a given order or regime. More democratically inclined governments may see movements as a potential source of political party strength, and therefore be more sympathetic within certain boundaries. The challenge for rural people is to build governmental systems which will enable them to associate, and to form movements which will support their active participation in policy and development processes. An enabling environment would include: constitutional and legal reforms protecting individual and collective rights; constitutional reforms decentralising powers and control over resources; and a recognition of when associations may be as effective a vehicle for the control of resources and provision of services as government or NGOs. Above all, an enabling environment implies that decision-makers have the attitude and flexibility to facilitate strong roles in development for popular organisations and movements.

Agriculture

One thing which marks out the new approaches – farming-system development, farmer participatory research, participatory technology development, etc. – from the old is the emphasis they all give to groups of farmers: farmer groups are the basis of any interaction with a development agency. Knowledge is increasingly seen as a common good, shared by a limited group to whom it is relevant. This applies particularly in the varied and 'difficult' environments which characterise most rural development situations, where social and environmental conditions are not uniform, so standard packages of technical knowledge rarely apply. Research is not, in this situation, a public good able to benefit a large number of farmers, and indirectly consumers; it is more like a common good. It is now recognised that in these typical differentiated contexts, it is farmers themselves who are actively generating new knowledge all the time, and effective research must be a partnership of some kind between farmers and researchers.

The problem for the agency (initially) and for the farmers is to identify groups which make sense to their members and are viable; and in which the interests of individual members or households are not overwhelmed by a dominant or average interest. A recognition that there are (perhaps informal) groups already in existence, or social networks which operate effectively, is usually a good starting point. This may then be combined with or checked against an analytical approach to identifying common interests around which a group can exist. Of the new approaches listed above, farming-system development, in its latest form does this most systematically. There are choices to be made between selecting a farmer expert to work with, using as a criterion the ability of that farmer to work with the wider client group, and relying on informal communication systems between farmer-expert and group; and working more directly with a (more formalised) group. Further choices concern the size, level and nature of the groups, and there are many social variables likely to affect choices: 'settlement pattern, social hetero-geneity, social stratification or factionalism, and the extent of seasonal migration. Gender analysis and planning for women's involvement introduce additional complexities' (Okali *et al.*, 1994: 88).

The focus on groups is necessary for socio-economic reasons as well. Farmer groups often benefit the less poor more, and may exclude women and marginal groups (see, for example, Bratton, 1986). However, the principle enables smaller farmers, farmers with less secure tenure arrangements, women farmers, farmers on the worst land, part-time farmers, backyard gardeners, and common land users to identify themselves as groups, to start to tackle their common problems, and to raise issues for public debate where there are differences between groups. In Zimbabwe there are three types of small farmer-group. Mutual-help groups share assets like plough animals or labour and often exchange in kind; these groups tend to serve women and the poorest farmers. Master Farmer clubs and marketing groups tend to serve better-off households with capital. Group development also enables the development of wider networks of groups facing similar problems across a number of communities or regions. Common interest networks, formal associations, and farmers' movements are thus the logical counterparts to the farmer group. It is they which will be able to take up lobbying functions effectively, and which will have the scale of resources to provide services to members on a sustainable basis.

At the interface between agencies and farmers there is a conver-gence of new approaches around small recommendation domains, small improvements in context, and involving farmers in the re-search or extension process from the beginning, all of which lessens the importance of the tools of conventional research which focus on scaling up and achieving statistical significance in research results.

The recognition of diversity is thus a liberation: good results can be appreciated for their own sake, not because they are going to solve wider problems.

The focus in the new approach has been on getting farmer participation in the research carried out by an agency, especially in problem selection and diagnosis, on-farm trials and dissemination. There is a rich diversity of experience reported in Okali *et al.* (1994: chs 4–6), though it is apparently too early to claim major successes for the approach. It is not a cheap approach, involving major commitments of time of farmers and researchers. Not everyone believes that the approach is the right one: 'Baker (1991) . . . is convinced that what farmers need are new options and that they are not seeking catalysts to their own innovative processes' (quoted in Okali *et al.*, 1994: 92).

This is early days for the new approach: there is still much current ideology claiming a role for farmers in research, but little clarity over what that role might be, especially when it comes to the issue of what farmers' independent role is (ibid: 99). Scientists are generally keen to see farmers contributing to their programmes, to make them more effective: this involves identifying what farmers are particularly good at – problem diagnosis, technology selection for particular niches, adapting the technology at farm level. Only occasionally are farmers involved in developing the technology itself. To date scientists have little understanding of farmers' own experimental processes. As research programmes move on to the other foot, with researchers assisting farmers to carry out experiments or develop technology, it will be necessary to develop new conceptual frameworks covering technical processes and social context (groups, networks, etc.) of farmers' own experimental processes. Okali *et al.* have made a start in the distinction they drew between farmers who consciously experiment – try new things and monitor the results – who usually have a reputation in the community as innovators; and the greater number of farmers who experiment in all sorts of small ways on a routine basis and carry in their heads ('reflection-in-action') the cumulative result of this less well-defined process, but do not specifically monitor impacts (ibid: 130). Much of this sort of experimentation is reactive, and happens as a result of hazard, which leads to practices which diverge from the norm.

Innovation happens in a social context: information is exchanged through networks, which may be quite complicated and extensive.

These need to be understood by agencies seeking to interact with farmers in the generation of new technology. The anthropological technique of network analysis may be useful here. There is glib talk of 'sideways extension' or 'farmer-to-farmer extension', but, in reality, considerable diversity in the extent to which this takes place. Beyond the local level, more formalised networking of farmer groups has potential in a situation where farmer groups are otherwise fragmented and narrowly based. In Tanzania, the Sokoine Agricultural University has facilitated several area-based networks, with an umbrella organisation focusing on information and technology transfer (Mattee and Lassalle, 1994).

What is missing in the debate on farmer participation in agricultural research is a significant debate about the implications it has for the organisation of research itself. Even the majority of 'farmer participatory research' is researcher-led in fact. This is unlikely to change unless the financing of research and the structuring of research agencies undergoes a dramatic shift. There are projects which have passed resources to farmers – for example 'a union of cassava producers in Ecuador uses USAID funds to contract research from the university and public sector' (Okali *et al.*, 1994: 85). These are, so far, isolated experiments. Significant reforms in this respect are occurring in the north. In Norway, for example, the government is in the process of passing over its entire field research system to farmer research circles in a phased manner. By 1992 about 400 farmer research circles were contributing 35 per cent of the budget of the research system, and, through meetings held with researchers during the long winter evenings, were beginning to have an impact on the design and implementation of the research programmes. Here the local researchers were beginning to work for the farmer members of the circles. Other northern reform processes are seeking to commercialise and then privatise agricultural research. While farmers may play a role in this process, it is likely that big capital with interests in the agricultural markets will come to dominate the field.

In the south, such institutional changes are likely to dominate the coming decade. In Mali, for example, following the successful example of research in cotton, whose success was attributed to the existence of a strong user organisation, farmers are now represented on national and local decision-making bodies in the public agricultural research system, through a structure of 'User Commissions', in which representatives of grassroots farmer organisations sit to debate agricultural research issues; these commissions delegate members to represent them on national and regional decision-making bodies. This has happened in an atmosphere of general democratisation and decentralisation in Mali, which has a recent history of increasingly powerful and well-organised farmers' organisations. Under a World Bank-funded project, the national agricultural research system is being made more accountable to farmers, through a system of contracts between the now autonomous research organisation, the individual scientists and the research funding body. A fund was also created to be available to farmer and processor organisations wanting to contract research from the system. Service NGOs were involved in selecting the farmers' organisations to represent particular socio-ecological zones, and in training in participatory research, though the latter was seen to need greater expertise than they had to offer. Communication came out as a key problem in the new system: which language to use? how to communicate scientific ideas in lay language? how to communicate what researchers can actually do? and so on. In Latin America for some time farmers' associations have formally contracted with research and extension agencies to carry out particular tasks.

There is mounting evidence that successful agricultural research requires to be demand-driven (Merrill-Sands and Collion, 1994). Tendler (1991: 75–8) argued that investors would be well advised to allocate a proportion of their research budgets to producers' organisations, who would make sure that research was relevant, and was done efficiently. In future, more and more farmer organisations can be expected to seek partnerships with research organisations (see, for example, Dugue, 1993). Links in many countries are currently haphazard and need to be institutionalised in ways appropriate to the particular situation.

However, farmers' organisations are no panacea. Gubbels (1993) has documented how democratisation and structural adjustment in West Africa have led to a mushrooming of local organisations led by retrenched civil servants, who tend to adopt 'traditional'(?) decision-making patterns which exclude women and the poor, and due to their inability to recognise differences among farmers may lead to increased conflict in the community. In Thailand, farmers' organisations are often used as vehicles for personal gain by village headmen and extension agents. In mixed membership organisations, it is the larger farmers who benefit; small farmers do not see their interests represented by these organisations. Changing this would require a much more subtle approach to group formation and village-level social and political relationships.

Capacity development is critical in a fast-changing situation. This is even true of national organisations, for example the National Farmers' Association of Zimbabwe, whose weaknesses were identified as: lack of leadership and management skills; poor financial management; dependence on external funding sources; weak internal accountability; and a rigid authoritarian organisational structure (Makumbe, 1994).

Despite the weaknesses, farmer organisations, of which there is now an astonishing variety in poor countries (Arnaiz *et al.*, 1995), offer the best promise that the gaps in agricultural research and extension created by public expenditure cuts and the organisational reforms of structural adjustment can be filled positively, and with the prospect of improved outcomes for small farmers. NGOs have entered the picture in a big way, especially in Latin America, in support of farmer organisations, many of which have only limited capacity for tasks such as organising research and extension. Farmer organisations often develop around other functions – political (e.g. price negotiation), marketing and associated activities – and capacity improvements are needed across a wide spectrum of activity, which would include village-level capacity since farmer organisations' strength and effectiveness will depend substantially on the strength and effectiveness of village-level branches. Farmer organisations are thus a potentially wide-ranging development instrument.

Health

The failure of primary health care systems to make a serious contribution to the health of the majority in many poor countries was discussed in Chapter 3. Because of this situation, rural people often have to take their health into their own hands. They patronise local healers and traditional or complementary medical practitioners in a private system; they use the private sector allopathic drug retailers; they top up the salaries of their community health workers; they pay for drugs and participate in revolving drug funds. Very frequently they have built or contributed to the building of health centres, and to their maintenance.

These tendencies have been formalised in the community health finance movement, focusing on various community cost recovery schemes, and the Bamako Initiative, which centres on payment for drugs. There is a range of community health financing mechanisms in existence: fees for consultation, for an episode of illness, for drugs or treatment; the establishment of community pharmacies. These mechanisms are generally part of a local health system in which ordinary people are involved in management committees, and decide on fees and price levels, on exemptions, and on what is done with the revenues (Carrin, 1992: ch. 10). The development of insurance schemes which include the rural poor has already been discussed in Chapter 3.

Once again we are dealing with a transition in perception. In the twentieth century, health has been viewed as a public good. More recent understanding is that many aspects of health are in essence individual; but a few aspects are of public significance (World Bank, 1993; and Chapter 3 above). Much of health is in fact achievable as a *common* good: this would include preventive health actions needed on a neighbourhood, area or community basis (e.g. in sanitation and sewage disposal); and curative services needed by individuals, but not available through public or private channels, or only available expensively or unreliably.

Moving from health as a public good to health as a common good creates important roles for groups, communities, local governments, associations and facilitating individuals. Cost recovery systems which keep revenues in common circulation are the foundation on which common strategies for health can be evolved. Currently, too much stress is laid on community involvement, rather than group, association or local government. This is partly an indication of how conservative and socially unaware health professionals are, but also a result of the desire to spread primary health services to all communities. One service (health centre, community health worker) per community has been the norm. Entirely predictably, women, marginalised groups (e.g. pastoralists) and the chronically ill and disabled have often not had the access (nor the quality of service) they need from this skeletal service. There is a case for conceiving of common services provided to groups with common interests which stretch across community boundaries. Women's reproductive and other health issues require somewhat specialised approaches and facilities; groups of women within communities, linking together across communities, may be in a better position to provide themselves with an appropriate service than they would get from a general community-based facility. This might be organised by an association of women's health groups.

Equity would be an issue for groups and associations, just as it is for a community. What policy should be adopted towards people who cannot afford to pay even the small amounts charged by health services which are already providing the cheapest services, as they use their scale to buy in bulk, or in the generic (or non-brand) drug markets? Making the service local and as cheap as possible is a good start – it includes more people. Cost recovery can be organised more or less equitably: a charge per illness, prepayment or insurance systems are more equitable than fees for drugs or consultations. Categories of people can be exempted (e.g. children, and long-term patients). Whatever the rules, it is important that users are involved in setting them, and reviewing them and their effects (e.g. service utilisation, incidence of good health, control of disease, etc.). However, the more complicated the system, the higher is the quality of management required. Management can be partly provided by a central association, or local government which can help to set up and monitor the accounting and management of revenues, the pricing of inputs and fee levels, and provide the knowledge of how to operate a simple insurance scheme (Carrin, 1992: 187–8).

Local government involvement in primary and preventive health is quite logical, but local governments often suffer from resource scarcities on an even greater scale than central Ministries of Health. Local government, with its local political constituency, is more likely to act in a responsive way to the requirements and demands of local groups and associations. Not having the same commitment to an anti-participatory professional ethic, local governments are far more likely to facilitate participatory structures than are Ministries of Health, which are dominated by doctors. The desire to keep control over the service will not be there in the same way. Local governments, provided they could be trusted, would be appropriate co-ordinators for drug revolving funds, for example.

Participatory methods

The study of health has emphasised the importance of a financial base for participatory structures, as well as a commitment to clarity about who is included as a beneficiary of a common service. Allowing popular control over budgets can be a more systematic way of encouraging participation: participants feel that their decisions are empowered. An interesting experiment in participatory budgeting in a number of Brazilian municipalities illustrates the potential. Here, special budget fora were established in the municipalities' zones to discuss projects and priorities. Conclusions from these were fed back to the municipality and became the foundation for a growing proportion of its budget over a period of several years. This led to a high degree of transparency in the budget process, so that citizens knew what was supposed to happen. Investment was based on agreed criteria, and local investment plans were documented. There were a number of limitations to the participatory process: it could be co-opted by the ruling party in a municipality; it distracted attention from building up party-based democracy; and took away energy from community organisations, as good local leaders tended to become delegates to the municipal budget council. This experiment represents one of the strongest examples of management by the poor, who were the majority in the local budget fora. Where rural (or urban–rural) municipal systems are strong enough, it is an attractive option (Mattheus, 1995).

Resources are one key (but neglected) aspect of the participatory decision-making process; the devolution of control over resources to local people is a procedure which has been too little tried in rural development and which fits well with the general approach to institutional development advocated in this chapter. Organisations with resources are generally anxious to keep control over them; a positive institutional development approach will use the devolution of resources to build local management capacity. The quality of interaction between professionals, managers, politicians and ordinary people is another, better developed, aspect of the participatory process. Here there has been a tremendous development of participatory techniques designed to bring outsiders and insiders to a closer understanding and respect of each other. Rural development has been so dominated by outsiders and their beliefs and values that this is a significant step on the way to ceding control over development processes to rural people. The most developed approach and bundle of techniques is Participatory Rural Appraisal (PRA).

PRA

There is a growing canon of literature on PRA, and a number of books and manuals on its applications. Readers are referred to Mukherjee (1993 and 1995) for South Asian focused textbooks, Leurs (1993) for a trainers' guide, the series of Rapid Rural Appraisal (RRA) (now Participatory Learning and Action – PLA) Notes produced by the International Institute of Environment and Development (IIED), and the recent articles by Chambers (1994 and 1995) and Leurs (1996).

PRA started as bundles of techniques derived from agroecosystem analysis, applied anthropology, field research on farming systems, rapid rural appraisal, and an approach derived from participatory action research (Chambers, 1993). At the time of writing it is a field of activity which absorbs a large number of rural development specialists and agencies both in the NGO and public sectors. In that the approach is intentionally participatory, can be socially perceptive, and has its roots in sustainability issues, it is very much at the active centre of the new paradigm. Ultimately it will be assessed not only by how much the approach benefits particular activities or agencies, but also by whether it fosters the germ of self-management by groups, communities, and associations. This is a tough criterion, but is one by which any initiative will be judged. 'PRA is a growing family of approaches and methods to enable local people to share [with each other? with outsiders?], enhance and analyse their knowledge of life and conditions, to plan and to act' (PLA Notes, 1995: 5).

As PRA expands it is getting difficult to define it. Is it a set of techniques (RRA), or a set of techniques wrapped up in a participatory approach (PRA), or a philosophy and approach to life for a professional's development? Its core lies in the development, adaptation and application of simple, structured interactive techniques based on game theory and social science research methods which produce accurate information through group work and dialogue. Their special merit lies in the visual nature of many of the exercises, allowing non-literate people to participate as well as literate. They also encourage professionals to keep their knowledge and opinions to themselves, at least temporarily, for the duration of the exercise. PRA allows popular categories to be used rather than planners' concepts. This is a beginning to the process of understanding indigenous objectives and knowledge. The result is models, sketch maps, preference ranks and matrices, historical time lines, seasonal calendars, transects, and so on. These are powerful tools with which any community can begin to plan its future. Some of the techniques help people to analyse as well as to collate information, to rank or prioritise. Problem trees and system diagrams ask participants to think about the links between cause and effect, and flows of energy or influence. The use of PRA is quite complementary with other holistic analytical techniques like Farming System Development (Chapter 6).

In the Himalayan examples referred to in Chapters 3 and 6, PRA approaches and techniques have been used to guide the village planning process. It has not been straightforward to introduce in the context of a public sector project organisation (see below), but where it has been applied seriously by staff and villagers it has had an astonishing impact: releasing the energies of local people including women, generating significantly increased awareness of and interest in the management of village natural resources, and changing the way that certain professions (in particular the foresters) went about their work. Villagers and junior fieldstaff gained considerably in confidence in the process. This promising initial impact has been reported for many similar efforts; the problem is to sustain the approach and impact in a hostile organisational environment. The key to this is institutional development in the villages (Shepherd, 1995).

PRA has been very technique-oriented: in this has lain its attraction for practitioners. It has taken some of the tools of applied social science, simplified them, and made them accessible to ordinary people – demystified them. This contrasts with classic methods of information gathering and analysis which are extractive, opaque and undermine ordinary people's knowledge. The positive reaction of practitioners, desperate for such a set of tools to improve interaction with rural people, has led to a very rapid adoption and widespread use of PRA, at least the techniques if not the approach. It has become a bit like a quick-fix solution to rural development agencies' problems – 'we're using PRA now, so we must be all right . . .' – and a requirement in many funding applications. Herein lie huge dangers: PRA will be used superficially, insensitively (with respect to social and gender issues, for example), without the action research which would enable learning to take place. Fieldworkers trained briefly in PRA may use the techniques ritualistically, without having the skill or the organisational flexibility to carry through a thorough

analysis of the information collated. Training needs to be continuous, and the organisation must also adjust its culture and procedures (see Chapter 9).

If there is no link between PRA work and institutional development, as described in this chapter, sustainability and equity will be
hard to demonstrate. A cynic might comment that the major
institutional development has occurred in the development industry
itself among those who can sell the PRA service; all sorts of
networks and reputations are being built on it. Despite the rhetoric,
institutional development in the communities where PRA is practised has been neglected. All these problems are recognised by the
core of PRA proponents (PLA Notes, 1995: 5–10). A further danger
is that the focus on a growing canon of techniques does not help to
focus on how local people themselves analyse and think about issues
– the temptation for the outsider is to go for the recognisable
product – the participatorily developed map, the preference matrix
or whatever. It is not helpful to have specific techniques so prominent in the overall approach, as this limits people's ability to
influence the agenda.

PRA practitioners will move beyond these difficulties as they
move into capacity development. This means: developing skills of
participatory planning and management in the village, and developing networks of local-level practitioners who can take the process
out of the hands of outsiders; and working with villagers to develop
their institutions – of formal government like village councils or
committees, of common property resource management, and of
more informal groups. The latter are important. Without them
people who are not accustomed to participation in public will be
left out – women, the disabled, minorities, the very poor. While
PRA leads in the direction of empowering local people, outsiders
working with villagers should never abandon their ability to ap-
praise the equity of village social structures, institutions and arrangements, without believing that they are in a position to alter the
power structure. The ideal is that insiders too will pick up these
capacities and concerns, and that they will be reinforced by legal and
institutional changes enacted by parliaments and assemblies.

Impact and constraints

There are perhaps unrealistic expectations of what PRA by itself can
achieve. It is a set of tools evolved by development practitioners at

the tail end of the 'development as outsiders' intervention' paradigm to share their control and authority with their clients. It has largely been used as a planning tool; uses in implementation, monitoring and evaluation are limited; as we have seen, the all-important institutional dimension is all but missing as yet. There is no reason why one set of tools should be a quick fix. But, combined with other aspects of the new paradigm, expectations can legitimately be raised significantly.

PRA proponents have identified changing behaviour and attitude as the foundation for the whole PRA approach (Chambers, 1993) – 'reversal of roles', 'transfer of power from outsiders to locals', and 'powerful to powerless' being key phrases used. The implications of a participatory approach are, however, much more far-reaching. The 'off the shelf' schemes which governments have offered to individuals, groups and communities in virtually all rural development programmes are challenged both by the specificities of the different environments, and by the adoption of a genuinely participatory approach. Allowing people to decide how they will manage their environments requires an ability to facilitate that process, not to dictate the nature of activities which will constitute that management process. Facilitators need to have the flexibility and creativity to encourage a variety of technical and managerial possibilities such that individuals and communities can choose what suits them best and can innovate.

Participatory rural development requires an intensive process of organisational change, of the kind illustrated by the Philippines NIA (see Chapter 9). The major lesson from a number of recent projects (Shepherd, 1995; Thompson, 1994; Kar and Backhaus, 1994) is that participation cannot simply be bolted to an existing project concept as an add-on. It has implications for the entire gamut of working practices of an organisation.

Conclusion

Ultimately participation is an aspect of political development. The success of associations and movements can be seen where their concerns are taken on board by established political organisations, or where they generate political organisations which influence policy and resource allocation. They are a critical link in making politicians and political systems more accountable and therefore more legitimate.

To what extent is there a role for outside stimulation of these processes beyond facilitating indigenous organisations where they emerge? At the small group level there is a strong role for outside facilitators, especially to assist the poor, women and marginalised people to get in on the act. Where there are conflicting interests, there are roles for outsiders as well as insiders in preventing and working through conflicts, and facilitating resolution. At the level of common property resource management there is a role for outside advisers to engage with resource users and other stakeholders to develop structures and processes which will lead to more satisfactory management outcomes, however these are defined. None of these roles need substitute for insider roles so long as they are seen as temporary, supplementary, and supportive. The likelihood is that the rich and non-marginalised will always be more articulate and dominant in any community or grouping. So outsiders can play an especially critical role in creating space for poor people, economically and environmentally, in terms of rights, access to services, and control over assets and services which the poor can provide to the rest of the community; and politically, by ensuring their inclusion in associations, helping them build networks and coalitions which will protect positions gained.

Participation in rural development is not then primarily about inclusion or involvement of the rural poor in development projects, but about the development of organisations and sets of organisations in which the rural poor can articulate their interests, defend what they have, and stake out new fields of promise. These organisations may be very small – groups of individuals – but these usually need to be linked with others in networks, associations and movements. What is clear is that the emphasis on organisations entails a concern with membership, boundaries, rules and the relationships between groups or organisations. This reduces the idealism inherent in the activist notion of participation, which is perhaps more appropriate at the level of movements and democratic politics. Rural development agencies' best role is to facilitate these organisational developments, and to link them with material, institutional and legal changes of benefit to the poor. How to do this is not always readily apparent. Just as technology development involves a learning process – an interaction among users, technologists, and investors – so institutional development happens as part of a learning process. This may be mutual – shared between two or more organisations one of which may sponsor another – or conflictual – where one organisation separates itself, or develops a legal or operational framework in distinction from and possibly in opposition to another.

8

Structuring Development Agencies

From the foregoing seven chapters I shall now extract a summary of organisational requirements in the new paradigm. The intention is to build up, inductively, a picture of what organisations need to look like if they are to play a positive part in rural development. It is often argued that the nature of an organisation goes a long way to determine what it can and cannot do (rather than the more logical converse). The development agencies engaged in rural development are usually organisations whose shape has been set in a wider context than that of rural development, as suggested above. As rural societies are often weak compared to others, organisations which have feet in the rural areas are usually not specifically designed for operation there. The circumstances of working in rural areas, and the nature of rural development work means that organisations originally designed for other tasks are rarely well set up for rural development work. It is for this reason that organisational structuring and organisational change figure high on today's rural development agenda.

The early blanket remedy of structural adjustment programmes for the problems of over-inflated public sectors was simplistic: it was believed that retrenching public sector workers, improving the pay and conditions of those remaining, divesting loss-making state-owned enterprises, and contracting out other state functions where possible would create an atmosphere where the private sector could flourish and become the engine of labour-intensive growth, which would in turn alleviate poverty. In the 1990s it has been realised that this simple recipe does not work in poor countries, is not enough to generate sustained economic growth, and that other more difficult measures are needed.

The 1990s global agenda for organisational reform now encompasses: legal and institutional change, including the repeal of anti-market laws and regulations and new pro-market laws, constitutional reforms focusing on the independence of the judiciary, the press and human rights; and moves to democracy. Organisational change is now concentrating on the reorganisation and strengthening of ministries, departments and agencies to reflect the importance of their residual functions (regulatory and enabling) in the wake of retrenchment and divestiture, reskilling of their workforces, and the introduction of new manpower policies and procedures to reflect the new roles of government. To a lesser extent there are also reforms and flows of aid funds to strengthen organisations of civil society: increased flows of funds to NGOs and greater acceptance of their role in advocacy and lobbying; and the strengthening of judiciary, police, press and human rights monitoring institutions. It is becoming a comprehensive and much more positive agenda from a rural development perspective, though in practice the initial reforms of structural adjustment (e.g. divestiture of state-owned enterprises) are sometimes so slowly implemented that attention of government and donors remains fixed on these for a much longer period than anticipated, and the slow pace of basic reforms gets in the way of the more difficult changes of the second phase. The second phase may well require a better organised internal constituency to see them through: this takes time to orchestrate.

Building rural development organisations for rural people

The core of conventional rural development services was the delivery of inputs of one sort or another – knowledge, fertilisers, drugs; the delivery model assumes that there is demand for whatever is being delivered. The new paradigm would enable demand to be expressed, and delivery to be organised as far as possible by the demanders or intermediaries. Intermediaries would normally be in the market or, if both the market and the demanders fail to organise delivery, a public agency or NGO. Development agencies in the new approach would thus be concerned with promoting private or collective solutions to problems, but only rarely providing the solution themselves. Clearly, it will often be to farmers' benefit if they can get together and develop their own solutions. Legislation needs to make it as easy as possible for farmers (or other rural client groups) to organise and supply themselves. Rural development agencies will need to lobby to bring about this situation.

Conventional rural development has focused investment on capital, and ignored labour (human capital) and quality of life issues. This corresponds to the still dominant theory that development happens as capital is invested; that poverty is a function of under-investment. Organisations have been geared up for capital investment as their prime function. This has limited the understandings of systems in which capital is but a component; and affected the criteria on which performance is often judged. Transfer of capital lends itself to the fixit and blueprint model of development: it also enables organisations to remain in control of the development process, defined as the process of transferring capital. Instead, in the new approach, organisations need to learn how to facilitate the multiple dimensions of change: the social/institutional/legal as well as the technical/technological/economic. Complex change processes cannot be simply characterised by inputs and outputs, measured in numeric information systems. They require a much more qualitative information system, focusing as much on process and the assumptions made in input–output models as on a limited investment act.

The urban orientation of most rural development policies and agencies has been commented on most trenchantly by Lipton (1977). It is time that rural development agencies were firmly rurally based. Again, modern communications systems will help; so will devolution of functions to local governance structures. Imposing the heavy weight of central government agencies on rural areas means that urban or core-region interests will dominate policy and even implementation in those agencies. In the worst cases, agencies act simply as employers of urban school-leavers, and do little rural development at all. At the opposite extreme there are a handful of extremely well-organised agencies and civil service departments doing excellent rural development work, but a huge number in the middle of the spectrum whose rural work is indifferent. These agencies, located in a remote urban area, are simply not under enough pressure from people to whom their work matters, unless a powerful politician supervises what they do. An agency located in a rural area, tied in multiple ways to its clients, is far more likely to be serious and dedicated and to work under pressure. Within rural development, it is entirely logical that central government should be 'rolled back' to a policy and framework-making function; leaving detailed development work to local agencies. Politicians and civil servants may still play an important role in terms of helping to set up the local agencies, develop and adjust their relationships with their clientele, and facilitate networks of local agencies.

Lobbying

These changes will create a platform from which agencies can lobby government or international agencies with a much more secure social basis. Lobbying to achieve desirable change in law, policy or trading structures is an increasingly important part of rural development. However, bodies too closely tied into the state cannot lobby; they may have some insiders' influence, but ultimately states must respond to pressures, and pressures need to be organised. The existence of substantial rural development bureaucracies has probably in the past reduced not only the scope for lobbying, but also the apparent need. Governments have been able to claim that issues are being dealt with, whereas in fact, the degree of effective support for most rural interests has been small. Bureaucracies can also be captured by elites; because they are relatively monolithic, the scope for representation of multiple interests is often limited. Local development agencies can also be captured; later sections will present the range of solutions to this problem.

Examples where lobbying will be very important in the coming years in order to get change in the interests of the majority of rural people are in the fields of promoting sustainable agriculture and fair trade. Here, small, non-bureaucratic NGOs have taken the lead in both north and south. Governments are slow to respond because vested interests are hurt, and because their carefully regulated structures do not encourage new initiatives or stepping out of line. Thus the weight of government should in coming decades be more sparingly used: where countries have seriously adjusted their public sectors, this is inevitable. Whether they use their power in a progressive way will depend on the structure of interests around them.

Organisation for sustainable agriculture

Agricultural extension agencies

The technical-fix approach of the Green Revolution fits well with a simple bureaucratic approach to organisation, a hierarchy down which information flows was always problematic even in its own terms, as it did not easily achieve the level of co-ordination required to establish the Green Revolution successfully through intervention. Agricultural development happens when a series of multiple and connected changes go hand in hand. Achieving the linkages – even simple links between input providers – was often difficult in the public sector, or in mixed public/private organisational settings. As a result, agricultural extension agencies often found themselves trying to provide all essential services to their clients. This inclusive approach ran into its own problems: in particular, information dissemination and feedback received low priority compared to getting supplies delivered; and the inclusive organisations set up were unsustainable. The Training and Visit (T & V) system developed and broadcast by the World Bank in the 1980s was a response to these issues: and an attempt to get agricultural agencies (in the public sector) to work in a efficient bureaucratic fashion, to deliver information to farmers, and feedback from them to researchers.

T & V focused exclusively on information transmission to and from contact farmers who were supposed to be representative of the farming community. It relied on Subject Matter Specialists (SMSs) in extension agencies who would interpret research results for field-level extensionists to pass on to farmers. The extensionists were linked with the SMSs through regular supervisory visits and training meetings – hence the name, Training and Visit. In the field, T & V has faced many difficulties: extensionists, under pressure to achieve targets of numbers of farmers adopting particular practices, chose contact farmers who would demonstrate the practices rather than those who were representative of the entire farming community. This led to social biases. To be effective, T & V relied on a stream of interpreted research results relevant at the particular season and for each different farming system: in many countries the research results were simply not there due to chronic underinvestment in research; in others the SMSs were not adequate in number. World Bank-supported projects to introduce T & V proved financially unsustainable as they have high incremental costs: this has led to a number of attempts to introduce charging for services. Above all, the T & V system is managerially intensive: large numbers of people have to be managed in a complex system, and the management resources to do this were often absent (Howell, 1994).

The T & V system may be quite effective where the resources are available to run it properly, where researchers are coming up with an adequate flow of research results to extend to farmers, and where the farming environment is sufficiently uniform to permit relatively uniform solutions and innovations – ideal for large, irrigated plains with little variation in soils and social conditions. However, most rural development work is done where these conditions do not apply. Furthermore, it is well recognised that hierarchically structured organisations may be good at delivery but cannot transmit information from the farmer upwards.

The organisational tasks required in the new paradigm are less to do with delivery (of inputs or information) and more to do with developing a systemic understanding together with groups of farmers through analysis, on-farm research work, and sideways extension. Interaction with farmers is critical; a systems perspective is critical; farmers' organisations at local level are critical. Professionals need to work fairly independently with farmers, networking with sources of information and necessary inputs, able to solve problems and refer problems to be solved, and able to live for extended periods in farming societies without looking down on farmers or rural life. The new paradigm requires professionals with considerable skills to be located at local level, running local services. In public agencies this can be achieved only if hierarchies are dissolved and highly trained generalists and specialists, even some researchers, are based working directly with farmers. Given the vested interests of many professionals in working in town – so that their children may go to better schools, so that they are near the centres of power and decision-making – this change would require the recruitment of many more sons and daughters from farm households into the agencies, as well as the creation of working conditions which encourage rural postings. These would often have to include special privileges – scholarships to good boarding-schools, transport and telecommunications facilities – to offset the disadvantages.

The discussion about the type of person required in the new agricultural development mingles with the debate about the organisation's structure. Current bureaucratic models of organisation severely limit the discretion allowed to front-line workers. What is needed is a structure which gives discretion to front-line workers who, after all, will be highly trained and experienced, and selected for their abilities to interact constructively with farmer and farm households. But, beyond discretion, which requires trust, front-line workers need to be involved in management.

Farming System Development (FSD) (FAO, 1990 and 1993b; and Chapter 6) is the basis for one such approach. In a discussion of its institutionalisation, a contrast was drawn between a classic Ministry of Agriculture structure and a reformed agricultural development agency capable of operating an FSD approach (Figures 8.1 and 8.2).

An essential part of the reformed organisation is the link to local participatory structures, whether farmer groups or local governance structures. These are necessary because the provision of local resources to pay the services of professional(s) will ensure that the services are accountable to the farmers or local representative structures. Only by this means will there be effective communication from the farmers to research organisations about problems and opportunities. Likewise the research organisations need to have their decision-making processes and budgets structured so that they respond increasingly to requests for work coming from farmers, farmer groups and professionals close to the farmers. Local professionals should have the capacity (training, resources) to engage in on-farm research.

Development agencies – currently typically centralised in management structure, and often large in scope: ministries being the obvious example – need to be 'unbundled'. This means, in this context, split up into small, probably area-based units which are manageable by the front-line workers involved in them. This implies a move from a hierarchical to a more collegiate model of organisation, in which most decisions are shared among the stakeholders.

The systems perspective, and the participatory approach means that the professionals working close to farmers need to be experienced, good generalists who are trained to analyse farm systems. The best of them can be encouraged to specialise and share their specialist knowledge with other generalists in a network. Specialists who have an interest in acting as generalists should also be encouraged to work at this level. With advances in modern communications this type of diffuse organisational structure will soon become possible even in the remotest corners of Africa.

An implication of this type of approach is that the armies of low-paid, poorly trained, often poorly motivated agricultural extensionists which the T & V system sought to build on will disappear. There is no point in their continued existence. The poor quality of much past rural development work can be attributed to the combination of demoralised, low-paid, poorly trained fieldstaff with a top-heavy bureaucracy where there is too much administration and too

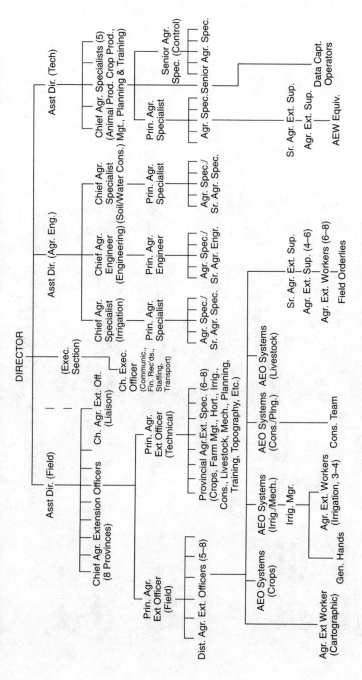

FIGURE 8.1 An agricultural agency's structure today
Source: FAO 1993b.

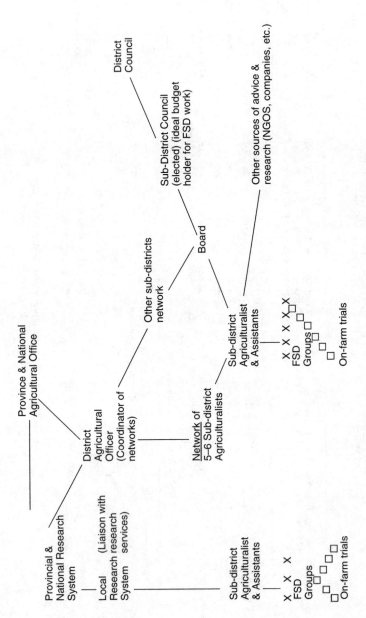

FIGURE 8.2 An agricultural agency's structure reformed for FSD
Source: FAO 1993b.

little management and opportunity for field-level professional work for senior staff. Retrenchment is thus a major issue in the reform of agricultural agencies. On the other hand, farmers (women and men) who are good communicators, who themselves research problems and are quick at identifying opportunities, can be incorporated in the new service – either as farmers, or farmer-scholars assisting the local professionals, or as farmer-professionals: part-time employees of development agencies. They would become temporary or permanent employees of local governance structures or farmer organisations. Some existing extension agents also have the capability to engage with the new approach; they an be assisted to make the transformation through training and work experience.

Finance

Financially farmers need to shoulder at least some of the burden of the research and advisory services they benefit from. There will always continue to be research and information dissemination for public benefit, for which public agencies will provide resources. However, the benefits of most research and extension work goes to farmers, and they should be involved in financing them. This is a difficult issue – especially in an era where there are also demands for people's involvement in the financing of health, education, water and other services. The approach adopted by the Norwegian Ministry of Agriculture in gradually transferring the financing of its farmer-managed research circles over a period of two decades from the state to farmers is instructive.

By the early 1990s the Norwegian Ministry of Agriculture had established over 400 farmer research circles, which met, together with local researchers assigned to the circles, in the long dark winter nights, to identify problems and potential solutions, and to plan a strategy for testing solutions. The state could also request circles to look at particular problems or issues. All research was done in the short Norwegian summer on farmers' fields, under farmer management, but with some financial and supervisory input from the circle. Funding for the research circles was increasingly provided by farmers: their share had reached about 35 per cent overall in 1991. They were willing to provide funds because the research was into issues they had identified as important to them. It helped, of course, that Norwegian farmers, though operating on a small scale, were not poor, due partly to the history of highly subsidised agriculture.

This type of transformation is not one which can be accomplished easily. Not only is poverty an obstacle: here development agencies have a role in helping farmers to foot the bill initially, but develop a capacity over time to pay, as with other services. But also, many decision cultures function in a diametrically opposed fashion to what is proposed here. The Norwegian decision culture is special: very local bodies are intimately involved in service provision; very local government (communes of small populations with wide powers) has been the historical norm. By contrast, many decision cultures are non-participatory, or exclusive to certain groups within both organisations and communities, and centralised. In such cases rural development efforts will be accompanied by an institutional reform movement, aiming to create (or strengthen) local organisations which are representative and have resources, or have the capacity to act.

Organisation for the common good

Chapter 3 has pointed out how important common goods are not only residually in poor societies and for the poor in many rural societies, but also in that there are new common goods created in the process of development. Development theory has been historically against common goods: the belief in state control and/or markets has dominated. Common goods are seen as a problem, to be replaced by superior forms of ownership and control. From the point of view of rural people, common goods are often a necessity, quite amenable in many circumstances to organisation, and in some cases the best way of organising ownership or management. The new rural development paradigm focuses on what is of common interest.

What is of critical importance, then, is to allow space for common goods: mentally and attitudinally especially among professionals; in law, by not discriminating against the organisation of common goods by making it impossibly difficult; and on a level with other forms of ownership and management. Legally there are often deep issues involved. Laws which allow a variety of collective bodies to have some legal status are relatively simple to add to the statute books. Examples exist in the Philippines and many other countries. Laws which nationalised land, forests, water and other common property resources (CPRs) are much more controversial and difficult to reverse, because vested interests are deeply involved. Here again, lobbying with its various activities of policy research, mounting legal challenges, defending the damaged interests of CPR users (pastoralists, forest users, etc.) are as much part of rural development as delivering services. Development agencies do not need to undertake these activities themselves but can work with the legal experts, the policy researchers in universities as well as governments. Capacity to liaise with and contract or partner other agencies or individuals is a key skill here. Where such capacities do not exist, a development agency can play a role in creating it: here the issue is whether it can be sustainably created within the development agency, or whether it is not better to help establish independent lobbying organisations, wherever possible linked to respected organisations (e.g. universities). Generally, lobbying is more powerful where it is linked to research and especially practical actions.

The legal and organisational frameworks created to permit or improve common goods management need to recognise that there are territorial and social limits to the benefits and costs of any activity, and that organisations need to be founded on appropriate boundaries. Where there is a different incidence of benefits and costs, geographically or socially, separate organisations of beneficiaries and those experiencing costs which can negotiate with each other may be the best way forward. Here, the law needs to supply a framework within which disputes may be settled. This too needs to be permissive: there are many informal ways of arbitration which people feel are legitimate; there are individuals and institutions (traditional leaders, for example) who are experts in dispute settlement. These issues are reflected in the notion of governance through polycentric institutional arrangements.

Take as an example the development and regulation of newly designated common forest. From a hierarchical and militaristic forest administration are culled 'new foresters' who are asked to work with forest users. From a regulatory approach the new foresters move to an inclusive, participatory approach, focusing on institutional development around the management of what is becoming a common good, with definable benefits and costs. The forester's target is to develop a self-regulating body or series of bodies in the local communities. These may be co-operative or competitive with each other, depending on the resource, how it is used and social relationships among participants. The forester needs skills of understanding and analysis, negotiation, conflict resolution and consensus building to take this project forward. He or she needs the backing of an agency which grants its front-line workers considerable autonomy, and adequate resources, or resource-raising capacities. These front-line foresters need to be able to interact with each other to keep tabs on what is working where, and why. Within this strategy particular groups of users would organise themselves to negotiate their interests with commercial loggers, government, and conservation organisations.

This model is an alternative to the conventional organisation of forest work where a rampant and exploitative private sector has been hopelessly inadequately regulated and policed by a weak and corruptible public sector. It is well known that this has led to the decimation of tropical and other forests, and to the absence of effective replacement through replanting or natural regeneration. The chainsaw brigade can only be stopped in its tracks by widespread public action, local and international, to defend these common and now global properties. Where countries depend heavily on timber for exports, employment and economic growth, the proponents of alternatives need to deal with these macro-economic issues: alternative export revenues and sources of economic growth are needed; forest employment can more easily be enhanced through investment in protection and replanting, and allocation of conditional title.

Organisation for poverty alleviation

The new generation of anti-poverty credit programmes work with groups (often of women as the lynchpin of the family) for mutual solidarity and peer review. They link up with social service provision or improvements either because borrowers borrow for social expenditures, or because the development agency also involves itself in these social development issues, or because it networks and lobbies. They draw poor people into the running of the schemes; they also stress poor people's abilities to reduce their own poverty, through mobilising savings, and most recently by applying commercial or above commercial rates of interest on loans. Loans are far less out of proportion with savings capacity in this approach.

The current orthodoxy is that this approach is best implemented by NGOs, sometimes in liaison with banks or official agencies, and that the NGOs will transform themselves into banks in the medium term. However, it is possible to go further than the current orthodoxy. If powerlessness is a central aspect of poverty, it follows that institutions which place poor people in charge of the process of poverty alleviation are central. Banks working on commercial principles will always tend to get drawn into financing the safe bets, especially when people's savings are involved. Control over the bank or other financing institution needs to be firmly vested in loan beneficiaries as well as savers. They may delegate their control to a management, or board, but accountability mechanisms should always be there. The more complex the financial scheme the more difficult it will be for poorer people to be in control: hence the attractiveness of simple savings and credit associations.

This model can be extended to other aspects of infrastructure for poverty alleviation. Development agencies can facilitate the development of social and physical infrastructure by providing advice, on organisation as well as technical aspects; and capital grants or soft loans where required. Whereas in the past the state has taken on the provision of many such services directly, it and its agencies can now vest their energies in promoting others to take on the direct provision function. This means that the skills of 'accompaniment' (working alongside) are at a premium. This may be done in a legalistic way, through contracting with associations, groups or the private sector; but it may also be done less formally by working alongside as a partner/stakeholder. In either case, the skills required of development agency personnel are those of advising on organisational development, management, democratic governance of the organisation, troubleshooting and conflict resolution, networking and helping to create a learning organisation in touch with its clientele – the consumers of services, the users of infrastructure. This type of backseat development agency is illustrated in Figure 8.3.

Individual development agents will specialise in different aspects of these tasks: they will know about the development of different types of organisation (credit, social service, education, etc.), and different aspects of management (bookkeeping, marketing, board development, accountability mechanisms, etc.). Some of the necessary skills may be passed on through training programmes; but much will have to be learnt on the job. Those individuals who do well in particular associations will quickly be in demand more widely to share their expertise; development agencies can facilitate the sharing – indeed development agencies will absorb some of the best association staff as advisers. However, the danger in this is that the

FIGURE 8.3   a Backseat development agency

success models are replicated way beyond their viability: advisers need above all to know what the options are and how to analyse particular situations and propose an appropriate option.

Returning to the idea that poverty is multidimensional – social, psychological, spiritual as well as economic and political – the typical approach followed from the 1970s in response to this perception was that of the integrated development project. However, these tend to breed complex multi-departmental bureaucratic organisations which concentrate power rather than diffuse it among poor people. It is much better for organisations to remain small, but to network with others, accepting the frustrations that others' actions are clearly beyond control, often beyond influence. A kind of market emerges in this situation where partnerships are forged among organisations which share approaches and can interact and reinforce each other positively. Coalitions and associations, temporary or permanent, are thus the key to advancing joint interests, whether in action or in lobbying.

Security

Poverty was seen to be as much conjunctural as structural in many places (Iliffe, 1987). The dominant model of preventing conjunctural poverty has been that pursued in South Asia since the 1950s, in turn leaning heavily on its colonial predecessors. This relies on state intervention in food and labour markets to prevent a slide into famine conditions. In societies with relatively strong states, capable of observing, analysing and reacting to local information, and with organised institutions of civil society – a free press, a democratically elected government – this interventionist model may still be successful. However, its transposition to societies and polities which do not have these qualities has not worked well (Curtis *et al.*, 1988). Furthermore, conjunctural poverty today is as likely to be caused by state breakdown and/or local anarchy and the civil disorder which follows as by the natural disasters for which interventionist security models were developed. If a cause of poverty (loss of assets, interruption of income flow, loss of labour due to illness, war, migration, loss of social organisation and psychological stability) is the collapse of state security mechanisms, we can hardly expect the state to step into the breach.

What has been neglected in the discussion of security is the importance of local security mechanisms, and local capacities to respond to insecurity. In a civil war situation it is these which tend to take over anyway, though by that point security is highly militarised and in today's world of collapsing states often takes on an ethnic social dimension, as society disintegrates too. Developmentally, what has proved important in preventing disintegration is strong local institutions. Even if disintegration occurs, strong local institutions help re-establish order and basic securities in the aftermath of conflict.

This offers development and relief agencies an alternative to two other possibly unsatisfactory approaches: reconstructing the central state apparatus which probably caused or contributed to the conflict in the first place; or themselves substituting for the institutions of governance. Here it is very easy for development agencies to slip into partisan roles, fuelling conflict. They then become extremely vulnerable.

The existence of strong local organisations used to dealing with the issues of social, food and personal security in peacetime will provide a good basis for the emergency situation. In poor societies, poor people suffer from conjunctural poverty all the time: poor people fall sick more frequently and their earnings stop as a result; poor people die earlier, rear more children, and so on. They are also more likely to be affected by disasters – fires, drought, floods – as their houses are built of poorer materials, and if they own land it is more vulnerable. The existence of mechanisms of social or financial insurance to protect against such conjunctures is a key to the alleviation of poverty. These mechanisms still exist as traditional mutual help organisations in some societies, but these fast disappear in modern commercial society. Development agencies can play a powerful role by stimulating the maintenance or new formation of such mechanisms: they would not be able to cope with widespread disaster or disorder but would not only be able to deal with isolated conjunctures, but also would provide an organisational and analytical basis for enhancing security at times of catastrophe.

The key to this sort of localised security is mutual reciprocity. Whereas in the past this has been provided by caste- or kinship-based networks, many states have actively sought to undermine these and the traditional leaders who 'manage' (or provide a focal point for) them. There is now a widespread realisation that these leaders have been done away with too easily, and that the state cannot substitute. This realisation has occurred in many African countries over judicial functions. Chiefs' judicial powers are being restored in many countries; customary law is gaining a new position of respect. The principles on which it often operates are those of accepted, legitimate authority; knowledge of individuals' circumstances and the consequent discovery of appropriate sanctions. This movement could be more widely extended into other aspects of security. Personal security is another area where there is considerable scope for innovative, common good solutions. Locally supervised and financed police forces are obvious examples. Where women are particularly victims of male violence, their defensive organisation, and lobbying the powers that be to remove the conditions for male violence, are logical directions for development. A challenge for future rural development practitioners is to work out schemes of insurance with appropriate forms of contract which will bind poor people together in modern forms of mutual reciprocity.

Politically, the centralised states of the world need to learn more about the concept of federation, as the rationale for centralised states wanes. Civil war is often flamed by central politicians seeking their own gain; local interests are often dragged reluctantly into conflict. If the local interests were more strongly organised in the entire spectrum of political actors, they would generally act as a considerable counter-war movement, since they would be well used to small-scale conflict resolution and compromise.

Equity

Where local common goods solutions are sought to problems of poverty and security, it is critical that the equity or distributional consequences are examined. One of the hesitations about devolving power to local government has always been that rural local government is often easily captured by local elites: the poor, women, and marginal social groups do not get a look in. This can be equally true in specific common goods organisations.

In some cases, these groups are well enough organised and recognised to ensure their participation at a formal level, and the political party in power is supportive; in other cases, more frequent perhaps in rural areas, the powerless are simply powerless, and any organisation is suppressed. Increasing the number of organisations involved in rural development increases the chances that poorer, marginal groups will have an opportunity to articulate their interests. Development agencies always have the dilemma of whether to back the elite, whose 'permission' is often necessary for an agency to work in an area, or to back a marginal group. Frequently, and inevitably, agencies try to sit on the fence and back both, recognising that they cannot only work with the poor or powerless, despite their mandate. Agencies rarely see it as their job to foment conflict; most would understandably rather pour water on the flames. This is also reasonable from the point of view of the poor and marginal, since they have to continue to live with the powerful beyond any agency's period of relevance.

It must also be remembered that poor people, and poor women especially, are usually very busy with daily survival tasks, and the energy they have for participating in organisations is very limited. What they participate in needs to be instrumental in improving their life chances; it is very important that initiatives for organisation be theirs, based on their analysis and priorities. For women, timing is also critical, as so many studies have shown. Structuring timetables of activities needs to be a participatory activity as a matter of course.

If part of the role of a development agency is to ensure representation of the poor, and articulation of their interests within a broader picture, what are the mechanisms for doing so? Clearly, formation or strengthening of separate organisations is one option, often quite a conflictual one, but also quite effective. Where the issue is inclusion in service provision it helps if there is divisible technology: several handpumps located in different parts of a village, looked after by different committees from the various neighbourhoods, offers a much greater chance of incorporating the poor in terms of access as well as participation. The Proshika solution of groups of poor people running irrigation water supplies for farmers is another integrated approach to service provision where different groups have varied stakes in one set of equipment. Here the unbundling of technology is 'vertical' as opposed to the 'horizontal' unbundling of the multiple handpumps. In education, a community can decide to provide a certain number of free places in one school, or, less satisfactorily, may run several schools for different categories of student. It is common to find enterprising teachers using school facilities to run evening classes or outreach activities for groups of students who find it hard to attend regular classes for financial or time reasons. Where basic education is increasingly self-funded, the poor may do better with a less-well-funded small school of their own than with the unwinnable struggle to keep up compulsory contributions or fees for a better-funded school. Separation can be seen as inequitable, the beginnings of apartheid, or it can be seen constructively as an opportunity for the poor or marginal groups to express their identities, develop management capacity, and find other less expensive ways to follow a syllabus.

If equity is to be achieved, there is little substitute for good social analysis. For instance, in farming-systems work, identifying innovations suited to very small farms or farms with particular resource problems (labour shortage, lack of access to working capital, lack of fertile valley bottom land) as a priority, will often benefit poorer households and women farmers. Likewise in the development of 'packages' of inputs, the smaller the quantity the less likely that distribution will be hijacked by the richer households. Outgrowers' systems often work well for the poor, partly for this reason. Decisions about which technology, crop, farming system to focus on have enormous implications for equity. The non-poor/marginal may also gain from the work, but will not be the main beneficiaries.

Development agents need the skills of imaginative organisational structuring and good analysis above all to ensure that the poor are included. In some cases standardised procedures can be developed, but agents should always have a raft of options which they can pursue within the standardised procedures: no blueprint will fit all situations, either in technological or organisational terms.

Processes

The discussion of process in Chapters 5–7 confirmed the critical nature of an agency's capacity to assess, together with rural people, the social, environmental and political consequences of development interventions and patterns. It confirmed too the importance of a systems perspective: where agents with different professional specialisms need to work together with rural people. Earlier chapters also confirmed that local managerial flexibility and accountability through a variety of mechanisms is a key characteristic of successful rural development. Activities should generally be (or aim to be) self-financing in principle. There is still an enormous need to reskill development agencies on notions of participation and institutional development. Ideas about 'community' have usually been a handicap, whereas working with groups and associations of groups was seen to be critical. In this section we will focus on how different types of development agency are dealing with these issues.

NGOs

NGOs are seen as cornerstones of modern rural development processes by many governments and financing agencies. This new perception contains great dangers for the people's movements which in many cases gave rise to the NGOs in the first place. NGOs while often at the forefront of criticism on many issues have, unfortunately, collectively sold their souls for money: offered the opportunities to bid for projects and roles in official programmes, most have taken these up with alacrity, going for organisational growth over and above all other values. The bigger international and national NGOs as a result have become the new rural development bureaucracies; they may still retain some comparative advantage over public sector bureaucracies, but increasingly this is in question, and definitely cannot be taken for granted. The bigger agencies necessarily move closer to their sponsoring agencies – usually national governments, whether in the north or the south. This means that they have to adjust their working culture: learn the language of projects, move with the fashions of the time, and probably subordinate their own values in the process. They may have been able to influence the official world to come closer to their values: this is the hope. But they are many and poorly co-ordinated, and often weakly linked to national politics and professional groups which are far more influential. They are more likely therefore to be influenced than to influence.

Just as the public sector has become over-inflated and unsustainable, this is also true of the NGO sector which has no tax base at all, but a small popular base in donations and charity. It can be argued that the medium sized and larger NGOs also need unbundling. They are far too often centralised in cities, close to sponsors and regulators, in with the elite, but far from their rural base. Their conditions of employment allow for more radical commitment than government or the private sector, but objectively NGO staff share many of the same interests. Few rural people ever get absorbed into the running of rural development NGOs; they are rarely run in conjunction with rural people's own organisations alongside. The latter may be called partners, but are usually subordinate. NGOs like to retain their independence above all else. Perhaps this is the best which can be hoped for from a redistributionist, urban-based development industry. On the other hand, where NGOs envisage being part of longer-term rural institutional development, their position could become much more powerful.

Whereas NGOs generally see themselves as development agencies, separate from their clients (individuals, groups, local organisations), they do now at least commonly perceive that developing the capacity of their clients beyond whatever particular activity they engage in is an essential part of development. This is a result of the painful awareness that NGO activities are often small-scale and unsustainable beyond the NGO's intervention. This notion needs to be radically extended, so that the very existence of an NGO working with a particular group of people leads to the improved capacities of those people. This can be achieved through collaborative social and institutional analysis, which identifies the problems, gaps, opportunities and options in capacity and institutional development. The role of the NGO is then to assist with achievable and sustainable (ultimately largely self-financed, self-managed) activities which promote capacity. There are NGOs already engaging in this type of support, sometimes as an explicit focus, sometimes as an adjunct to more output-oriented investments and programmes. However, far more work is still done by NGOs in partnership with government or local government in situations which develop the capacities of those institutions but not of the grassroots: it is difficult to do both simultaneously.

If an NGO adopts this line of thinking it will avoid building up its own technical and managerial resources, as these are unsustainable. It will encourage grassroots organisations to make use of public or private sector technical expertise and to develop their own management abilities. NGOs which attempt to provide a comprehensive service will need to unbundle themselves. Their employees will find good employment as development consultants, whose expertise can then be hired by grassroots (and other) organisations. In order to do innovative things, NGOs may wish to employ particular professionals for limited periods, but this should rarely develop into permanent employment. Professionals could rather organise themselves into small NGOs capable of providing services to others.

Some international NGOs are unbundling themselves in another way by creating country offices which are loosely federated to replace the centralised, northern-dominated structures of the 1980s. This definitely represents progress, but the changes should not rest there. The country offices need to find ways of associating themselves much more closely with their rural grassroots and the rural social movements. This can come about with a blurring of the boundaries between agency and rural community, through openness to influence, exchange of personnel, blurring of the boundaries of particular activities and so on.

A further imaginative way of unbundling northern NGOs working with official bi- or multi-lateral development funds in the south is to move towards a purely monitoring role. Under this arrangement, southern NGOs would be direct recipients of official development funds, but they would be obliged to contract with northern NGOs to monitor and/or provide some technical assistance where necessary. As more funding of NGOs is provided by official agencies in the south, and more goes directly to southern NGOs, withdrawal of northern NGOs to a monitoring and capacity building role is inevitable.

Networks

Networking is often seen as information exchange and, loosely, 'keeping in touch'. Here we can give it a much deeper meaning. Where development agents are working closely with rural people, they require a support structure. That support structure can be conceived as a network rather than a hierarchy. Development agents support each other in this network, as in the FSD example above. Financing agencies may be part of the network, stakeholders, but without explicit authority. They negotiate with development agents and grassroots groups and organisations, but cannot impose their whims. Control cannot be achieved by any one party in a network; funding agencies need to recognise that control is neither possible nor desirable.

Networks pose risks. In social anthropology networks were conceived as particularistic social relationships, based on kinship or patron–client principles. These do not sit well with a modern organisational ideology where merit should determine recruitment and advancement. There are certainly dangers of corruption, so accountability is a key issue. Accountability needs to be negotiated, and is ideally primarily to rural people and their organisations. Where there are legal requirements for accountability to funding agencies for money spent, these two accountability requirements sit together uneasily, and auditors and regulators need to be brought along as far as they will go towards accepting accountability measures which satisfy rural people. Where auditors put the fear of God into development workers, as in some government and some NGO systems, they will be a key part of the organisational change process necessary to advance the new paradigm.

Groups and associations in rural areas are increasingly networking their activities. Again, this is not only for information exchange purposes, but will also strengthen and improve capacities and contribute to the evolution of social movements, which are far more powerful in generating social change than the isolated impact of NGOs. The external environment is critical to the success of development activities, creating a spectrum of incentives, demands, sanctions and urgency. A networked movement is a far more powerful actor in that environment than an NGO or a consortium of NGOs – though these too may have their power. A networked movement is also more powerful in negotiating with development agencies. Networking in this sense allows for the fact that many development agencies are one-person outfits. It accepts that fact, but creates an infrastructure within which those one-person outfits can operate more successfully and accountably. This is especially so when mutual evaluation becomes the centrepiece of a network.

Networks will never be trouble-free: conflict is an ever-present reality. However, a network is a device for containing conflict, as different interests learn to tolerate and respect each other's different positions. Networks formed explicitly around conflict issues in conflict situations, however, may falter sooner than those formed around developmental issues.

Communication

Communication will become a central focus for capacity building: and telecommunications provide the physical means for greatly enhanced communication. It will soon be quite unnecessary for development agencies to base their activities in capital cities, though they may still keep presence there to enable lobbying. For the time being in many countries the limited reach of the communications infrastructure will continue to dictate a small town basis for rural development activities, with small towns as the hubs of networks. As telecommunications spread this limitation will disappear.

In the information age the technology exists to link rural people with information centres, with each other, and with professional advisers in an unprecedented way. Woods (1993) has outlined the potential of decentralised digital software delivery systems for transcending the limits of the existing information systems. Because the technology is so flexible it 'has the capacity to help people – all people! It permits mass personalisation of information, regardless of location, level of education, social background or economic status. The challenge before us is to realise the technology's potential' (Woods, 1993: 112). What this requires is a public informatics system to be installed – like a national road network, or telecommunications system. Indeed the public informatics system uses these other infrastructures, and gives especially the telecommunications infrastructure much greater importance in development than it has so far been afforded. Once the public delivery system is there, a whole variety of uses can be made of it.

Examples of how digital software delivery systems are used in practice in rural development are isolated as yet. The USA has led the field with its Education Utility System, which has three parts: a central store of software, local storage and processing capacity in institutions, and access for local users into these institutions. India is designing a system which will reach at least some of its 640,000 villages with software which will make use of symbols, graphics and sound, thus not requiring literacy.

Indian authorities believe that many people in typical, moderately sized villages can pay small amounts for a range of uses of the system and that a variety of governmental and other agencies such as banks, traders and NGOs would use it too. Together these could make the system financially viable. Its use could then be made free of charge for formal education and either free or at reduced rates for poorer segments of communities. (Woods, 1993: 95)

This could be a model for the rest of the world.

The cost of the digital technology is coming down, and its capacity to transfer material – data, video – is increasing all the time. Initiative for the application of digital technology to public information is likely to come from the software and hardware industry as it perceives the benefits from such a system to itself. Governments will play a co-ordinating role, getting the different user ministries and agencies together to agree on the parameters of the system, and regulating the system – deciding on the principles for inclusion of particular software, for example.

The software for development purposes is not in place, though the capacity to create it is. It is not there because it has not been commercially viable to date, precisely because of the absence of a mass market. Public informatics systems would create that mass market. The benefits of such systems would be many. Face-to-face interaction, and therefore transport requirements of development agencies could be reduced; rural people would have greater choice of information sources, at times and places of their choosing; the time of professionals could be saved for more analytical, problem-focused advisory work rather than simple transfer of information; the number of lower-level extension staff could be reduced as a result.

Developing capacity for evaluation and research

Information and its assessment are also critical parts of rural development. Earlier chapters stressed the importance of evaluation, and downplayed planning as the central intellectual activity in rural development. It was argued that this was the only way to institutionalise the concept of the learning organisation. Ongoing participatory evaluation requires a change in emphasis in development agencies: from the current ideologically based thinking (where certain approaches or activities are promoted irrespective of situation) to a more objective understanding of trends and patterns and the role of particular activities within those wider patterns. Whereas the activities of a project currently have the greatest importance to most of the stakeholders, in the evaluative mode the overall pattern of development would have the greatest intellectual significance, and the activities and their specific measurable results only become significant because of the wider context.

The stress on evaluation would tend to avoid large-scale investments, as these, with their urban-industrial focus, typically externalise social, environmental and other costs on to rural people. The existence of networks and information systems would help the process of evaluation, as sympathetic but non-involved professionals and people from elsewhere can get involved, together with local people, in the process. The constitution of evaluative teams would be one of the functions of networks, and evaluation seen as a supportive, developmental activity promoting accountability but also comparison and, automatically, ideas for the future. Evaluation is in fact the key intellectual activity for which capacity needs to be developed: it is the activity *par excellence* where donors and NGOs can help develop the capacity of local development agencies and groups.

Implications for managers

Managers require skills in strategic thinking, relating means to purposes. They need to be capable of managing the central learning and evaluation function, the dissemination of information within the organisation and the building of consensus around the consideration of options. And they need to be capable of fostering these skills in their partner organisations. Putting senior, experienced staff in the front line should make it easier to create systems of accountability to that front line, and in turn to the development agency's rural constituency. Managers need to be open to working in networks and movements, fostering a culture of co-operation rather than competition. Contracts with partners need to be supported by close co-operative relationships. Managers need to know how to scale down, withdraw and terminate activities as well as build them up.

Implications for professionals

The implications of the new paradigm for development professionals are becoming apparent. In agriculture and natural resource management, professionals are having to come to terms not only with a far more complex, interrelated world where issues can no longer be evaluated singly, but also with pressures to develop technical systems which do not require perpetual subsidy or public management. In irrigation, for example, public sector water engineers are having to learn private sector disciplines and be more supportive of farmer organisations at the same time (FAO, 1993a: 296). In agriculture, agriculturalists are having to adapt from transfer of technology models to farmer-first procedures, involving role changes to support farmers in analysis, choice and experiment. In turn these new roles need to be supported by institutional changes – including the decentralisation of resources and the reshaping of incentives and rewards (Chambers, 1989: 180–95). Foresters have had to give up power to local forest users' groups, working with them to facilitate appropriate management strategies (Poffenberger, 1990). Health professionals are finding their medical model of health increasingly challenged, and are being persuaded to take seriously notions of participation and local management of health (MacDonald, 1993). The changes required of professionals have clear implications in terms of training, retraining, and the restructuring of professional rewards to support appropriate behaviour.

Chambers (1986, 1987, 1993) advocated the need for a new type of professional to engage in participatory rural development. Normal professionals are drawn away from serving the poor through deep preferences for 'first' or 'core' values: focusing on wealth, comfort and power, interacting with respected male leaders, associating with prestige investments, and seeing their roles as teachers. The new professional is committed to working with poor people, often those of low status, as collaborators. The professional becomes a consultant to these people, rather than powerful organisations. These changes clearly require that the poor clients have some resources at their command with which to hire the consultant; respect should not be only because of an individual's commitment. Again, the realisation of the concept of new professionals depends on the empowerment and institutional development of the poor.

New rural development professionals need to go beyond the attitudinal and behavioural changes highlighted by Chambers. They need to be able to work with holistic approaches and methods, to have a competence in the field of institutional development, and to be continually involved in actual fieldwork, especially as they become more senior and experienced. These requirements imply significant organisational changes.

Implications for central governments

The major implication for central government is that it either has to restructure its ministries, departments and agencies in a fundamental way, or (the easier course) reduce its involvement in the direct provision of rural services and the organisation of development in favour of agencies with greater appropriate capacity. Restructuring, the tough option, would include serious decentralisation of resources and decision-making; internal reorganisation to create a new, collegiate management culture capable of strategic and participatory management; the removal of all kinds of irksome controls and access obstacles, and the development of partnerships with grassroots groups and associations, ceding power to these organisations as they mature. This would require organisational structures and cultures which are different from the normal hierarchical civil service or public corporation. These might more easily be achieved in the context of local government, though typically local governments also reflect the wider national public sector culture.

Current orthodoxy in civil service reform is conservative, advocating a return to the classic administrative values and activities. The aims of structural adjustment programmes' civil service reform have been primarily to reduce cost and increase efficiency. Retrenchment and reduction of intervention, and the rationalisation of recruitment and civil service careers, and salary increases have been the major measures. More recently, the development of capacity to regulate (monitor, educate, inspect, sanction) and to enable (analyse and remove restrictions, provide finance, inform, explore markets, encourage linkages) has become an explicit focus. This has led to the reorganisation of ministries and agencies around the residual functions governments are left with, but not to any critique or substantial challenge to the principles on which civil services are organised. These remain those of the rule of law, hierarchy, segmentation and specialisation of tasks, and an ethic of public service which includes strong notions of impartiality and upward accountability.

These Weberian principles, while admirable in their own way, represent a polar opposite of the management approach outlined above as appropriate in rural development. This would suggest that the role of central government in rural development should be minimal. It should do no more than establish legal frameworks within which decentralised organisations with strong grassroots constituencies can operate, a legal framework for partnership and contracting, together with supportive legal and enforcement institutions and a legal framework to encourage self-regulation of economic and other activities, with minimal state involvement in arbitration where conflicting interests cannot be reconciled. Central governments have enabling roles too: information provision being a critical function for the successful operation not only of markets but also of networks and movements for change.

Governments will require a variety of new capacities to play these roles. For rural development the capacities particularly important are those of allocating resources in response to citizen demand, and in some cases ensuring equity or minimum levels of access (Campbell and Fiszbein, 1994); and the creative capacities to learn, adapt, innovate and encourage the taking of risks (North, 1990: 80). The first capacity governments need in the new era is to restructure themselves (Chapter 9). The second is to decentralise across a wide spectrum of activities, not just to local government, but to a variety of single purpose authorities and organisations as well.

Education: an example

An example would be the need to decentralise education services in the context of developing contracts for local management appropriate to particular situations and conditions. The propensity of central policy-makers to retain substantial control over key policy issues – for example, in education, the content of the syllabus, or teachers' conditions of service – needs to be substantially reduced, while developing a strong monitoring role around a set of broadly agreed principles. Resources need to flow to enable decentralised decisions to be made: these will be partly local resources, linked to particular schools or education processes, in the case of education, but partly also central government expenditures. Central government auditors will need to accept that accountability for the use of these resources is as much to local institutions and their objectives (e.g. parent–teacher associations, boards of governors) as to central government. To make a reality of this sort of decentralisation, government policy has to become permissive rather than universalist. It will have to permit (encourage) cultural differences (Gould, 1993: 91) which will foster ethnic identity within an accepted national framework. It will have to accept that inter-regional inequalities cannot be redressed merely by imposed central standards, though provision of disproportionate resources to under-developed regions may remain to counter inequality to the extent possible. Above all, rural societies need flexibility to adjust curricula, the language of instruction in the early years of education, and school opening times and dates, and they need to play a role in the recruitment of teachers (Gould, 1993: 121–2).

Implications for local government

Rural development thinkers in many countries have for some time in principle given strong support to the idea of local government, as important in terms of citizen participation, as a counterweight to the centrally sponsored rural investments which most governments and donors have preferred (Uphoff, 1986; Curtis, 1991). However, there is a major problem with the advocacy of rural local government. The prevalent model of local government, at least in the English-speaking world, is of urban government. Rural local governments are set up as pale reflections of their urban counterparts. Functionally they are supposed to equalise rural–urban disparities in services and the provision of physical infrastructure, which they can rarely do as they are not adequately resourced. Revenues are much easier to devise and collect in town; a much higher proportion of the rural population is absolutely poor in most poor countries. Towns are politically volatile concentrations of people, far better able to press for investment than the disconnected, less powerfully led and often remote villages of their hinterlands. In rare cases have central governments been so serious about developing rural local government that significant resources have been decentralised to them: the current exceptions are in the Philippines, in Brazil, and incipiently in Ghana. The key features of these stories are: a strong central government commitment, for its own political or ideological reasons; a strong measure of resource devolution; and a considerable measure of autonomy. In all three cases towns are not separated from their hinterlands, making internal resource generation and redistribution easier.

Much more usual is the picture of a rural local authority which has had personnel but not resources transferred to it; as a result local governments are widely seen as employment generators rather than service providers. Frequently such local governments pay out 70 per cent of their budgets in salaries to people who have very little capacity to deliver any kind of resource-intensive service. These local governments usually cover a wide geographical area, and are not seen as legitimate units by their constituents. As a result their locally collected revenues are poor.

Even the positive examples given above may run down in the absence of continued central support on which they must rely, unless they can generate a constituency for local government which prevents central governments from taking away resources. Central governments' confidence in local government is rarely so great that it rapidly increases the resources available to local governments. Other mechanisms are necessary.

Polycentric institutional arrangements

Local governments can easily develop the wrong culture of bureaucracy, inaccessibility and elitism. The only way to counter this is to ensure a wide sharing of local governance (a broader concept than government) among all kinds of local institutions. The model is one of local governments as one actor in a network of actors of equal legal status, sharing governance with very local, village and sub-village organisations, decentralised arms of central government, citizen associations and federations of associations. Many of these may take on functions which in the classic model of local government would be performed in-house, by the local government. They do so with their own resources, sometimes supplemented by local government resources, whether human or financial. With this approach in mind, local, like central government, does not need to be a big employer: it needs to be staffed by officials who are excellent at communication and liaison, who know where to find specialist skills – in the rural communities, in central government institutions, in the private sector, in NGOs – and who are paid accordingly. The small number of officials ensures that the majority of revenues go into services, unlike the typical case where, for example, market taxes are collected but markets never experience any physical improvements unless a traders' association makes a special collection. As far as possible in this model, activities are further decentralised to very local levels (the market association, in this example) wherever there is capacity to carry them out. Where capacity is lacking, the function of local government should be to build capacity by linking the very local level with the relevant expertise or resource, and develop the very local level's systems so that next time it can provide the resource itself.

What is being advocated here is a version of Ostrom and Wynne's polycentric institutional arrangements (1993: 177ff). This could be summarised in the statement that there is too much government but not enough governments. Given that 'there is likely to be a greater homogeneity of demand within small groups than over broad segments of society' (Ostrom and Wynne, 1993: 182), the proposition is that such homogeneous groups should be able to create single- (or even multi-)purpose authorities in a particular area according to demand. In poor countries there is a variety of indigenous institutions (see Chapter 3) which provide a basis for thinking that multiple authorities established by demand would have a legitimacy much greater than the systems of government which were imposed by imperial powers, or of local government where these were imposed by unpopular central governments. Not only do indigenous institutions provide principles for the management of such authorities, they also sometimes suggest mechanisms for resolving the inevitable disputes between authorities. There would have to be 'independent forums for dispute resolution' which would preside over the rule of a hierarchy of law (Ostrom and Wynne, 1993: 209).

Conclusion

This chapter has drawn out the radical implications of the previous chapters for organisation. The nature of rural development organisation is changing, with more emphasis being given to people's organisations, NGOs, networks of development agencies, and joint government–people organisations where professionals play a facilitating, advisory role. Development organisations need to be rooted in the communities they serve, and be encouraged to develop locally appropriate services which can be at least partly sustained by local energy. As a result the common public objective of uniform standards of service provision implemented through a bureaucratic approach is under challenge. In future these will at least have to be negotiated with a range of organisations involved in policy and service provision. Where there is a public value in uniformity, resources will need to be committed to ensure it. Otherwise variation and destandardisation should be accepted as the price for a more sustainable pattern of development.

9

Organisational Change

The rural development agenda outlined in the previous eight chapters indicates that the late 1990s and early twentieth century are and will be an era of substantial change in institutional arrangement and organisational policies. It is an era for radical decisions. One of the skills rural development managers will need is that of promoting and managing organisational change. This is true in all agencies – donors, governments, parastatals, NGOs and the private sector. In donors, governments and the private sectors, organisational change appropriate to the new paradigm in rural development will be heavily constrained by other overriding political and organisational objectives. Part of the challenge will be to influence these wider organisations to change their practices insofar as they have an impact on rural development. Given the unbundling which is now characteristic of public sector reform, this should not prove impossible.

It is clear that bureaucracy in either its classic or its degraded form cannot work well in the new paradigm. The possibility of reform is affected by contexts and culture. In South East Asia, where the influence of the private sector is strong, reform of bureaucracy is likely to be more rapid compared with South Asia where a public sector culture dominates even the private sector to a degree. A strong public sector may vary considerably in its culture and functioning. The key difference is the degree to which it is rule- and procedure-bound or led by purposes to which the rules are subordinate. Success in rural development invariably requires a degree of risk-taking (innovation, rule-breaking, etc.) which is very difficult to achieve in a rule-bound working environment. In several Sub-Saharan African countries the public sector has been so decimated and become so donor-dependent, that reform of structures has become a way of life. However, the reforms introduced so far have not done much for development, being aimed largely at other objectives like cost-cutting and retrenchment (Larbi, 1995).

A rejection of the bureaucratic mode does not imply rejection of all its features. Accountability is a critical issue, but can be assured in ways other than upward reporting and accounting. Horizontal (peer review) and downward communication (accountability to community) is more important. Balancing accountability upwards and downwards, and mutual understanding between financing agencies and participating groups, communities and organisations is a challenge for organisations working in the new paradigm. Merit recruitment systems are vital, but can be achieved more effectively in rural development without the centralised, bureaucratic procedures associated with a massive public service. Criteria such as local experience, trust of local people and use of local language, which are not normally considered appropriate may be of greater relevance.

Hierarchy, as a principle of organising, however, is rejected. Even the hierarchy implicit in contracting is often inappropriate. Contracts (public–private; donor–NGO; government–NGO; NGO–Community-based Organisation, CBO; CBO–group/community) are useful devices for clarifying and regulating inter-organisational relationships. However, the development of trust and partnership in a relational contract is usually important in rural development. Trust is mutual, and implies a lessening of hierarchy, if not a total absence of it.

Organisational change in rural development is directed at generating an interactive, outward-looking organisation, able to promote the capacity and institutional development of partners especially at the local and associational levels, as well as its own. Management needs to recognise the requirements of different organisations and avoid the tendency to create mirror organisations. Organisations should value individuals in key positions especially those in the field, giving them high levels of discretion and support. Organisations need to generate, participatorily, useful information about their activities: this is the key to their strategic thinking process. The latter sounds very grand, and can be very complex, but may also actually be quite simple. It needs to be simple in many situations. An outward-looking organisation will seek to involve others in its functioning, through, for example participation on an Executive or Advisory Board, or through establishing an external monitoring team, or simply by participating in discussions and networking. This is important not only in renewing the ideas and energies available to the organisation, but also in explaining its functioning to others, and in seeking to work with other agencies.

The creation of capacity for change

Organisational change is about the creation and destruction of capacity. It should be recognised that there are negative capacities – the capacity to block criticism, debate and change, delay action, deny access, restrict information, exclude stakeholders. Change is as much about removing negative capacities as creating the positive ones which this book has focused on. Change can be seen as a process, with a specific content, in a particular context. The content may be straightforward – one simple, easily achievable goal; start easy but get difficult – an initial change which necessarily leads to others; or be difficult from the outset – with multiple goals and purposes which change as time passes. The capacity for change is variable within organisations – between departments and between individuals – as well as among organisations linked in a hierarchy or network. Change leaders need to understand why this is so, and develop their strategies for change in the light of this analysis. Content and context interact in a process.

Content of change

There are many types of change highlighted in this book. None of them is straightforward; most involve sets of interrelated changes, and deep change in attitude and professional ideology as well as in organisational structures and procedures. Such is the nature of a paradigm shift. An example will illustrate some of the problems. Oxfam is recognised as a leading agency in the introduction of gender issues into its own work, as well as in the wider development debate. Its Gender and Development Unit (now Team) was formed in the mid-1980s to drive a process of organisational change. Conceptually, integrating gender issues into development work is not very complicated: knowledge about gender differences and their significance has been widely available for some time. However, it has proved a slow process, even within a reputedly progressive organisation like Oxfam. A review of work in 1994 on gender issues in 30 countries where Oxfam operates, claimed many successes, including increased women's participation in Oxfam projects, strengthened women's organisations, and better awareness of gender issues among partner organisations. There were also many lessons learnt from a decade of experience: training staff and getting issues understood by Oxfam staff and partners takes time; the issues challenge people personally, and working through these challenges also takes time. There are powerful religious and cultural forces arrayed against change in unequal gender relationships, and as a result the profile of research and advocacy on issues like women's rights, legal status, and violence against women needs to be raised if there is to be any effect. Men and women need to be involved in, rather than excluded from, each other's projects if change is to be achieved. Gender aware project management procedures are needed. Women were also excluded from debate by the widespread use of English as the only language.

Problems identified by Oxfam staff included: a failure to influence men, and the resistance of some male staff; a lack of time to carry out the time-consuming work that gender issues require, because workloads in other areas are heavy; the difficulty of translating concepts developed in headquarters to different contexts around the world; and the repeated failure of women's income-generating projects (a key strategy) to improve women's status or access to decision-making and resources (Wallace, 1994). The risk is that an organisation retreats from a problematic change process; a more useful conclusion would be to narrow down what can be achieved to a more practical agenda, and allow time and resources for difficult changes.

Contexts of change: government

Critical capacities for government in rural development include: a capacity for self-restructuring, and organisational change; a capacity for public education and information, to foster self-regulation and the development of social movements which will support self-regulation; a capacity to abandon the search for control over detail, but to orchestrate consensus behind purposes; a capacity to evaluate together with stakeholders; a capacity to value individuals who are central to networks rather than seeing them as a threat; and finally, and most problematically for government, a capacity to allow dissension, political campaigning, and the emergence of counter-vailing interests.

But governments have critical incapacities: they are inflexible with respect to staffing and financial management; the pace of work is often too slow due to low productivity and low motivation; unmotivated staff are overly concerned with their own survival and perks; hierarchy and concentration of decision at the top make devolved management impossible; central ministries retain control at all costs. These fundamental incapacities mean that change in government has to be structural as well as cultural: there are very big decisions which have to be taken at ministerial level. Devolution of rural development functions to local government is one approach, but beware creating the same incapacities there. Delegation to specialist, autonomous bodies is another approach, much tried in the era of integrated rural development, but which may gain a new lease of life in the new paradigm, where fieldworkers are highly prized, experienced staff. They may be organised in small, autonomous, collegiate bodies, reporting to a devolved government. Each autonomous body may have a small secretariat, but not the armies of office and fieldworkers typical of integrated rural development projects. If extra people are required they will have to be hired, on contract, preferably with local backgrounds as well as relevant skills. Or work may done through partnership with local associations or NGOs.

The management of organisational change involves various capacities: the capacity to retrench, redeploy and destroy large parts of the public sector. Destruction and retrenchment may sound very negative, but public sector organisations have become so overburdened with the wrong kind of staff and the wrong sort of culture that in many cases retraining, redeployment and restructuring will only bring substantial benefits if accompanied by considerable retrenchment and destruction. This would apply particularly to central ministries and centralised organisations based in capital cities. Only a very small percentage should remain in those locations: senior policy-makers, policy analysts, information system managers, and legislative experts. These types of change would affect ministries of agriculture, departments of primary and preventive health, departments of primary and secondary education, rural industry departments, and so on.

The capacity to retrench is complemented by a capacity to develop rolling relational (trust-based) contracts with other agencies or individuals, or even within the organisation. Performance on these contracts then needs to be monitored by both or all parties.

However, the contract culture needs to be tempered with commitment and a long-term perspective on the development of capacity at very local level. In most poor countries' rural areas there is no private sector waiting to take contracts from development agencies: contracts inevitably take on the characteristics of partnerships in this situation.

Radical restructuring would offer early retirement to civil servants, with benefits, especially those without appropriate skills; offer experienced workers responsible field postings with allowances to compensate for hardship, and scholarships for their children; create a framework in which they retire to their villages (early) and work for development organisations in their villages, perhaps competitively; privatise and regulate those services which can be, for example, veterinary, where demand is strong; move in a phased way towards creating autonomous bodies for extension and research, and service provision (schools, hospitals, clinics, water supply systems), giving networking responsibilities to these decentralised bodies; and create links of accountability to local democratic bodies, as well as direct client groups.

Contexts of change: NGOs

The call for NGOs in recent years has been to 'scale up' – spread and grow in order to have a wider impact. This may be done through lobbying and advocacy, or by growing organisationally. The message of this book is that it is rather scaling down which is required: unbundling, becoming properly rooted in society, working with partners in networks, at all costs avoiding the errors of past organisational empire-building strategies.

The empowerment of local organisations, CBOs, and associations does not require the long-term presence of a sustainable southern or northern NGO; success in developing the capacities of grassroots organisations and their associations would enable intermediary NGOs (or government departments charged with capacity-building) to disappear, or at the least to change role, or move on. As a contribution to the development of civil society NGOs are clearly often a positive development, but they may be male and elite-dominated, and highly opportunistic and career oriented in a situation where careers are hard to come by, and where northern NGOs provide much needed opportunities. How much better that enthusiastic, skilled individuals find employment with locally rooted agencies.

The intermediary NGO is an unsatisfactory and temporary form of organisation, a creature of the aid industry. Much more significant, because rooted and sustainable, are associations, and other organisations which find their *raison d'être* in the political economy, not as semi-outsiders. The real capacity-building of southern NGOs is, then, their transformation into rooted organisations, which the northern capacity development strategy outlined above only steps towards. There are few role models here. Grameen Bank is one example (see Chapter 4), Bancosol another, of NGOs which have become commercial, poverty-oriented banks.

The best-known case of an NGO transforming itself into a bank is that of Prodem (Foundation for the Promotion and Development of Microenterprises) in Bolivia, which created Bancosol. Prodem was established by the local business community, supported by USAID grants, at a time when Bolivia's formal banking system was in disarray, so that there was a large demand for reliable savings and credit facilities, especially from the informal microenterprise sector. Prodem developed with quite a commercial orientation, but by 1988 had only 3,300 customers. To expand this client base Prodem converted itself into a commercial bank, leaving behind its research and development wing as an NGO. This took four years, and involved building up its capital to a minimum threshold laid down by government, developing an effective blend of voluntary and compulsory savings in a savings-poor economy, and establishing commercial rates of interest against the prevailing culture of banking. In this it was supported by a number of organisations: USAID, the American NGO Accion International, and the Calmeadow Foundation. This group, together with key Bolivian businessmen, raised the necessary capital from a wider group of international organisations. Client deposits were increasingly replacing the more expensive bonds and inter-bank loans; these were mobilised through small groups of savers and borrowers mobilised by the bank (Mosely, 1995).

In NGOs the process of organisational change has been characterised by fission, with new NGOs being set up by discontented staff from established NGOs. Such staff could exercise greater imagination as they build their new organisation, exploring the scope for rooting the new organisation as a sustainable institution bound to a local membership or client group. There will always be a role for service agencies – agencies which provide services to membership organisations – but the priority today is to build the membership base organisations just as much as, if not more than, the service agencies.

Changing from an organisation which provides services to one which builds membership into the process of provision involves continually identifying demand, adapting to identified demand, involving members in decision-making on a regular basis and generating at least some resources internally (i.e. within the membership): the skills of building democratic broad-based organisations managing common properties and providing services. New attitudes are required of leaders: they must be able to shape membership opinion, but also be disciplined by it. Skills of consensus-building and managing change when consensus is absent will be at a premium.

Managing organisational change

A textbook recipe for managing organisational change derived from western private sector practice would talk about strategy and process, and entails a belief that change can be managed, and does not simply derive from changes in the wider society or economy. Steps in developing a strategy for change would include: a participatory analysis of the present situation (strengths, weaknesses, opportunities and threats); the formation of focus groups, involving different stakeholders to generate commitment from the beginning; a review of the impact of external developments (for example, using the Delphi technique of calling in experts to help diagnose these and their impacts); a specification of the desired future (formalised in a mission statement, a statement of how the organisation wants to be perceived – a vision statement, a statement of core values, or strategic objectives); and a strategy for managing the transition.

Managing the transition involves identifying leaders, establishing key tasks ('mini-projects'), and clarifying responsibilities. Throughout the process there is a need to gain and maintain support for the process. Workshops to define the change, to decide what is included and what excluded, are best carried out in an inclusive way. The organisation of change will depend on how big it is, and whether its impact is large or small. A small change with a big impact could be managed by a co-ordinator, ensuring that the change is achieved and that everybody knows about it and can handle the impact; a big change with a big impact needs a project team to manage the process. A big change with restricted impact can be handled by a specially assigned project manager (Lovell, 1994).

Change in the public and non-government sector is usually more complicated as organisations tend to have several and sometimes diverse goals. Consensus around corporate goals and values may not be so easy. Incentives and sanctions can often not be manipulated by managers to secure compliance either. People's participation tends to increase the objectives which need to be fulfilled, as these will vary from one place and time to another.

There is a low level of understanding of the management of change in development organisations (Blunt and Jones, 1992: ch. 10). Applications of western theory or practice are much more common than attempts to deepen understanding of change processes. Here we will take some key points developed in western management, and examine their application. The case-studies which follow are a small attempt to plug a gap.

Leadership

Leadership is at the heart of thinking about planned organisational change. This field is dominated by the 'Excellence' tradition (Peters and Waterman, 1982), which suggests that decentralised, project-based organisations which give central place to the roles of individuals within the organisation succeed. This tradition is strongest in the American private sector, but has influenced thinking about management across a wide spectrum of organisations, including those involved in rural development. Leadership is supposed to substitute for rules, quotas and targets. Leaders can be trained to be competent across a wide variety of competences to play different roles. Here is one prescription for the 'master manager'. He or she should be able to play the following roles:

1. The director role. Taking the initiative. Goal setting. Effective delegation.
2. The producer role. Personal productivity and motivation. Time and stress management.
3. The co-ordinator role. Planning, organising, controlling.
4. The monitor role. Writing effectively. Reducing information overload.

5. The mentor role. Understanding oneself and others. Effective inter-personal communication. Developing subordinates.
6. The facilitator role. Team building. Participative decision-making. Conflict management.
7. The innovator role. Creative thinking. Living with and managing change.
8. The broker role. Creating and maintaining a power base. Effective negotiation and influencing skills. Effective oral presentation (Wilson, 1992: 106)

These roles tend to focus on the internal environment of change, whereas change may have much more to do with the interactions between leaders or innovators and the external environment. Aspects of the external environment may also have to be managed: in fact, since rural development organisations rarely have much autonomy they will need to pay considerable attention to changing the external environment if organisational change is to stick. This is illustrated by the case-study of Integrated Watershed Management in India below.

Leadership is a culturally relative notion, and development agencies should attempt to reveal its characteristics in any particular place. Some societies value a much more collective style of leadership, than predominates in the west, for example. The NGO Ashoka was established to identify and support leaders whom it calls social innovators or entrepreneurs. Its criteria for searching and selecting these leaders are: creativity both in goal-setting and in follow-up problem-solving; entrepreneurial quality – they are possessed by an idea and the mechanics of implementing it; the social impact of the idea – the idea should be capable of having a national impact; and ethical fibre – the leader should be trustworthy. In South Africa a study by the New Economics Foundation (1995) found that those selected tended to be already clearly leaders (rather than as intended, potential leaders), and that more were white and male than these categories were represented in the population. The process of selection was criticised for the following reasons: that it gave undue importance to ability to speak and write good English; that it was selecting advantaged people who were helping disadvantaged rather than seeking out role models for the disadvantaged themselves; that leadership in South Africa was often, if not collective, validated by a complex process which the selection of an individual could not recognise, and indeed could undermine; and finally, that requiring a national impact excluded many people from disadvantaged backgrounds whose focus was at the community level (New Economics Foundation, 1995: 50–5). This illustrates the difficulty of cross-cultural discussions of leadership.

Leadership is not only about possessing competences: it is also an interactive process. Followers have to be led, willingly, but usually with incentives and sanctions, and some support from both the narrow organisational and the wider culture. Effective innovators are rare as a result, and should be cherished.

Innovators and organisational culture

The role of the innovator is 'one of the most compelling, and yet least understood, of the eight leadership roles' (Quinn *et al.*, 1990: 237). Innovators need to be tough-skinned, driven by wider objectives, and supported by conviction based on reality that what they are doing is right and feasible. In practice, innovators are often threatening to others, and come under a lot of pressure to work at a more widely accepted pace and in a less demanding style. However, there are different cultural styles which will be appropriate. Whereas the innovator in a western organisation will often be quite ruthless in pushing through new ideas, an innovator in a more paternalistic culture will need to combine innovation with a caring, family work orientation. This is an uneasy combination, very difficult to balance. Without it, the innovator loses legitimacy. In either case, support from top management or headquarters organisations is vital.

Innovations may be encouraged or discouraged by factors in the internal and external environments of the organisation. These are: the degree of vision present and the degree to which interest groups identify with that vision, and the degree to which the vision is achievable within given financial and human resource frameworks. Linked to the development of a shared vision is the evolution of a leadership cadre committed to change. Pressures from the environment – financial crisis, or pressures to proceed in a certain way – can speed up or slow down the change process. The process of change itself can also exert an influence: for example, simplicity and clarity of goals will help widespread understanding, and understanding is perhaps the first step to commitment.

Organisational culture is often an inherently conservative force in the face of necessary change (Schein, 1986). This is why so much emphasis has gone into developing organisational cultures which enable learning, adaptation and innovation as a matter of course. In rural development, change is now pervasive. Adapting to pervasive change should be easier for organisations which are newly established compared with more long-lived agencies with stronger cultures of their own. Many rural development organisations are new, and have less formalised divisions of labour and procedures of operation. Where cultures are better established it is likely that structures, procedures and attitudes will need change. Resistance to change has several sources:

1. The preference of staff (and other stakeholders) for stability and predictability. This is probably greatest in economies where uncertainties are also great.
2. The cost of change: accountants' cost-conscious views often stand against proponents of change.
3. Long-term external agreements and contracts may be seen to restrict, or complicate the process of change.
4. Groups perceive change as a threat to their positions and power. Since rural development involves power sharing, this is a critical dimension. (Mullins, 1989)

The stronger the culture opposing change the more likely it is that it will be imposed on individuals. This is why changing the culture through training and other activities which facilitate individual growth may smooth the way. Involving key players in creating the process of change – bringing out their latent creativity insofar as possible – helps spread the sense of ownership of the change. Getting the material incentives (pay, security, workload) right helps to break resistance. These would include factors which enable employees to meet social expectations – assistance to family members, for example – if this can be done without compromising organisational objectives.

Process of organisational change

The process of organisational change is likely to go through several stages. The best known model of this in the context of participatory development is Korten's (1980). He talks about phase 1 where the organisation learns to be more effective through action research. It learns to accept past errors and learn from them; how to involve people in decision-making, and how to translate learning into action, creating a culture of learning. In this phase, staff work with a small number of communities, adjust to using local knowledge, work out the issues behind conflicts of interest and try new approaches both technical and social.

In phase 2 the organisation uses the new methods derived from phase 1 more widely, and adapts them to suit available resources. Once 'acceptable levels of effectiveness and efficiency have been obtained' expansion and replication begins. This is phase 3 (Korten, 1980).

In rural development, change in one organisation is generally interlocked with change in others: rural development practice is multi-level and multi-organisational. In order to accomplish change several models of 'good organisation' may be needed to fit each organisation's needs and tasks. One organisation's change will prompt, demand and support change in another. Change in one without supportive changes in others may be useless. Even worse, changes may be mutually contradictory, in which case negotiation and separation will be necessary strategies which will also lead to changes.

Rural development organisations are at different stages in the organisational change process. For many, the changes to adapt to the new paradigm are quite major: involving what they do as well as how they do it, who they typically interact with and the quality of their external relationships. They are also far-reaching, involving retrenchment, unbundling, redeployment, reskilling, new recruitment and reorganisation. Such major change applies more to large public sector organisations than smaller NGOs, but aspects of it apply to NGOs too.

Case studies of organisational change

We will briefly examine three cases of rapid and significant organisational change. Readers are encouraged to go to the original sources for two of them. The Philippines National Irrigation Administration (NIA) is perhaps the best-known and only well-documented case (Korten and Siy, 1989). The approach employed there has been used elsewhere (e.g. Bangladesh), with some success. Organisational change in the public sector in India has proved much more problematic (Shepherd, 1995). NGOs by contrast, if they are not heavily donor dependent, should present a much more conducive organisational environment for change. Some reflections on the recent experience of Plan-Nepal confirms this.

The NIA changed from a classic infrastructure development government department to a semi-autonomous, self-financing servant of the farming community over a period of fifteen years. The key change introduced in the development of small and medium-scale irrigation was a substantial and participatory planning phase in which the farmers likely to benefit from an NIA investment collectively sort out their differences and agree a plan of action. This is facilitated by a cadre of NIA workers, the Community Organisers. Accommodating this cadre and the painstaking preparatory work it performs have been the major changes the NIA has had to adapt to. A key supportive change has been the progressive requirement that the NIA raise more and more of its own revenue from the farmers it serves. This ensures that the work it does is what the farmers want. Even more critical was the formation and persistence over a long period of a group of key leaders and supporters of organisational change, both inside and outside the NIA.

Our second case-study, the Watershed Management Directorate (WMD) of the Indian state of Uttar Pradesh, presents a different image. Funded by the European Union and government of India, and charged with reducing erosion and raising incomes in the Himalayan foothills, this organisation attempted to develop a participatory, gender-sensitive approach, making use of PRA. In this it has been partially successful in a short period of time. Significant changes in the behaviour of front-line staff with villagers were recorded. The principle of village-level identification and negotiation of priorities was accepted. Village women were involved to a greater degree than in any previous governmental development effort. However, there were obstacles to radical change. The government's strong culture of target orientation and achievement eroded the space which was available early on for participatory planning: pressure to spend money escalated after the establishment phase. This pressure came largely from the state Finance Ministry and other state-level officials, and was not always resisted by senior project personnel, who are of course assessed by the degree to which targets are achieved. The target culture was reinforced by the common understanding that aid money would be lost if not spent. Retrospectively, the original project plan was also at fault. This gave indicative physical and financial targets which were quite incompatible with the slow initial rhythms of a participatory approach.

These were of course seized on by officers anxious to have targets to fulfill.

Radical change was achieved in Plan-Nepal, our third case-study, through a combination of changes in personnel, the drawing-up of a country strategic plan, and the opening of the organisation to outside influences. Plan-Nepal was a very conservative NGO, like its international parent; providing services to the families and communities of sponsored children in a reactive and dependency-creating way. The appointment of two women to senior posts, and a regional director from outside the organisation, paved the way for a significant move towards a more thoughtful, participatory and gender-sensitive approach. The geographical and topical focus of the agency's work has changed significantly, with a new willingness to work in poor, remote areas and to confront difficult social issues like child prostitution. Again the use of PRA has significantly changed project-level operations. Nevertheless, with its incredibly successful child sponsorship financial treadmill, which has supported unprecedented organisational growth during the last decade, there are pressures to spend money in Plan-Nepal too: these will undoubtedly limit the freedom of Plan-Nepal staff to retain the quality of their new approaches.

A wide variety of organisations is involved in rural development: only a tiny selection is represented here. What is impressive in all three cases is that positive change can be accomplished even in large bureaucratically managed organisations. The implementers' degree of autonomy clearly makes a big difference to the extent that change can be implemented: the NIA and Plan-Nepal having much greater autonomy than the WMD. In all three cases a key element of success was the existence of a group of people who realised the need for change, and whose thinking about the direction of change was complementary. These groups have to be created, need to be seen as legitimate, and their influence needs to be accepted. Without support from key organisational processes – like finance, changes in rules and regulations or legislation, and strategic management – these groups will not prevail over sceptical opponents who can mobilise a hostile organisational culture. External orientation is vital – to rural people through their associations and via participatory planning and evaluation techniques; and to the wider development community of movements, intellectual forces and media which can help to influence decision-makers with power over the key organisational processes mentioned above.

The NIA experience has been influential elsewhere in South East Asia and beyond the irrigation sector. In the rural sector, forestry bureaucracies have been especially interested in facilitating local management of forest resources by community groups because staff and financial resources are so limited while forest areas are so enormous (Poffenberger, 1990). In the process, forest bureaucracies have had to give up some of their authority in order to empower local groups. This has required a high level of commitment to devolution of power. Increasingly community involvement is sought in the core business of the forestry organisations: protecting and developing the state forests. This has required shifts in policy and law, procedures and attitudes.

In the Philippines, Indonesia and Thailand these changes have been achieved through a combination of factors. Both insider and outsider facilitators have been employed by organisations where there is already some awareness of the need for change. These facilitators get things going – meetings between insiders and resource persons, discussion groups to exchange ideas. Insiders are key in determining the pace of change: they will build the necessary coalition to support change among colleagues, and will represent the changes to the outside world. Outsiders usually need time to adjust to the realities of the organisation before they can make a useful contribution. Some outsiders may be suspicious – staff from NGOs, for example, asked to work with a government agency. Above all, the interaction worked better where no one claimed superior expertise in how to do it: all can work with the idea that joint exploration is required.

Working groups

The forestry bureaucracies took up the use of working groups following the example of the NIA, and with the assistance of the Ford Foundation. The composition of these groups changed as their role changed; in particular, university researchers in the early phases were replaced with rural development practitioners in the later phases. Working groups commonly experienced communication problems among members, and with remote areas; regular meeting schedules could be difficult to maintain.

The function of the working group is to learn from the field, digest the learning and offer suggestions to management. Learning mechanisms include field research, in particular looking at the existing relationships between agency and community; routine review of field reports; and process documentation, which produces regular reports on the agency–community interactions in the field. The working group can also create situations in which junior staff can communicate field problems directly to senior staff; if this process can be institutionalised it is probably the biggest single contribution facilitators can make to the process of organisational change. Exchange visits to neighbouring or especially selected projects can also be helpful.

For a successful expansion process, communication with staff is vital. Staff need to understand and believe in the new approaches. Training and workshops help middle-level managers to keep up with the change: they can easily get left behind by senior managers interacting enthusiastically with field staff during the learning phases. The performance of field staff is critical in the new approach: they must be carefully selected, retrained, and training curricula need to be revised. Good staff need to be rewarded, and career opportunities opened for them. This may involve difficult changes in criteria of hiring and promoting. For example, forestry bureaucracies often excluded women and non-foresters who proved the most successful community organisers (Poffenberger, 1990: 114).

It helps the expansion process if pilot projects are designed to be implemented under as normal as possible management conditions. This allows the testing of new ideas without excessively favourable conditions. Senior decision-makers need to be in command of the expansion process so that changes made are consistent with policy. The speed of change needs to be carefully gauged: too rapid change can lead to dilution of results. Too slow change leads to loss of momentum. In the cases reviewed, the collapse or poor performance of previous systems meant that managers were generally faced with intense pressure to speed up change before they could properly cope with it.

Working groups represent one method of achieving change: others include technical assistance teams, newly recruited staff, and co-opted staff from other agencies. What is impressive about the working group approach is the amount of learning these groups were able to achieve, probably because of the good institutional links with research organisations, whose facilities could be used in research. This is probably a factor which makes distinguishes the South East Asian experience from that in South Asia.

One of the reasons why NGOs may be gaining such an important place in rural development is their greater capacity to change rapidly. Comparing Plan-Nepal with the Indian Integrated Watershed Management project one can sense that this capacity is partly the result of the comparative autonomy of an NGO with its own sources of funds. The external environment of the public sector organisation is much more complex, and in the context of Indian government structures, much more inhibiting of change. Consequently, a successful public sector strategy of change would need to rely much more on a positive external orientation than is the case with an NGO.

Conclusion

Organisational change will be a major issue for rural development in years to come. Skills in managing organisational change are now at a premium. Would-be leaders can to some extent learn these skills, though there is a dearth of documented experience to learn from. Both internal and external environments are critical, and both have to be managed in rural development. Some aspects of the external environment may be extremely difficult to manage: a stakeholder analysis would suggest that it has merely to be 'appreciated'. However, where the changes are radical, organisations need to develop a strategy for exerting influence externally – through alliances with significant resource persons or movements, use of the media, getting aid donors to exert pressure on government or vice versa.

In dealing with change in the public sector, internal and external environments are, of course, not completely distinct. Personnel may work under general civil service rules, and the organisation's culture may be informed by general practice as much as its specific objectives and strategies. Hence the inevitable attempt to get away from civil service regulations by setting up autonomous bodies. Change in an NGO context is likely to be more achievable: though even there the example of introducing a gender dimension to Oxfam's work indicated the limitations and difficulties. And NGOs strongly committed to organisational growth may find that they become more hierarchical and centralised in the process, which could in turn inhibit more positive forms of change.

Overall, we can conclude that while there are no well-researched recipes for organisational change, it is a vital aspect of the wider shift to the new paradigm, an aspect which urgently needs researching, documenting and public debate.

10

Conclusion

The retreat of the state

Fundamentals in the new paradigm are not difficult to discern. One absolute fundamental is the retreat of the state. The early critique of conventional rural development focused on the state (Heyer *et al.*, 1981). It was seen as serving the particular interests of national and international dominant social groups rather than general interests. Stated objectives of rural development were often undermined by actual implementation, which was environmentally ruinous and socially regressive. States and the international organisations set up by states played the greatest role in rural development from the 1960s through to the 1980s, and therefore must take the blame for the widespread negative impacts of development on rural societies. As the international concern for poverty and redistribution waned in the 1980s, for a mixture of political and economic reasons, and was transformed into a concern for macro-economic management, so the role of the state has diminished, and the volume and importance of aid (an indicator of the commitment of states) has also lessened.

Structural adjustment programmes are ensuring that the state withdraws from many areas of production and provision. In some cases withdrawal from urban-industrial involvements may free up resources for rural investments. This would be the case if the World Bank's health agenda were implemented, as this argues for a shift of public resources from hospitals to primary and preventive health care (World Bank, 1993). This shift is only likely to happen, however, where there is a favourable political structure to steer it past the inevitable opposition of the urban middle classes. In countries whose rural areas remain largely poor the withdrawal of the state need not be regretted, as it will open up opportunities to meet needs in different ways, either through the private sector, or the institutions of civil society.

With the withdrawal of the state from a spectrum of service provision and enterprise management roles, space is recaptured for much more serious attention to policy issues, and policy processes. Rural development has for far too long been seen as a set of interventions, guided or, more usually, implemented by the state (or by aid agencies). The withdrawal of the state from such interventions allows a useful return to an earlier notion about development happening as a result of a complex flow of forces for change in which states and agencies can play important but rarely determining roles. This is because states and agencies are usually representative of certain interests; if not captured by them, they are subject to their veto. Policies then become 'critical points of debate and potential conflict. There is usually a small number of very important issues over which the state has a significant degree of influence: beyond macro-economic management, it may be to do with setting universal prices or standards, with legislation about the powers of organisations, or with investments in education and information.

Parallel to the decline of the state as an interventionist force, aid is dwindling into a termination phase, due to 'aid fatigue' in some rich countries, the emergence of other spending priorities (e.g. Eastern Europe), and due to its lacklustre performance. The decline of aid also represents an opportunity: less money for aid means less pressure to spend it, which opens the door to a less linear approach to investment. With less pressure to spend, there should be more scope for participatory, holistic, gender-sensitive work, incorporating much more reflection and evaluation than hitherto. The quality of development work will increase as a result, if the aid agencies and recipients allow it to, and will contribute to the achievement of the much talked of high-quality growth. If aid is moving into a termination phase how long should it be? In the poorer countries there is a need for a 25–50 year perspective. The content of aid can be read from the themes of this book, though it must be emphasised that the ideas in this book cannot simply be translated into programmatic statements, irrespective of context. The book has stressed over and over again the importance of understanding and analysis together with action.

The question is now, what takes the place of the state and aid in rural development? The answer could be: the private sector, and the market. However, in poor rural societies the private sector is often limited, as capital tends to drain out of the system; and the market is distorted by many imperfections. While there is little room any more for state productive enterprises, and even state service provision has been costly and inadequate, the private sector does not supply instant growth and certainly will not of itself remove or even alleviate poverty in many situations. In fact the organised, capitalised private sector is often experienced by ordinary rural people as a predatory force, against which a defence has to be mounted. This is as true today as it was in the post-war period when it gave rise to widespread state intervention. At the very least, states will now need to play the complicated and difficult roles required to ensure a competitive private sector, in rural situations which may provide the circumstances which encourage monopolies.

Part of the answer to this conundrum is to be found in the promotion by the state (and affiliated organisations) of the 'third sector', organised civil society, so that it can compete with the private sector in trade, service provision, and production. So, local institutional development including the development of legitimate local governments as well as a range of decision-making authorities rooted in local society, the collective management of common goods, the development of economic associations as service providers to their members, including the service of marketing – all these are activities which will promote a competitive market in rural areas where the private sector may be disinterested, or only interested under exploitative or monopolistic conditions.

Under structural adjustment programmes the hope was that the local private sector would develop rapidly to take over tasks previously performed by the state. There was also the hope that, with a liberalised pattern of trade, the international private sector would come in to do some of these things, in partnership with national capital. However, results have thus far been disappointing in the poorer countries. States are increasingly encouraged to deal with the failure of the private sector to take up opportunities created by the withdrawal of the state (privatisation, contracting out, budget limitations) by setting up programmes to develop the skills and capitalise the same private sector. To realise the paradigm shift it is probably necessary that such efforts should go not into promoting the private sector but into the promotion of competition for the private sector from the third sector. The collapse of the public sectors and the lack of interest or capacity of the international private sector in poor countries has created an extraordinary opportunity for the promotion of the third sector. This is, however, heavily constrained by the incapacities of the state.

Liberalisation and structural adjustment are creating a related set of opportunities for rural development, not as an interventionist process, but as a pattern of change. To the extent that they remove the biases of the public economy which largely favoured urban-industrial and elite groups these policies have increased the importance of rural development in poor countries, as well as the possibility of generating a positive process of rural change. However, these gains are fragile: coalitions of powerful interests can easily build up against them. For example, in Ghana, as this is written, the pressure is mounting in a pre-election year for a return to agricultural input subsidies. The commercial farmers want them, as does the Ministry of Agriculture (MacBright, personal communication). The absence of subsidies has enabled NGOs in Ghana for the first time in decades to work in a sustainable agriculture medium: a return to subsidies would threaten this position. Non-farm enterprise can be promoted without having to compete in a distorted market which favoured an excessive allocation of labour and capital to agriculture. Poor rural communities have regained access to common land which had previously been put under the plough on a large scale by commercial farmers taking advantage of subsidised inputs and artificially cheap access to land. Strategies for common property resource development have become thinkable. This situation would be threatened again by the return to subsidisation. The development of a predatory style of state-sponsored capitalism contributed to the present-day violent conflicts over land in northern Ghana: a return to subsidies would undoubtedly make the resolution of those conflicts more difficult, as they would benefit the same predatory social groups. For all these reasons, NGOs and CBOs working on these issues need to attempt to ensure that subsidies are kept off the electoral agenda.

Thus it can be argued that liberalisation and structural adjustment bring about the conditions for a sustained effort in rural development, with the primary objective of enabling rural people and societies increasingly to determine their own trajectories, in the context of a complex world where there are many ideas about development, and where one person's development may be another's disaster.

Structure of the new paradigm

By this point in the book I hope it is evident to the reader that the new paradigm is a set of closely interconnected and broadly complementary clusters of ideas, or theories. Start with one of them, and you should find it possible or even necessary to move around the circle. There should be strong links between the 'what', the 'who' and the 'how'. For example, start with a participatory approach. The use of participatory methods to structure dialogue between outsiders and insiders would normally lead to the exposure of indigenous ideas about resources and their management. These could be further explored using a holistic method such as farming systems development, or, if common goods are involved, a common property resource framework. Issues to do with local-level organisation are likely to emerge from the latter. The participatory exploration of the constraints and potentials of a system together with the women of a community might identify surplus family (especially female) labour at particular seasons of the year, which could lead to identification of income-earning opportunities or scope for employment generation. On the other hand, the women might insist that their labour-time was already over-committed, and their real problem was that their husbands spend too much of the family income on drink. The coming together of women to analyse their problems might lead to some initiative to form a women's network to combat drink and associated problems like wife-beating. Having made an impression on this issue, this women's network would also begin to address the natural-resource management issues of special concern to women – drinking and washing water, protecting the sources of that water, woodfuel supplies, and fodder for small stock. And many womens' groups might establish literacy classes. At this point their confidence in their capacity to manage development would be much greater than at the beginning of the process. This process could not have been planned from the outset; it would require a flexible and evaluative response from any development agency accompanying the process. It would take place over a number of years. Expenditure would be small, in lumps now and then. The development agency could respond best to this situation if it possessed experienced and responsible fieldworkers able to take decisions and harness human and other resources to the problems and issues which emerge.

The results of this process were that: over a period of ten years, the drinking problem was considerably reduced, men put in more effort into household activities, including farming, and women from very poor households with little land began to explore possibilities for additional income earning activities. Some women's groups had evolved into savings groups, and these were now interested in increasing their resources to enable more sizeable investments. These were not only in small enterprises, but also in social and environmental improvements – schooling, latrines, and agro-forestry. Some of the poorer groups were the most successful. After the literacy classes it was realised that there was a complete dearth of reading material in the village; a number of women got together to start a mobile library on a cost-recovery basis, which in turn led to a number of small static libraries in a number of villages, run by library committees, with contributions from readers able to pay, and a grant from the state education authorities. The grants petered out soon after this, however. Each library charged readers an additional tiny fee which went into a fund administered by a federation of libraries, and was available to member libraries for matching grants. After twenty years, this was only a small part of the story, which it would take another book to tell completely. There was evident change in the area as measured by a number of indicators, most of which were recorded locally through services provided locally. Above all, there was a sense that people in the area had taken a grip on their own development, and had addressed the issues of importance to them. There was still a role for development agencies and service providers from outside the community, but this was minimal compared with twenty years previously.

Such stories are the stuff of development in the new paradigm. Others would illustrate different combinations of elements. Apart from withdrawal of the state, the fundamentals in these stories are likely to be: participation and institutional development, ensuring that efforts are sustained and the process of development has added dynamism; an expanded arena for common goods management, around which institutional development frequently takes place; and affordable and sustainable technological development so that even poor people can involve themselves. The development agency may start by giving a degree of direction, but should rapidly allow direction to be taken from it, and move into responsive mode.

Development theory

The entire notion of development is under challenge in much of this writing. It has been 'opened up' for debate, but the debate is currently muted. It is clearly no longer just economic growth, and redistribution is unfashionable (but probably inescapable). 'High quality' growth begs the question of who will judge quality – it has generally referred to the issue of whether the poor are included. But what about women? Ethnic minorities? Environmental conservation? They should be included too. Economic growth and war can co-exist; certain aspects of economies (and certain individuals and companies) thrive in war. What value peace? And, since we already speak of cultural development, is there not a spiritual dimension too? Like environmental conservation, spirituality can easily be a casualty of growth.

These are not simply rhetorical questions for the amusement of development philosophers, but real doubts in the minds of rural development practitioners. This crisis of confidence spells the beginning of the end of external intervention as a mode of doing development; external intervention cannot be sustained as a long-term project without a mission: that has now been lost. The new paradigm provides an exit for practitioners, development agencies and the concerned public: it provides an agenda for the reduction of external intervention. In Chapter 6, I suggested that development could be replaced by the concept co-evolution. This is perhaps too radical a step at the present time: the notion of development is still a powerful one in terms of orchestrating a human response, mobilising resources, and getting things done. It will no doubt continue to be for some time to come. However, the meaning of development has changed and is continuing to change: this is now an unstoppable process. No longer is it economic growth, or even growth with redistribution. It includes an idea of sustainability, gives value to peace and democracy, and is validated by the quality of women's personal life experiences as well as by (usually male) statistics. Even the statistics have changed – girls' education being reported on next to economic growth rates. Within this spectrum individuals and interest groups can legitimately define development in their own way: they may not be powerful enough to persuade others to accept their definition, but it may still find a place in terms of determining action.

Hettne (1995) (see also Chapter 1) summarises this situation in a classic Hegelian thesis–antithesis–synthesis. The realisation that western social science is not as universally applicable as claimed nor as innocent in causing the rich world's problems as might be thought, has led to an indigenisation of social science around the world, an emancipation of social scientists from western development paradigms, and in turn to a more self-critical self-appraisal among western social scientists themselves. These twin processes of indigenisation of thinking about development and reconsideration by western thinkers are 'the basic points of departure for the emergence of a more universal conception of development'. This is not a forecast but a project for development theorists (Hettne, 1995: 259).

The future of rural development

The new rural development paradigm does not yet (nor ever will) constitute a rural development theory: rural development, in my view, is necessarily too context-specific to be encompassed in one grand theory. However, the new paradigm does present an approach and a set of interconnected theories and ideas which can be used to address most of the issues and problems faced by policy-makers and programme managers.

Rural development has matured to the point at which it is possible to perceive of solutions to many of its long-standing problems which pass the tests of sustainability, equitability, and efficient use of resources. The remaining question is whether development agencies, governments and non-government organisations have, can or will bring the new paradigm into the mainstream. It has already been argued that this is unlikely to happen in some cases. The World Bank should leave this 'softer' end of development to other agencies less bound by expenditure pressures and an ideology which is too restrictive. At the other end of the spectrum, one would expect NGOs to be working in the new paradigm. Some no doubt are, or are trying to; but at least in the north NGOs have generally gone for growth themselves over the last decade and a half, mainly through increasing their dependence on official aid sources. It is argued elsewhere that organisational growth achieved by this means is in conflict with much of the new paradigm, because of the demands it places on the organisation and its component parts and activities in the field (Wallace *et al.*, 1997). NGOs are increasingly not looking as though they are the major vehicle for the new paradigm. Hopefully, reading this, they will ask themselves deeper questions about the consequences of their own development as organisations for the kind of development work they purvey. In the north, the sector needs a major reorganisation; in the south, lured by resources and growth opportunities, NGOs will increasingly face the same dilemmas. The conclusion would be that they can still be useful intermediaries, but that their self-interest can easily get in the way. Donors and governments can help significantly here: by creating incentives for NGOs to use their resources to promote local institutional development, and by reducing their insistence on the achievement of targets and preference for the delivery of services in favour of a more participatory, process-oriented and analytical approach to development. This can be done by giving NGOs the room for manoeuvre they need – especially in terms of time; and by encouraging them to switch from an emphasis on planning and appraisal to evaluation as the guiding tool in development.

As states democratise either under pressure from their international partners or from internal sources, rural development will spring back on to the political agenda. Where viable states continue to exist, politicians will no doubt want to respond to rural demands for services in a conventional way. They will find the new paradigm useful when it comes to improving the quality of services and administration. However, political parties seeking a high degree of control will find the new paradigm does not help them. Where states have become weaker, the new paradigm offers ways of providing services, or rather allowing services to be provided by the third sector, or the private sector; states can contribute not only permissions but also resources into this process of developing partnerships with local bodies. Does all this require a massive purposive reorientation of officials and politicians? Undoubtedly reorientation, through training, debate in the media and so on, will help, but it needs to be backed by the existence of pressure for change from emerging or well-established local bodies.

Local government can easily get in the way of this process: local governments are often so poorly resourced that they see themselves as competing for resources with other local bodies – associations, community-based organisation, and NGOs. However, local government can also be the pivot around which partnerships evolve: this is generally the only way to make their extremely limited resources go further. It is usually the central state which determines what sort of role local government will play. The key to this role is that it should spread rather than concentrate power within its area of jurisdiction: this is something many central governments would like to see, so that local governments do not compete politically with the central government.

Rural development professionals face a challenging future: one where they will be combining their skills with those of the unrecognised professionals living and working in rural areas. There is an increasing number of funding and implementing organisations which are serious about this: but the organisational implications – adjusting incentives and pressures, changing work patterns – have rarely been worked out adequately. This is a major task for the coming generation of rural development work.

Organisational change is a major neglected task. While its importance cannot be overestimated (and has been underestimated in the past) there are no easy guidelines which can be offered. Cultures vary greatly (Hofstede, 1980; 1991) in the ways in which people interact, learn and are motivated and constrained; universal prescriptions about management tend to have limited validity. The field is more dominated by approaches and ideas culled from American and other business organisations than are other aspects of rural development; this is not particularly helpful since the tasks faced by rural development workers are so different from the commercial and production tasks of business. Nevertheless, some of the more recent management development ideas do have relevance in rural development, insofar as they are attempts to deal with an uncertain or chaotic business environment for which innovation and being close to the customer are important. There is still much further intellectual work remaining to be done in the coming years to define how organisations working with the new paradigm should operate.

Ultimately, even though process is much more important in the new paradigm than it was in the old, rural development actions stand or fall on what they achieve, on their content. The evidence suggests that rural development actions have often not been highly appropriate, effective, or led to sustainable and equitable outcomes. However, Chapters 2–4 of this book outlined a set of approaches and principles on the basis of which appropriate actions can be developed. These are based on the premise that economic growth is necessary, but that if development agencies and policy-makers are to take seriously notions like high-quality growth which is socially progressive and environmentally sustainable, the content of development programmes and policies needs to be significantly adjusted.

The message is that the approaches to and methods of investment in agriculture, services, infrastructure and non-farm businesses which will achieve this sort of growth are increasingly known. Where they are not known, the principles on the basis of which relevant strategies can be developed are known and can be used in experimental activities. The rural development profession has matured beyond the panic which characterised its earlier phases: that mass starvation was just around the corner and could only be averted by a massive technical fix; that poverty could only be eradicated through enormous aid programmes and subsidies; that growth could only be assured through enormous infrastructure investments and substantial social and technological transformation.

The new rural development is in fact leading the way towards a new conception of development as a whole. It is giving substance to notions like high-quality growth. In its practice it is increasingly able to reconcile growth with equity, and development with environmental sustainability. In its shift towards participatory approaches it is giving space to a much greater diversity of values to underpin the development process, replacing earlier exclusive concern with material progress. It is able to work with and see value in different knowledge systems, and allow their co-evolution; there is no longer the immaturity expressed by the assertion of one right way. There is thus every chance that, over the next half century, the problems of poverty, food insecurity, exclusion, and environmental degradation which have dogged large parts of the world can be usefully addressed by purposive development programmes and policies.

Bibliography

Agency for Co-operation and Research in Development (ACORD) (1991) *Operationality in Turbulence: The Need to Change* (London: ACORD).

Arhin, D.C. (1991) 'The Health Card Insurance Scheme in Burundi: A Social Asset or a Non-Viable Venture?', *Social Science and Medicine,* vol. 36, no. 6.

Arnaiz, M., Merrill-Sands, D. and Mukwende, B. (1995) *The Zimbabwe Farmers' Union: Its Current and Potential Role in Technical Development and Transfer* (Overseas Development Institute, Agricultural Research and Extension Network Publications).

Ashby, J.A. and Sperling, L. (1994) *Institutionalising Participatory Client-Driven Research and Technology Development in Agriculture*, (London: Overseas Development Institute, Agricultural Administration (Research and Extension) Network Paper 49).

Ashish, S.M. (1993) 'Decentralised Management of Natural Resources in the UP Hills', *Economic and Political Weekly*, 28 August.

Aziz, S. (1978) *Rural Development: Learning from China* (Basingstoke: Macmillan).

Aziz, S. (1990 *Agricultural Policies for the 1990s* (Paris: Development Centre of the Organisation for Economic Co-operation and Development).

Bagadion, B.U. (1989) 'The Evolution of the Policy Context: An Historical Overview', in Korten and Siy (1989).

Baker, D. (1991) 'Reorientation not Reversal: African Farmer Based Experimentation', *Journal of Farming Systems Research-Extension*, vol. 2, no. 1, pp. 125–47.

Balkenhol, B. and Gueye, E.H. (1994) 'Tontines and the Banking System – Is There a Case for Building Linkages', *Small Enterprise Development*, vol. 5, no. 1 (March).

Barber, M. and Ryder, G. (eds) (1993) *Damming the Three Gorges* (London and Toronto: Earthscan Pubs Ltd).

Barratt Brown, M. (1993) *Fair Trade: Reform and Realities in the International Trading System* (London: Zed).

Bates, R. (1981) *Markets and States in Tropical Africa: The Political Basis of Agricultural Policies* (Berkeley and London: University of California Press).

Bawden, R. (1992) 'Systems Approaches to Agricultural Development: The Hawkesbury Experience', *Agricultural Systems*, 40, pp. 153–76.

Beaumont, P. (1993) *Pesticides, Policies and People* (London: The Pesticides Trust).

Bernstein, H. *et al.* (1992) *Poverty and Development* (Milton Keynes: Open University).

Besley, T. (1995) 'How do market failures justify interventions in rural credit markets' in *Finance against Poverty: Challenges and Advances in Banking with the Poor*, University of Reading: Conference Proceedings.

Bingen, J. *et al.* (1995) *The Malian Union of Cotton and Food Crop Producers: Its Current and Potential Role in Technology Development and Transfer* (London: ODI Agricultural Research and Extension Network Discussion Paper).

Birgegård, L. E. (1975) *The Project Selection Process in Developing Countries* (Stockholm: The Economic Research Council).

Bisset, R. (1988) 'Developments in EIA Methods', in P. Wathern (ed.), *Environmental Impact Assessment: Theory and Practice* (London: Allen & Unwin) pp. 47–60.

Biswas, Asit K. and Qu Geping, (1987) *Environmental Impact Assessment for Developing Countries* (London: Tycooly International for United Nations University).

Blake, R. R. and Mouton, J. S. (1964) *The Managerial Grid* (Houston, Texas: Gulf).

Blunt, P. and Jones, M. L. (1992) *Managing Organisations in Africa* (Berlin and New York: Walter de Gruyter).

BMA (British Medical Association) (1993) *Complementary Medicine, New Approaches to Good Practice* (Oxford: Oxford University Press).

Boserup, E. (1965) *The Conditions of Agricultural Growth: The Economics of Agrarian Change under Population Pressure* (London: Allen & Unwin).

Bouman, F. J. A. (1995) 'Rotating and Accumulating Savings and Credit Associations: A Development Perspective', *World Development*, vol. 23, no. 3 (March).

Bratton, M. (1986) 'Farmer Organisations and Food Production in Zimbabwe', *World Development*, 14 March.

Brinkerhoff, D. W. and Ingle, M. D. (1989) 'Integrating Blueprint and Process: A Structured Flexibility Approach to Development Management', *Public Administration and Development*, vol. 9, issues nos 1–5, pp. 487–503).

Brown, L. R. (1970) *Seeds of Change: The Green Revolution and Development in the 1970s* (New York and London: Praeger).

Bull, D. (1982) *A Growing Problem: Pesticides and the Third World Poor* (Oxford: Oxfam).

Burkey, S. (1993) *People First: A Guide to Self-Reliant Participatory Rural Development* (London: Zed Books).

Buturo, N. 'The Governance of Indigenous NGOs in Ghana: A Case Study Approach', University of Birmingham: PhD thesis, forthcoming 1997.

Caiden, N. and Wildavsky, A. (1974) *Planning and Budgeting in Poor Countries* (New York, London, etc.: Wiley Interscience).

Campbell, T. & Fiszbein, A. (1994) 'Local Government Capacity: Beyond Technical Assistance' (draft Washington: World Bank).

Carloni, A. S. (1987) *Synthesis Paper. Part of Women in Development: A.I.D.'s experience 1973–1985, Vol. 1* (Washington DC: Agency for International Development).

Carlsson, J. Kohlin, G. and Ekbom, A. (1994) *The Political Economy of Evaluation: International Aid Agencies and the Effectiveness of Aid* (New York: St Martins Press).

Carrin, G. with Vereecke, Marc (1992) *Strategies for Health Care Finance in Developing Countries: With a Focus on Community Financing in Sub-Saharan Africa* (Basingstoke: Macmillan).

Carson, R. (1963) *Silent Spring* (London: Hamish Hamilton).

Case, D'A.D. (1990) *The Community's Toolbox: The Idea, Methods and Tools for Participatory Assessment, Monitoring and Evaluation in Community Forestry* (Rome: Food and Agriculture Organisation, Community Forestry Field Manual 2).

Cernea, M. M. (ed.) (1985) *Putting People First: Sociological Variables in Rural Development* (New York and London: published for the World Bank by Oxford University Press).

CGIARTAC (Consultative Group on International Agricultural Research, Technical Advisory Committee) (1989) *Sustainable Agricultural Production: Implications for International Agricultural Research* (Rome: FAO).

Chabot, J. *et al.* (1991) 'National Community Health Insurance at Village Level: The Case from Guine-Bissau', *Health Policy and Planning*, vol. 6, no. 1, pp. 46–54.

Chambers, R. (1974) *Managing Rural Development: Ideas and Experience from East Africa* (Uppsala: Scandinavian Institute of African Studies).

Chambers, R. (1983) *Rural Development Putting the Last First* (Harlow, Essex: Longman Scientific & Technical).

Chambers, R. (1986) *Normal Professionalism, New Paradigms and Development* (Brighton: University of Development Studies (IDS) Discussion Paper No. 227).

Chambers, R. (1987) *Sustaining Rural Livelihood* (Brighton: Institute of Development Studies, Commissioned Study, No 7).

Chambers, R. (1992) *Rural Appraisal: Rapid, Relaxed and Participatory*, University of Sussex, IDS Discussion Paper 311.

Chambers, R. (1993) *Challenging the Professions: Frontiers for Rural Development* (London: IT Pubs).

Chambers, R. (1994) 'The Origins and Practice of Participatory Rural Appraisal', *World Development*, vol. 22, no. 7.

Chambers, R. (1995) 'Making the Best of Going to Scale', *PLA Notes*, no. 24.

Chambers, R., Pacey, A. and Thrupp, L. A. (eds) (1989) *Farmer First; Farmer Innovation and Agricultural Research* (London: IT Publications).

Checkland, P. and Scholes, J. (1990) *Soft Systems Methodology in Action* (Chichester: Wiley).

Christen, R. *et al.* (1995) 'Maximising the Outreach of Microenterprise Finance: The Emerging Lessons of Successful Programs', in *Finance Against Poverty: Challenges and Advances in Banking with the Poor* Reading University, Conference Proceedings.

Christiansson, C. (1991) 'Use and Impacts of Chemical Pesticides in Smallholding Agriculture in the Central Highlands', in C. Folke and T.

Kåberger (eds), *Linking the National Environment and the Economy* (Amersterdam: Kluver Academic Publishers).

Cleaver, H. M. (1975)'The Origins of the Green Revolution', PhD thesis, Stamford University.

Cochrane, G. (1979) *The Cultural Appraisal of Development Projects* (New York: Praeger).

Cohen, J. (1978) *Land Tenure and Rural Development in Africa* (Cambridge, Mass.: Harvard International Institute for Development).

Colchester, M. and Lohmann, L. (eds) (1993) *The Struggle for Land and the Fate of the Forests* (London: The Ecologist).

Conway, G. R. and Pretty, J. N. (1991) *Unwelcome Harvest: Agriculture and Pollution* (London: Earthscan).

Conyers, D. (1982) *An Introduction to Social Planning in the Third World* (Chichester: Wiley).

Cosgrove, D. and Petts, G. (eds) (1990) *Water, Engineering and Landscape: Water Control and Landscape Transformation in the Modern Period* (London: Belhaven Press).

Costanza, R. (ed.) (1991) *Ecological Economics: The Science and Management of Sustainability* (New York: Columbia University Press).

Coulter, J. (1994) *Liberalization of Cereals Marketing in SSA: Lessons from Experience*, NRI Marketing Series 9 (Overseas Development Administration).

Coward, E. W. (1980) *Irrigation and Agricultural Development in Asia: Perspectives from the Social Sciences* (New York and London: Cornell University Press).

Curtis, D. (1980) 'Small Scale Industry Promotion: Report on a Field Project', University of Birmingham, Development Administration Group, Paper in the Administration of Development.

Curtis, D. (1991) *Beyond Government. Organisations for Common Benefit* (Basingstoke: Macmillan).

Curtis, D. *et al.* (1979) *Participation and Basic Needs* (Geneva: ILO World Employment Paper).

Curtis, D., Hubbard, M. and Shepherd, A. with contributions from Clay, E. *et al.* (1988) *Preventing Famine: Policies and Prospects for Africa* (London: Routledge).

de Boef, W., *et al.* (1993) *Cultivating Knowledge: Genetic Diversity, Farmer Experimentation and Crop Research* (London: IT Publications).

de Luisa, I. (1995) 'Entrepreneurship in Mexico: The Management of Information in Rural Small-Scale Firms', PhD thesis, Development Administration Group, Birmingham University.

Demery, L. (1994) 'Structural Adjustment: Its Origins, Rationale and Achievements', in G. Cornia and G. Helleiner (eds), *From Adjustment to Development in Africa* (Basingstoke: Macmillan).

Dhawan, B. D. (1993) 'Ground Water Depletion in Punjab', *Economic and Political Weekly*, 30 October.

Dinham, B. (1993) *The Pesticide Hazard: A Global Health and Environment Audit* (London: Zed Books).

Doornbos, M. *et al.* (1990) *Dairy Aid and Development: India's Operation Flood* (New Delhi; and Newbury Park, California: Sage Pubs).

Dreze, J. and Sen, A. (1989) *Hunger and Public Action* (Oxford: Clarendon).

Duffield, M. (1994) 'Complex Emergencies and the Crisis of Developmentalism', *IDS Bulletin; Linking Relief and Development*, vol. 25, no. 3 (October).

Dugue, P. (1993) 'The Sengalese Institute for Agricultural Research (ISRA) and the Fatick Region Farmers', Association', in K. Wellard and J. Copestake (eds) *NGOs and the State in Africa* (London: Routledge).

Duncan, A. and Howell, J. (1992) *Structural Adjustment and the African Farmer* (London: ODI in association with James Currey).

Ellis, F. (1993) *Peasant Economics: Farm Households and Agrarian Development* (Cambridge: Cambridge University Press).

FAO (1993a) *The State of Food and Agriculture* (Rome: FOA).

FAO (1993b) *The Institutionalisation of Farming Systems Development* (Rome: FAO).

FAO (Food and Agriculture Organisation) (1990) *Farming Systems Development, Guidelines for the Conduct of a Training Course in Farming Systems Development* (Rome: FAO).

FAO (Food and Agriculture Organisation) (1991) *Den Bosch Declaration and Agenda for Action on Sustainable Agriculture and Rural Development* (FAO and Ministry of Agriculture, Nature Management and Fisheries of Netherlands).

Farmer, B. (1984) *Understanding Green Revolutions: Agricultural Change and Development Planning* (Cambridge: Cambridge University Press).

Farrington, J. *et al.* (1994) *Reluctant Partners: NGOs, the State and Sustainable Development* (London: Routledge).

Fernanda, D. (1991) 'Towards Projects as the Enabling Edge of Development: A Preliminary Study of the Impact of the Project on Development Administration in Indonesia', MSocSci thesis, Development Administration Group, University of Birmingham.

Feuerstein, M-T. (1986) *Partners in Evaluation: Evaluating Development and Community Programmes* (Basingstoke: Macmillan).

Fowler, A. (1988) *Non-Governmental Organisations in Africa: Achieving Comparative Advantage in Relief and Micro-Development* (Brighton: IDS).

Freebairn, D. K. (1995) 'Did the Green Revolution Concentrate Incomes? A Quantitative Study of Research Reports', *World Development*, vol. 23, no. 2, pp. 265–80.

Frimpong, A. O. (1994) 'The Konkomba Factor', No. 3992, 4–10 April.

Fujisaka, S. (1994) *Will Farmer Participatory Research Survive in the International Agricultural Research Centres?* (London: International Institute for Environment and Development, Gatekeeper Series, No. 44.

Fukuoka, M. (1992) *The One Straw Revolution: An Introduction to Natural Farming* (Mapusa, Goa, India: The Other India Press).

Gabriel, T. (1991) *The Human Factor in Rural Development* (London: Belhaven Press).

Gadgil, M. and Guha, R. (1993) *This Fissured Land: An Ecological History of India* (Berkeley: University of California Press).

George, S. (1985) *Operation Flood: An Appraisal of Current Indian Dairy Policy* (Delhi: Oxford: Oxford University Press).

Gibbons, D. S. and Kassim, S. (eds) (1990) *Banking on the Rural Poor in Peninsular Malasia* (George Town: Centre for Policy Research/Asian and Pacific Development Centre).

Gilbert, E. (1995) *The Meaning of the Maize Revolution in Sub-Saharan Africa: Seeking Guidance from Past Impacts* (London: Overseas Development Institute, Agricultural Administration (Research and Extension) Network Paper 55).

Gittinger, J. P. (1982) *Economic Analysis of Agricultural Projects*, 2nd edn (Baltimore, Md.: Johns Hopkins University Press).

Goldman and Smith (1995) 'Agricultural Transformation in India and Northern Nigeria: Exploring the Nature of Green Revolution', *World Development*, vol. 23, no. 2 (Feb).

Gould, W. T. S. (1993) *People and Education in the Third World* (Harlow, Essex: Longman Scientific & Technical).

Grieshaber, C. (1994) *Step by Step: Group Development* (Germany: DSE/ZEL).

Gubbels, P. (1993) *Peasant Farmer Organisation in Farmer-First Agricultural Development in West Africa: New Opportunities and Continuing Constraints*, Agricultural Research & Network Extension Paper, No. 40, July (Overseas Development Institute).

Guha, R. (1989) *The Unquiet Woods: Ecological Change and Peasant Resistance in the Himalaya* (Delhi; Oxford: Oxford University Press).

Guha, R. and Gadgil, M. (1993) *This Fissured Land: An Ecological History of India* (Berkeley: University of California Press).

Gurung, S. B. and Roy, P. (1988) *Planning with People, Decentralisation in Nepal* (New Delhi: Orient Longman).

Hailey, J. (1994) 'Capacity Building for Southern NGOs', presentation at DSA Study Group Meeting, 23 November 1994, unpublished.

Halim, N. and Lohani, B. N. (1987) 'Recommended Methodologies for Rapid Environment Impact Assessment in Developing Countries: Experiences Derived from Case Studies in Thailand', in Biswas and Qu Geping (1987).

Hammer, M. and Champy, J. (1993) *Re-engineering the Corporation* (London: Nicholas Brealey).

Harkaly, A. (1991) 'Is There a Way Out for the (Small) Farmer in Developing Countries?', in B. Geier, C. Haest and A. Pons (eds), *Trade in Organic Foods* (Germany: International Federation of Organic Agriculture Movements).

Haroun, A. M. (1992) 'Determinants of Agricultural Development in Northern Ghana', University of London, Ph.D.

Harper, M. (1989) 'Training and Technical Assistance for Micro-Enterprises', Cranfield School of Management, SWP 8/89, Cranfield University, Bedford.

Hecht, S. and Cockburn, C. (1989) *The Fate of the Forest: Developers, Destroyers and Defenders of the Amazon* (London: Verso).

Hettne, B. (1995) *Development Theory and the Three Worlds* (London: Longman).

Heyer, J. *et al.* (1981) *Rural Development in Tropical Africa* (Basingstoke: Macmillan).

Hill, P. (1963) *The Migrant Cocoa Farmers of Southern Ghana: A Study in Rural Capitalism* (Cambridge: Cambridge University Press).

Hill, P. (1970) *Studies in Rural Capitalism in West Africa* (Cambridge: Cambridge University Press).

Hinton, W. (1990) *The Great Reversal: The Privatisation of China* (New York: Monthly Review Press).

Hofstede, G. (1980) *Culture's Consequences: International Differences in Work-related Values* (Beverly Hills; London: Sage).

Hofstede, G. (1991) *Cultures and Organisations: Software of the Mind* (London: MacGraw-Hill).

Hogwood, B. and Gunn, L. (1984) *Policy Analysis for the Real World* (Oxford: Oxford University Press).

Holcombe, S. (1995) *Managing to Empower: The Grameen Bank's Experience of Poverty Alleviation* (London: Zed Books).

Honadle, G. and Cooper (1989) 'Beyond Coordination and Control: An Interorganisational Approach to Structural Adjustment, Service Delivery and Natural Resource Management', *World Development*, 17 Oct.

Honadle, G. and Rosengard, J. (1983) 'Putting Projectised Development in Perspective', *Public Administration and Development*, vol. 3, pp. 299–305.

Hossain, M. (1988) *Credit for the Alleviation of Rural Poverty: The Grameen Bank in Bangladesh* (Washington: International Food Policy Research Institute (IFPRI), Bangladesh Institute of Development Studies Research Report 65).

Howell, J. (1988) *Training and Visit Extension in Practice* (London: Overseas Development Institute).

Htun, N. (1988) 'The EIA Process in Asia and The Pacific Region', in P. Wathern (ed.), *Environmental Impact Assessment: Theory and Practise* (London: Allen & Unwin) pp. 225–38.

Hubbard, M. (1995) *Food Security* (London: Intermediate Technology Publications).

Hubbs, V. *et al.* (1992) *The Gender Information Framework* (Washington DC: Office of Women in Development, USAID).

Hulme, D. and Turner, M. M. (1990) *Sociology and Development: Theories, Policies and Practices* (Hemel Hempstead, Harvester: Wheatsheaf).

IFPRI (1990) *Technology Policy for Sustainable Agricultural Growth* Washington: International Food Policy Research Institute Briefs 7).

IIED (International Institute of Environment and Development) (1994) *Whose Eden? An Overview of Community Approaches to Wildlife Management* (London: IIED).

IIED (1995) *PLA Note: 5* (London: IIED).

Iliffe, J. (1987) *The African Poor* (Cambridge: Cambridge University Press).

Inayatullah (1972) *Co-operatives in Asia* (Geneva: United Nations Research Institute for Social Development (UNRISD)).

Israel, A. (1987) *Institutional Development: Incentives to Performance* (Baltimore and London: Johns Hopkins University Press for the World Bank).

Ives, J. D. and Messerli, B. (1989) *The Himalayan Dilemma: Reconciling Development and Conservation* (London: Routledge).

Jackson, J. C. and Collier, P. (1991) 'Incomes, Poverty and Food Security in the Communal Lands of Zimbabwe', in N. D. Mutizwa-Mangiza and A. H. J. Helmsing (eds), *Rural Development and Planning in Zimbabwe* (Aldershot: Gower).

Jaffee, S. and Morton, J. (1995) *Marketing Africa's High Value Foods* (Washington: World Bank).

Jazairy, I., Alamgir, M. and Panuccio, T. (1992) *The State of World Rural Poverty* (London: IT Publications for the International Fund for Agricultural Development).

Jazayeri, A. (1995) 'Village Banks', in *Finance Against Poverty: Challenges and Advances in Banking with the Poor* (University of Reading, Conference Proceedings).

Jodha, N. S. (1991) *Rural Common Property Resources: A Growing Crisis* (London: International Institute for Environment and Development, Gatekeeper Series, No. 24).

Johnson, C. (1994) 'Notes on WaterAid's Experiences of Capacity Building', paper presented to DSA study group meeting, 23 November 1994, unpublished.

Kabeer, N. (1994) *Revised Realities: Gender Hierarchies in Development Thought* (London: Verso).

Kar, K. and Backhaus, C. (1994) 'Old Wine in New Bottles: Experiences with the Application of PRA and Participatory Approaches in a Large-Scale, Foreign-Funded Development Programme in Sri-Lanka', draft, June 1994.

Karam, M. (1981) 'Dispute Settlement Among Pastoral Nomads in the Sudan', University of Birmingham, M.Soc.Sci. thesis.

Kitching, G. (1982) *Development and Underdevelopment in Comparative Perspective* (London: Methuen).

Kofi, T. (1995) *Structural Adjustment in Africa – a performance review of World Bank policies under uncertainty in commodity price trends: the case of Ghana* (Helsinki: United Nations University World Institute for Development Economics Research).

Korten, D. C. (1980) 'Community Organisation and Rural Development: A Learning Process Approach', *Public Administration Review*, 40 (Sept-Oct) pp. 480–510.

Korten, D. C. (1984a) 'People-Centred Development: Towards a Framework', in D. C. Korten and R. Klauss (eds), *People Centred Development* (West Hartford, Connecticut: Kumarian Press).

Korten, D. C. (1984b) 'Rural Development Programming: The Learning Process Approach', in D. C. Korten and R. Klauss (eds), *People Centred Development* (West Hartford, Connecticut: Kumarian Press).

Korten, D. C. (1990) *Getting to the 21st Century: Voluntary Action and the Global Agenda* (West Hartford, Connecticut: Kumarian Press).

Korten, D. C. (ed.) (1987) *Community Management: Asian Experience and Perspectives* (West Hartford, Connecticut: Kumarian Press).

Korten, F. F. and Siy, R. Y. (eds) (1988) *Transforming a bureaucracy: The Experience of the Philippine National Irrigation Administration* (West Hartford, Conn: Kumarian Press c 1988).

Kottak, C. P. (1985) 'When People Don't Come First: Some Sociological Lessons from Completed Projects', in M. M. Cernea (ed.), *Putting People First: Sociological Variables in Rural Development* (New York and London: Oxford University Press).

Kuhn, T. S. (1962) *The Structure of Scientific Revolutions* (Chicago and London: University of Chicago Press) 1970.

Kurian, N. J. (1987) 'IRDP: How Relevant is it?', *Economic and Political Weekly*, vol. 22, no. 52, pp. A161–76.

Lamb, D. (1990) *Exploiting the Tropical Rainforest* (Paris: UNESCO, Man and the Biosphere series, vol. 3).

Larbi, G. (1995) 'Implications and Impact of Structural Adjustment on the Civil Service: The Case of Ghana', Birmingham University, Development Administration Group, Role of Government in Adjusting Economies, Paper 2.

Last, Murray and Chavundukwa, G. L. (1986) *The Professionalisation of African Medicine* (Manchester: Manchester University Press in association with the International African Institute).

Lawrence, P. (1987) 'The Green Revolution in Africa: Stagnantion or Diffusion', Paper to Department Studies Association Conference, Manchester.

Leurs, R. (1993) 'A Resource Manual for Trainers and Practitioners of Participatory Rural Appraisal (PRA)', Papers in the Administration of Development, No. 49 DAG, Development Administration Group, University of Birmingham.

Leurs, R. (1996) 'Current Challenges Facing Participatory Rural Appraisal', *Public Administration and Development*, vol. 16, no. 1.

Lewa, P. M. (1995) 'The Politics of Grain Market Reform in Kenya: A Study of the Maize Milling Industry', PhD thesis, Development Administration Group, Birmingham University.

Lipton, M. (1977) *Why Poor People Stay Poor: Urban Bias in World Development* (London: Unwin Hyman).

Lipton, M. and Longhurst, R. (1989) *New Seeds and Poor People* (London: Unwin Hyman).

Loewinsohn, M. E. (1987) 'Insecticide Use and Increased Mortality in Central Luzon, Philippines', *The Lancet*, No. 1, pp. 1359–62.

Lovell, R. (ed.) (1994) *Managing Change in the New Public Sector* (Harlow: Longman).

MacDonald, J. (1993) *Primary Health Care: Medicine in Its Place* (London: Earthscan).

Makumbe, J. (1994) 'The National Farmers', Association of Zimbabwe: Its Structure and Function', *African Rural and Urban Studies*, vol. 1, no. 1, pp. 111–40.

Maninfeld, K. (ed.) (1989) *Sustainable Agriculture in Semi-Arid Areas* (Amsterdam: ETC Foundation).

Markandya, A. and Pearce, D. (1991) *Beyond the Green Revolution* (London: Earthscan).

Mathur, H. M. (1981) 'Experts of the United Nations in Third World Development', in D. Pitt and T. G. Weiss, *The Nature of UN Bureaucracies* (London: Croom Helm).

Mattee, A. Z. and Lassalle, T. (1994) *Diverse and Limited: Farmers', Organisations in Tanzania*, Agricultural Research and Extension Network Paper 50 (London: ODI).

Mattheus, H. (1995) 'Urban Management, Participation and the Poor in Porto Alegre/Brazil', Birmingham: university of Birmingham PhD Dissertation.

Mawhood, P. (ed.) (1993) *Local Government in the Third World: The Experience of Decentralisation in Tropical Africa* (African Institute of South Africa).

McCracken, J. A., Conway, G. R. and Pretty, J. N. (1988) *An Introduction to Rapid Rural Appraisal for Agricultural Development* (London: IIED).

Meinzen-Dick, R. *et al.* (1994) *Sustainable Water User Associations: Lessons from a Literature Review* (Washington DC: World Bank/IFPRI).

Merrill-Sands, D. and Collion, M-H. (1994) 'Farmers and Researchers: The Road to Partnership', *Agriculture and Human Values*, vol. 11, nos 2 and 3.

Michaud, M. (1995) 'Fair Trade and Organic Agriculture', *New Farmer and Grower*, no. 47, Summer.

Mold, T., Blake, G. H. and Becker, L. A. (1991) 'Goal Oriented Medical Care', *Family Medicine*, vol. 23, no. 1, pp. 46–51.

Mooney, P. R. (1983) 'The Law of the Seed', *Development Dialogue* (1988) 1–2, Uppsala: Dag Hammarskjold Foundation.

Moore, M. and Harris, J. (1984) *Development and the Rural–Urban Divide* (London: Cass).

Morgan, E. P. (1983) 'The Project Orthodoxy in Development: Re-evaluating the Cutting Edge', *Public Administration and Development*, vol. 3, pp. 329–39.

Moris, J. (1977) 'The Transferability of Western Management Concepts and Programs: An East African Perspective', in J. E. Black *et al.* (eds), *Education and Training for Public Sector Management in Developing Countries* (New York: Rockefeller Foundation).

Moris, J. (1981) *Managing Induced Rural Development* Bloomington, Indiana: International Development Institute, Indiana University).

Morss, E. R. and Gow, D. (1981) *Integrated Rural Development: 9 Critical Implementation Problems* (Washington: Development Alternatives Incorporated).

Mortimore, M. and Turner, B. (1993) Crop–Livestock Farming Systems in the Semi-Arid Zone of Sub-Saharan Africa (London: Overseas Development Institute, Agricultural Administration (Research and Extension) Network Paper 46).

Mosely, P. (1995) 'Metamorphosis from NGO to Commercial Bank: The Case of Bancosol in Bolivia', in *Finance Against Poverty: Challenges and Advances in Banking with the Poor*, University of Reading: Conference Proceedings.

Moser, C. (1989) 'Gender Planning in the Third World: Meeting Practical and Strategic Gender Needs', *World Development*, vol. 17, no. 11.

Moser, C. (1994) *Gender Planning and Development* (London: Routledge).

Mosher, A. T. (1966) *Getting Agriculture Moving: Essentials for Development and Modernisation* (The Agricultural Development Council).

Mosley, P. *et al.* (1991) *Aid and Power: The World Bank and Policy Based Lending*, vols 1 and 2 (London: Routledge).

Mosse, J. (1993) *Half the World, Half a Chance: An Introduction to Gender and Development* (Oxford: Oxfam).

Mukherjee, N. (1993) *Participatory Rural Appraisal: Methodology and Applications* (New Delhi: Concept Publications).

Mukherjee, N. (1995) *Participatory Rural Appraisal and Questionnaire Survey* (New Delhi: Concept).

Mullins, L. J. (1989) *Management and Organisational Behaviour* (London: Pitman).

Mushita, A. J. (1993) 'Strengthening the Informal Seed System in the Communal Areas of Zimbabwe', in de Boef *et al.* (1993).

Narayan, D. (1993) *Participatory Evaluation* (Washington DC: World Bank).

National Research Council US (1989) *Alternative Agriculture*, Committee on the Role of Alternative Farming Methods in Modern Production Agriculture, Board on Agriculture (Washington DC: National Academy).

Norgaard, R. B. (1994) *Development Betrayed: The End of Progress and a Coevolutionary Revisioning of the Future* (London: Routledge).

North, D. (1990) *Institutions, Institutional Change and Economic Performance* (Cambridge: Cambridge University Press).

O'Donovan, I. (1995) *The ODA's Process Approach to Projects: Experiences in India, Lessons for Project Management* (University of Birmingham: Development Administration Group).

Oakley, P. (1994) 'People's Participation in Development: Reviewing the Balance Sheet', unpublished.

ODA (1995) *A Guide to Social Analysis for Projects in Developing Countries* (London: HMSO).

ODA (Overseas Development Administration) (1995) *Social Development Handbook, A Guide to Social Issues in ODA Projects and Programmes* (ODA, Social Development Department).

ODI (Overseas Development Institute) (1995) 'NGOs and Official Donors', ODI Briefing Paper.

Okali, C., Sumberg, J. and Farrington, J. (1994) *Farmer Participatory Research: Rhetoric and Reality* (London: IT Publications).

Onumah, G. and Shepherd, A. (1997) *The State and Agricultural Markets in Ghana* (Development Administration Group University of Birmingham).

Ostrom, E. (1990) *Governing the Commons: The Evolution of Institutions for Collective Action* (Cambridge: Cambridge University Press).

Ostrom, L. S. and Wynne, S. (1993) *Institutional Incentives and Sustainable Development: Infrastructure Policies in Perspective* (Boulder, Colo.; and Oxford: Westview Press).

Page, S. (1994) *World Trade Reform: Do Developing Countries Gain or Lose?* (London: Overseas Development Institute).

Paranjpye, V. (1990) *High Dams on the Narmarda: Studies in Ecology and Sustainable Development* (Indian National Trust for Art and Cultural Heritage).

Participatory Learning and Action (PLA) Notes (1995) London: International Institute for Environment and Development.

Pearse, A. (1977 'Technology and Peasant Production: Reflections on a Global Study', *Development and Change*, vol. 8, no. 2, pp. 125–60.

Pearse, A. (1980) *Seeds of Plenty, Seeds of Want* (Oxford: Clarendon Press).

Pearse, A. and Stiefel, M. (1979) 'An Inquiry into Participation: A Research Approach', mimeo, UNRISD (United Nations Research Institute for Social Development) Geneva.

Perrings, C. (1991)'Reserved Rationality and the Precautionary Principle: Technological Change, Time and Uncertainty in Environmental Decision-Making', in Costanza (1991) pp. 153–67.

Peters, T. (1987) *Thriving on Chaos* (London: Pan Books).

Peters, T. and Waterman, R. H. (1982) *In Search of Excellence* (New York: Harper Collins).

Petts, G. and Cosgrove, D. (1990) *Water, Engineering and Landscape* (London: Belhaven Press).

Poffenberger, M. (ed.) (1990) *Keepers of the Forest: Land Management Alternatives in SE Asia* (West Hartford, Conn.: Kumarian Press).

Pohl, G. and Mihaljek, D. (1992) 'Project Evaluation and Uncertainty in Practice: A Statistical Analysis of Rate-of-Return Divergencies of 1015 World Bank Projects', *World Bank Economic Research Digest*, vol. 6, no. 2, pp. 255–77.

Porter, D. and Bryant, A. (1991) *Development in Practice, Paved with Good Intentions* (London: Routledge).

Potter, D. (1994) 'Democracy and the Environment in Asia', Economic and Social Research Council Global Environmental Change Programme, Working Paper No. 2 The Open University.

Powell, J. M. and Williams, T. O. (1993) *Livestock, Nutrient Cycling and Sustainable Agriculture in the West African Sahel* (London: International Institute for Environment and Development, Gatekeeper Series, No. 37).

Pretty, J. (1995) *Regenerating Agriculture* (London: Earthscan).

Prior, J. (1994) *Pastoral Development Planning* (Oxford: Oxfam).

Querol, D. (1993) *Genetic Resources: A Practical Guide to their Conservation* (London and New Jersey; Penang, Malasia: Zed Books. 3rd World Network).

Quinn, R. *et al.* (1990) *Becoming a Master Manager: A Competency Framework* (New York and Chichester: Wiley).

Rahman, M. A. (1990) *Qualitative Dimensions of Social Development Evaluation: Thematic Paper in Evaluating Social Development Projects*, Development Guidelines, No. 5 (D. Marsden and P. Oakley eds) (Oxfam).

Rao, A. (ed.) (1991) *Gender Analysis in Development Planning: A Case Book* (West Hartford, Conn.: Kumarian Press).

Reed, D. A. (1996) *Structural Adjustment and the Environment* (London: Earthscan).

Reijntjes, C., Haverkort, B. and Waters-Bayer, A. (1992) *Farming for the Future: An Introduction to Low-external Input and Sustainable Agriculture* (London and Leusden: Macmillan ILEIA).

Remenyi, J. (1991) *Where Credit is Due: Income Generating Programmes for the Poor in Developing Countries* (London: IT).

Rondinelli, D. A. (1983) *Development Projects as Policy Experiments: An Adaptive Approach to Development Administration* (London: Methuen).

Rondinelli, D. A. (ed.) (1977) *Planning Development Projects* (Strousberg, Pa.: Dowden, Hutchinson & Ross).

Sahara, T. (1989) *A Learning Process Approach versus a Command Control Approach in Institution Building* (University of Manchester: Institute of Development Policy and Management).

Sahn, D. E. (ed.) (1994) *Adjusting to Policy Failure in African Economies* (Ithaca, NY, and London: Cornell University Press).

Sandford, S. (1983) *Management of Pastoral Development in the Third World* (Chichester: Wiley).

Save the Children Fund (1994) *Toolkits: Assessment, Monitoring, Review and Evaluation* (by L. Gosling and M. Edwards) (London: Save the Children Fund).

Saxena, N. C. (1995) *Towards Sustainable Forestry in Uttar Pradesh Hills* (Uttar Pradesh Forestry Dept. and ODA UK).

Schein, E. H. (1986) *Organisational Culture and Leadership* (San Francisco: Jossey Bass).

Shaw, R. R. and Griffin, C. C. (1995) *Financing Health Care in Sub-Saharan Africa Through User Fees and Insurance* (Washington: World Bank).

Shepherd, A. (1979) 'The Development of Capitalist Rice Farming in Northern Ghana', PhD thesis, University of Cambridge.

Shepherd, A. (1981) 'Agrarian Change in Northern Ghana: Public Investment, Capitalist Farming and Famine', in J. Heyer, P. Roberts and G. Williams (eds), *Rural Development in Tropical Africa* (Basingstoke: Macmillan).

Shepherd, A. (1983) 'Capitalist Agriculture in the Sudan', *Development and Change*, vol. 14, no. 2 (April).

Shepherd, A. (1993) *Women's Development, Creativity Requirements in the Project Process* (Development Administration Group, Papers in the Administration of Development in FAO (1993b).

Shepherd, A. (1995) 'Participatory Environmental Management: Contradiction of Process, Project and Bureaucracy in the Himalayan Foothills', *Public Administration and Development*, vol. 15, pp. 465–79.

Shiva, V. (1991a) *The Violence of the Green Revolution: Third World Agriculture, Ecololgy and Politics* (London: Zed Books).

Shiva, V. (1991b) *Ecology and the Politics of Survival: Conflicts over Natural Resources in India* (New Delhi: Sage).

Shiva, V. and Ramprasad, V. (1993) *Cultivating Diversity: Biodiversity, Conservation and the Politics of the Seed* (Dehra Dun: Research Foundation for Science, Technology and National Resource Policy).

Simpson, I. G. and Simpson, M. C. (1978) *Alternative Strategies for Agricultural Development in the Central Rainlands of the Sudan*, University of Leeds Rural Development Study, No. 3.

Simpson, M. C. (1981) *Large Scale Mechanical Rainfed Farming Developments in the Sudan*, in Centre of African Studies, *Post-Independence Sudan*, Edinburgh: University of Edinburgh.

Slater, R. P. (1991) *From Farm to Firm: Rural Diversification in the Asian Countryside* (Aldershot: Avebury).

Slater, R. P. and Watson J. R. (1990) 'Regional Needs and Poverty Alleviation in India', in R. Rothermund (ed.), *Regional Disparities in India:
Rural and Industrial Dimensions* (New Delhi: Manohar).

Slater, R. P. and Watson, J. R. (1992) 'Decentralised Planning and the
Reform of IRDP', in Y. Raju and R. Hooja (eds), *Decentralised Planning
in a Multisectoral Perspective* (Jaipur: Rawat).

Smyke, P. (1991) *Women's Health* (London: Zed Press).

Sowa, N. K. *et al.* (1992) *Small Enterprises and Adjustment: The Impact of
Ghana's Economic Recovery Programme on Small Scale Industrial Enterprises* (London; and Accra: ODI: University Ghana Dept Economics).

Stewart, F. (1975) 'A Note on Social Cost Benfit Analysis and Class
Conflict in LDCs', *World Development*, vol. 3, no. 1 (Jan) pp. 31–9.

Stewart, F. (1994) 'Are Short Term Policies Consistent with Long Term
Development Needs in Africa?', in G. Cornia and G. Helleiner (eds),
Structural Adjustment in Sub-Saharan Africa (London: Macmillan).

Stiefel, M. and Wolfe, M. (1994) *A Voice for the Excluded: Popular
Participation in Development, Utopia or Necessity* (London: Zed, in
Association with the United Nations Research Institute for Social
Development).

Tait, D. (1961) *The Konkomba of Northern Ghana* (Oxford: Oxford University Press).

Tendler, J. (1991) *Dynamics of Rural Development in NE Brazil: New
Lessons from Old Potatoes* (Washington, DC: World Bank).

Thompson, J. (1994) 'Participatory Approaches in government Bureaucracies: Facilitating the Process of Institutional Change', *World Development*, vol. 23, no. 9, p. 154 ff.

Thurston, H. D. (1991) *Sustainable Practices for Plant Disease Management
in Traditional Farming Systems* (Boulder, Colo.; Oxford: Westview Press).

Tiffen, M. (1987) *The Dominance of the Internal Rate of Return as a
Planning Criterion and the Treatment of O and M Costs in Feasibility
Studies* (London: Overseas Development Institute, Irrigation Manage-
ment Network).

Tiffen, M., Mortimore, M. and Gichuki, F. (1994) *More People Less
Erosion: Environmental Recovery in Kenya* (Chichester: Wiley).

Toffler, A. (1981) *The Third Wave* (London: Pan, in association with
Collins).

Tolba, M. *et al.* (eds) (1992) *The World Environment 1972–92: Two Decades
of Challenge* (London: Chapman & Hall on behalf of UN Environment
Programme).

UNDP (United Nations Development Programme) (1994) *Sustainable Human Development and Agriculture* (New York: UNDP).

UNICEF (1987) *Adjustment with a Human Face* (G. Cornia, R. Jolly and F.
Stewart eds) (Oxford: Clarendon Press).

UNNGLS (United Nations Non Government Liason Service) (1994) *Sustainable Agriculture and Rural Development* (Geneva: Environment and
Development File, Vol. III, No. 8).

Uphoff, N. (1986) *Local Institutional Development: An Analytical Source-
book with Cases* (West Hartford: Kumarian Press).

Uphoff, N. and Korten, D. C. (1981) *Bureaucratic Reorientation for Parti-cipatory Rural Development* (Washington: National Association of Sectors of Public Affairs and Administration).

Wallace, T., Crowther, S. and Shepherd, A. (1997) *The Standardisation of Development: Influences on UK NGOs', Policies and Procedures* (Oxford: Worldview Press).

Walsh, K. (1995) *Public Services and Market Mechanisms: Competition, Contracting and The New Public Management* (Basingstoke: Macmillan).

Wangwe, S. (1994) 'New Trade Issues: Traditional Versus Non Traditional Exports', in G. Cornia and G. Helleiner (eds), *From Adjustment to Development in Africa* (Basingstoke: Macmillan).

Wathern, P. (ed.) (1988) *Environmental Impact Assessment: Theory and Practice* (London: Allen & Unwin).

WCED (World Commission on Environment and Development) (1987) *Our Common Future: Development and International Co-operation* (New York: United Nations).

Welbourne, A. (1994) Presentation, Workshop on *Development in Conflict* Developing Administration Group, University of Birmingham.

West Africa 1994a and 1994b 1994c.

Williams, G. (1981) 'The World Bank and The Peasant Problem', in J. Heyer, P. Roberts and G. Williams (eds), *Rural Development in Tropical Africa* (Basingstoke: Macmillan).

Wilson, D. (1992) *A Strategy of Change: Concepts and Controversies in the Management of Change* (London: Routledge).

Winpenny, J. T. (1991) *Values for the Environment: a Guide to Economic Appraisal* (London: HMSO).

Wood, C. (1988) 'EIA in Plan Making', in P. Wathern (ed.), *Environmental Impact Assessment: Theory and Practice* (London: Allen & Unwin).

Wood, G. D. and Palmer-Jones, R. (1991) *The Water Sellers: A Co-operative Venture by the Rural Poor* (London: IT Publications).

Woods, B. (1993) *Communication, Technology and the Development of People* (London and New York: Routledge).

Worede, M. and Mekbib, H. (1993) 'Linking Genetic Resource Conservation to Farmers in Ethiopia', in de Boef *et al.* (eds) (1993).

World Bank (1975) *Rural Development: Sector Policy Paper* (Washington DC: World Bank).

World Bank (1981) *Agricultural Research: Sector Policy Paper* (Washington DC: World Bank).

World Bank (1987) *Rural Development: World Bank Experience 1965–1986* (Washington DC: World Bank Operations Evaluation Department).

World Bank (1989) *Sub-Saharan Africa: From Crisis to Sustainable Growth: A Long Term Perspective Study* (Washington DC: World Bank).

World Bank (1990) *World Development Report; Poverty* (Oxford University Press).

World Bank (1991) *Gender and Poverty in India* (Washington DC: World Bank).

World Bank (1992) *Himalayan Watershed Managment Project. Field Report*, 20–24 July 1992 and letter 14 Aug 1992.

World Bank (1993) *World Development Report (1993) Investing in Health;
World Development Indicators* (Oxford: Oxford University Press for
World Bank).

Young, K. (1994) *Planning Development with Women* (Basingstoke: Macmillan).

Zhaoquian, W. (1991) 'Ecological Agriculture in China', *New China Quar-
terly*, August.

Index